WHITE FLANK

WHITE FLANK

*Organizing White People
for Racial Justice*

CHANDRA RUSSO

STANFORD UNIVERSITY PRESS
Stanford, California

Stanford University Press
Stanford, California

© 2026 by Chandra Russo. All rights reserved.

No part of this book may be reproduced or transmitted in any form or by any means, electronic or mechanical, including photocopying and recording, or in any information storage or retrieval system, without the prior written permission of Stanford University Press.

Library of Congress Cataloging-in-Publication Data
Names: Russo, Chandra author
Title: White flank : organizing white people for racial justice / Chandra Russo.
Description: Stanford, California : Stanford University Press, [2026] | Includes bibliographical references and index
Identifiers: LCCN 2025030664 (print) | LCCN 2025030665 (ebook) | ISBN 9781503640641 cloth | ISBN 9781503644380 paperback | ISBN 9781503644397 ebook
Subjects: LCSH: Showing Up for Racial Justice (Organization) | Anti-racism—United States | Racial justice—United States | White People—United States—Politics and government | White people—United States—Attitudes | United States—Race relations
Classification: LCC E184.A1 R784 2026 (print) | LCC E184.A1 (ebook)
LC record available at https://lccn.loc.gov/2025030664
LC ebook record available at https://lccn.loc.gov/2025030665

Cover art and design: Jan Šabach

The authorized representative in the EU for product safety and compliance is: Mare Nostrum Group B.V. | Mauritskade 21D | 1091 GC Amsterdam | The Netherlands | Email address: gpsr@mare-nostrum.co.uk | KVK chamber of commerce number: 96249943

Contents

	Acknowledgments	vii
ONE	Organize Your Own	1
TWO	We Stepped into a Long History	37
THREE	White Privilege Is Not an Organizing Strategy	72
FOUR	The Thing That Will Get Us Free	109
FIVE	Accountability Is an Active Thing	150
SIX	What If We Get Called Out?	190
SEVEN	Fight for Our People	228
	Appendix: Methods	239
	Notes	251
	Index	283

Acknowledgments

What right do we have to our fears? We have promises to keep.
—TA-NEHISI COATES[1]

Writing this book has depended upon many interlocutors, both the movement intellectuals whom I met through the course of study as well as fellow scholars with whom I have shared ideas and drafts. Their support and occasional provocations have been invaluable to shaping this book. It is my hope that I have provided an account and set of insights commensurate to the energy, talents, and vulnerability that so many have shared with me.

First and foremost, I thank each of the study participants, both named and unnamed. Anne Dunlap played a special role in helping this research begin. Carla Wallace and Pam McMichael each made space in their busy lives for hours of recorded conversations with me, followed by tens of written correspondences. They reviewed my analyses and my writing, helping me to ensure factual accuracy as well as correct matters of emphasis. Jason David similarly allowed me to interview him over many hours and many months and has continued to be in relationship and conversation with me in the years since. Others whose investments of time and thought in this research went above and beyond include: Clare Bayard, Sonja DeVries, Josie Diebold, Cameron Levin, Liz Sutton, Shelly Tochluk, Scott Winn, and Vitaly.

Many colleagues have listened to me ramble and fret, offering listening, support, feedback, and motivation. They include: Catherine Corrigall-Brown, Crystal Fleming, Emily Mitchell-Eaton, Annie Ferguson, Cate Fosl, Justin Helepololei, Kristen Miller, Paula Miller, Michael Nishimura, Eileen O'Brien, Alicia Simmons, Becky Thompson, and Maura Tumulty. I am also thankful to everyone in the Department of Sociology and Anthropology at Colgate University and the Social Movements Writing Group who read and offered feedback on drafts and, later, titles. A few scholars deserve mention for having read and responded to numerous drafts. David Myers sat with me during some of the murkier moments of this project, offered frank and necessary feedback, and helped me to find my voice. Jessie Daniels, whom I met through this research, has been particularly generous as well as grounding, conferring the reminder when I needed it that, really, "a book is just a book." James Thomas gave enormous doses of enthusiasm since being presented with the paragraph version of this research idea. His deep engagement with the full monograph, and with many draft chapters in between, has been formative.

George Lipsitz has been a most valued mentor and conversation partner for over fifteen years. George read and commented on each of this book's chapters, often through multiple revisions, and his insights have deeply informed the book. I know I am not alone in being a beneficiary of George's tremendous talents and generosity. I have ineffable gratitude for his intellect, wisdom, and kindness.

Scholar and beloved friend Emma Gargroetzi has accompanied me on every aspect of writing this book, from the first seeds of an idea to the final ruminations over the matter of a title. She has offered careful listening, enormous compassion, and important advice when I hit obstacles in the research and writing processes. Thank you, Emma.

I am grateful to grant monies from Colgate University's Social Sciences Division and the Research Council that allowed me to cover my research needs for this project. Colgate also ensured I had a number of students to help keep data and literature organized over the past four years. These students include: Anthony Garcia, Nya Herron, Carrie Huang, McKena Mathews, and Anna Unger.

Two students engaged with this work in truly profound ways. Leah Boykin spent a summer and then several semesters helping me think and talk through emerging findings. I thank her for her work ethic and sharp insights. Olwethu Ezell participated in this research more deeply than I suspect either of us predicted she might. Her endless interest in the book's subject matter as well as her active commitments to collective dignity and justice were contagious, helping me to sustain my own ability to think and write. This book is deeply informed by you, Olwethu.

In moving towards publication, I am immensely grateful to Marcela Maxfield at Stanford University Press, who has read drafts, offered important suggestions, and shepherded this manuscript through the various stages of review and approval. I also thank the anonymous reviewers who helped me to further clarify the book's stakes and contributions. Thank you to the many people who worked on the book's production, including SUP's design team as well as Chris Peterson, Justine Nicole Sargent, Melissa Jauregui Chavez, and Jennifer Gordon.

I also thank the editors, peer reviewers, and journals that challenged and encouraged me as I explored early claims and evidence. Material from Chapter 1 appeared in Chandra Russo, "White People's Activism in US-Based Social Movements for Racial Justice," *Sociology Compass* © 2023 John Wiley & Sons Ltd. https://compass.onlinelibrary.wiley.com/doi/10.1111/soc4.13098). Portions of Chapters 1 and 3 were previously published in Chandra Russo, "White Privilege . . . Is Not an Organizing Strategy": Shifting Frameworks in White People's Antiracist Efforts, *Sociology of Race and Ethnicity* 11, no. 2 (2024): 176–190. Copyright © 2024 American Sociological Association. (http://journals.sagepub.com/doi/10.1177/23326492241265946). Ideas and examples from Chapters 1, 3, and 4 are derived in part from Chandra Russo, "Beyond the Book Club: White Antiracist Organizing Before and After the 2024 Election," *Ethnic and Racial Studies*, © 2025 Taylor and Francis (http://www.tandfonline.com/doi/full/10.1080/01419870.2025.2482715).

While the aforementioned organizers, intellectuals, and institutions have allowed this book to make it into the world, my family has offered me a steadfast foundation during the tumult of research and writing. My mom has given me all her love even as our lives have taken us to different ends of the continent. Diana Blue has offered unconditional support and insight, helping me see that sometimes taking a break, and working on a jigsaw puzzle, can be the solution to a particularly distressing bout of writer's block. Andy Pattison's resolute confidence in me, even when I lack it, is a gift. His political acumen, intellectual breadth, humor, and love keep me anchored among the waves. In some sense, I wrote this book for our most kind and empathetic Sabine. It will be many years before she can engage with its more complex ideas. Still, I hope the stories of resistance we collect today will give her and her cohort some helpful tools, and a dose of inspiration, amidst all that is yet to come.

1 ORGANIZE YOUR OWN

AROUND FIFTY PEOPLE GATHER in Ashland, Kentucky's Central Park on a warm and overcast Saturday afternoon in mid-April for a meeting of Kentucky People's Union (KPU). Handwritten butcher paper posters are duct taped around the pavilion where we meet on picnic benches, mapping out "Long Term Vision" and "Campaign Next Steps." Jill,[1] a white woman in her early twenties, opens the meeting, asking us to share: "How did you find KPU, and why are you here?" Reed, who walks with a cane—also in their early twenties, white, and trans—explains with some emotion being homeless when "KPU found me." This group, they explain, has offered a sense of community, hope, and purpose. Other group members snap in validation. Leilah, a Black woman in her thirties, explains how she is a renter but also works with the homeless. She therefore feels the lack of safe and affordable housing on multiple fronts. Different group members continue to articulate their reasons for seeking housing justice. Many discuss living in substandard conditions. They describe friends and family afraid to complain for fear they will lose their homes. Some in attendance are formerly incarcerated, have been impacted by the opioid crisis, or are living, as one member puts it, "one paycheck away from being out on the streets."

This is the opening of the monthly membership meeting of KPU, which brings together people from this predominantly white region of Central Appalachia to fight for the living conditions their community deserves. Ashland, Kentucky, where this meeting is held, sits just across the river from rural Ohio and less than ten miles north of the state border with West Virginia. Ashland, a town of 20,000, once had a strong union tradition, with a local steel mill being the locus of great prosperity during the mid-twentieth century. Today, it is a community with a deep heart and imaginative spirit, even as its population, like many communities throughout the region, has been economically and environmentally decimated by the coal industry, coupled with capital flight and state abandonment that began in the 1970s.[2] This is precisely the kind of community where those in this study want to be organizing.

This book asks how U.S.-based movement efforts might bring more white people into politically impactful, antiracist action. My search for answers took me to places that range from major coastal cities to America's rust belt to Central Appalachia. KPU engages in one such effort and is a project of the national organization Showing Up for Racial Justice. I begin with this snapshot of KPU because it challenges common assumptions about what white people's antiracism might look like while demonstrating important aspects of the approaches explored in this book. The notion of white people's antiracism, if it is not dismissed outright as an oxymoron,[3] tends to evoke images of book groups and discussion circles, perhaps people attending protests as they arise. We likely predict that members of white antiracist groups are urban and suburban residents, people with college degrees and class privilege, social progressives inclined towards political involvement. We are less likely to conjure an image of poor and working-class people in rural Appalachia, or much of the South for that matter. While this study will also explore the work of urban groups populated by white progressives, formations like KPU help us to think across a broader range of possibilities for bringing more white people into practical antiracist action.

The question of what it might take for significant numbers of white people to divest from white supremacy and invest in multiracial democracy is as urgent as ever. The first decades of the twenty-first century have seen a resurgent white nationalism earn broadening support, part and parcel of a long tradition of white rage and violence in the face of racial progress.[4] Today, a major political party routinely promotes antidemocratic policies and authoritarian candidates in an explicit appeal to white racial grievance. Meanwhile, a bipartisan consensus, undergirded by racialized fears and anxieties, has endorsed policies that divest from public goods and invest in mass imprisonment, militarism, and corporate welfare for over half a century.[5] This occurs as the material returns of racial whiteness are diminishing for everyone but a tiny elite.[6] Yet policies that authorize increasing levels of collective destruction—in the form of economic abandonment, antisocial contracts, and mounting levels of environmental destruction—find broad support, particularly among those who continue to invest in their racial whiteness and believe it to be under threat.[7]

At the same time, new iterations of longstanding racial justice struggles agitate for different politics, social arrangements, and collective ideas about what is possible.[8] Indigenous communities in North America are at the forefront of environmental justice struggles that reveal the enduring impacts of settler colonialism.[9] Migrants the world over draw attention to the contradictions of state systems that invest in human containment while protecting the mobility of capital.[10] The occupied and their allies vocally and bodily oppose militarism, war-making, and humanitarian assaults undergirded by the logics of racial and religious dispossession.[11] One of the more visible and resonant of these movement efforts has been the rise of the Movement for Black Lives, this generation's instantiation of the centuries-long Black freedom struggle.[12] Within this confluence, evidence demonstrates that white Americans are today both more aware of and differentially invested in their whiteness.[13]

The project of seeking to bring more white people into multiracial struggles for collective liberation is not new. If those raced as white can certainly be found within freedom struggles led by Black, Indigenous, and people of color (BIPOC) in the United States,[14] their numbers have generally been exceedingly small. By way of contrast, white majorities have been repeatedly and successfully recruited to align with their whiteness at the cost of subordinated racial groups' safety, dignity, and welfare.[15] Leaders in radical movements for racial justice ranging from the civil rights era to more recent efforts for Indigenous sovereignty, immigrant justice, and the Movement for Black Lives understand these odds. For generations they have asked their white allies to organize for racial justice where racism is most actively reproduced: in the white community.[16]

One organization that has sought to heed this call and has done so at a scale not previously achieved in U.S. history, is Showing Up for Racial Justice (SURJ). SURJ therefore offers a useful window into the tactics, strategies, and logics being wielded in the attempt to bring a critical mass of white people into movement work for racial and economic justice. Through interviews, fieldwork, and relevant media, this study endeavors to explore these approaches, to identify in which contexts they are most helpful, as well as when and how challenges might arise. More specifically, I examine the work of three of SURJ's urban groups, termed "chapters": in Buffalo (New York), Louisville (Kentucky), and Los Angeles, along with two of its projects in the rural South, one based in Ashland (Kentucky) and the other in Shelbyville (Tennessee). I contextualize these more local investigations within the national organization's evolving assessments and activities. My fieldwork, most of which took place with the urban chapters, included over a hundred hours in group meetings, trainings, and campaign activities. I also interviewed fifty-eight racial justice activists, sometimes sitting with the same individual across many months and many hours. Those interviewed include founders and staff of the national organization, participants in the local groups I study, organizers in the Black and Latinx-led organizations with which these groups partner, and activists outside of the organization able to give important additional context regarding the history and contemporary landscape of white antiracist efforts.

In what follows, I begin by tracing how the Black liberation movement and concomitant political developments over the past half century shape the current context for antiracist organizing in U.S. white communities. I pay special attention to the final years of the civil rights era, and to the dissolution of the Student Nonviolent Coordinating Committee (SNCC) in particular, as the moment in which the call to white people to "organize your own" was first most clearly and publicly articulated. I also attend to the rise of dominant liberal approaches to white antiracism as it is against this backdrop that the efforts in this study seek to pose a meaningful alternative. This history allows me to introduce the key concepts and central questions guiding this study before turning to case selection, the organizing approaches examined in this book, and my own orientation to the study.

CALL TO THE WHITE LEFT

It must be offered that white people who desire change in this country should go, where that problem (of racism) is most manifest. That problem is not in the Black community. The white people should go into white communities where the whites have created power for the express purpose of denying Blacks human dignity and self-determination.
 —SNCC Position Paper for the Vine City Project[17]

The idea that white people might best serve the cause of Black liberation by organizing against racism in their own communities was widely publicized in the August 5, 1966, issue of the *New York Times*. Most readers, unfortunately, did not interpret the call as such. In its decision to publish a somewhat fringe, leaked, and unofficial SNCC document, the *Times* was arguably trying to gin up a sense of newsworthiness for its largely white liberal readership; the *Times* seized an opportunity to distort the concept of the Black Power movement as one that summarily dismissed white participation.[18]

Like many newsworthy fabrications, the leaked paper nevertheless held an ounce of truth. There were, in fact, growing concerns within SNCC, the civil rights movement's most grassroots and arguably radical organization, about the perils of an increasing number of white participants—often students who came from outside the South and had a good deal of class privilege.[19] More specifically, the leaked paper suggested that in sending these young white organizers into Black communities, centuries of white supremacist socialization were being reproduced. This was both through expressions of white superiority and paternalism as well as in the deference Black communities were demonstrating toward these white organizers. The paper established its aim, then, as outlining a rationale for the Black Power movement: the right to Black self-determination, self-respect, and collective empowerment through race-based organizing. It also suggested that a new strategy for white involvement was necessary for a new political moment. White volunteers had played an integral role in earlier moments of the struggle for civil rights, the paper suggested, naming specifically the Freedom Summer effort of 1964, but that form of white participation was now "obsolete." The paper acknowledged that while something like "'coalition politics'" might be a useful model for work in the future, "it is meaningless to talk about coalition if there is no one to align ourselves with, because of the lack of organization in white communities."[20]

Since its inception, SNCC had always employed a small number of white organizers. They were generally committed movement participants who understood their role in the Black-led organization as building connections to the dominant, white-led organizations to which they had access, such as universities and service organizations.[21] Moreover, the idea that white people should organize in white communities was not a new proposal. Even Bayard Rustin, no great proponent of the Black Power stance, had called on white people in SNCC to "'go into white communities, work as hard as any Black SNCC worker, to convince white people to support' the civil rights movement."[22] As early as 1961, SNCC itself had invested in small-scale efforts to organize in white southern communities, though with limited success.[23] These experiments are generally forgotten when compared to 1964's Freedom Summer, which introduced white participation to the organization, and to the movement, in ways that were both quantitatively and qualitatively distinct from other efforts.[24]

Freedom Summer was a mass voter registration campaign and a carefully calculated escalation tactic. It brought a substantial number of white, middle-class college students, generally not from the South, into Mississippi's Black communities. Leaders in the southern movement correctly predicted that media coverage of police and vigilantes menacing white, middle-class young people would garner national attention and response in a way that the brutalization of Black people had not. The costs of the campaign, however, were not weighed lightly. Many understood that incidences of racist attacks would go up. There was also substantial consternation about bringing large numbers of unseasoned white activists into a Black-led organization, and even more so about introducing such participants to the embattled communities in which the long-term, careful work of organizing was taking place. Insofar as organizers predicted both great benefits and high costs, they were correct. Freedom Summer was pivotal in the struggle to secure national civil rights legislation. The campaign may have also precipitated SNCC's ultimate demise.[25]

Some historians warn that overemphasizing the racial tensions that arose in SNCC misses the much more important story: white people were welcomed into the southern movement with a remarkable level of grace and generosity.[26] Their experiences in interracial movement would transform them as well as their future activist trajectories.[27] The proposal, then, that there should be what Amy Sonnie and James Tracy term "a racial 'division of labor' within the Left" was not unanimous but signified "the tactical difference between the civil rights and Black Power movements."[28] It also evinced a movement at the crossroads.

A significant set of demands for civil and legal rights had been won in the passage of civil rights legislation in 1964 and 1965. Many in the movement, however, did not envision the right to be integrated into the liberal state and capitalist market as their ultimate ends. If organizations and their leaders certainly differed in regards to questions of strategy, many drew clear connections between racial oppression at home and the murderous operations of war and imperialism abroad.[29] There was also a growing analysis that racial justice could not be achieved separately from wide-ranging economic justice, not just for aggrieved racialized communities but for poor whites as well.[30] As Paul Le Blanc and Michael D. Yates argue, "the activist wing" of the civil rights movement had always understood the fight for legal recognition as the first stage in a much longer vision for societal transformation, which included tackling issues of economic justice, channeling the struggle against the Jim Crow system into an even more massive struggle (through a coming together of the anti-racist and labor movements) for jobs for all, an end to poverty, and democratic regulation of the economy, which would involve a transition from capitalism to socialism.[31]

By this account, the most visionary and active sectors of the Black liberation movement were also anti-imperialist and anticapitalist in their aims. Movement leaders understood that white racism can manifest as personal prejudice, collectivized hatred, and institutional exclusion and violence. They also assessed whiteness as a political project, one that had effectively won large groups of people—those raced as white—to align with a system that costs white people significant moral and psychic injury,[32] while harming majorities, undercutting democracy, and forestalling broad-based movements that can win a different social contract.

THE PROBLEM OF RACIAL WHITENESS

The problem of whiteness to movements for collective liberation is embedded in the creation of the white racial category itself. In North America, scholars demonstrate how a small planter elite in (settler) colonial Virginia enshrined whiteness in law, custom, and norms so as to prevent the relatively common rebellions being staged by European and African workers, who united to resist their conditions.[33] Suppressing such resistance required a long-term, multipronged strategy. In addition to shifting the labor pool away from indentured Europeans and toward kidnapped Africans, the creation of racial categories served as a logic of exploitation and extraction and a methodology of social control. The making of the "Negro" rendered African people as property. The making of the "Indian" authorized slaughter and land theft. "Whiteness," by contrast, became the unique indicator of full humanity.

For European settlers, a consolidating system of white supremacy offered an incentive structure for aligning with the planter elite. In a society organized around enslavement, whiteness allowed some to oversee plantation workforces and run slave patrols. Measures were taken to prevent both marital intermixing and competition between free white labor and the labor of enslaved Africans. Even poor whites had the privilege of acquiring Native American lands as personal property.[34] If the terms of white supremacy evolve and shift, what Charles Mills termed "the racial contract" remains intact.[35] The vast majority of those eligible for whiteness collectively align with a political system that elevates those deemed white over everyone else.

Following the formal abolition of slavery, W. E. B. Du Bois assessed how racial whiteness dashed the promise of multiracial democracy that was briefly glimpsed in the reconstruction era. As one of his more famous insights, Du Bois identified the "public and psychological wage" afforded uniquely to white people. Whites alone were allowed to serve on juries and testify in courtrooms. They made up police forces and received more lenient treatment under the law, especially in response to vile and violent acts against "the Negro." They were granted entrance to the best schools and social clubs. They were addressed by title. Such a wage could only be had through both insult and injury to "the Negro"; the result, as Du Bois put it, was "two groups of workers with practically identical interests who hate and fear each other so deeply and persistently and who are kept so far apart that neither sees anything of common interest."[36]

The creation and reification of racial categories has thus been a very successful effort to thwart worker unity. The concept of racial capitalism nevertheless insists we understand race beyond just an elite tool to divide the working class by demonstrating how racial categorization and capital accumulation are co-constitutive. This is because capitalism requires that wealth be extracted from people's labor, land, and resources; it relies upon logics that "separate forms of humanity so that they may be connected in terms that feed capital."[37] Thus even before European settlement in the Americas, and the construction of whiteness and Blackness as such, early capitalist development in mercantilist Europe accentuated existing social differences so as to support economic relations.[38] What the historical record suggests is that there has never been, nor can there be, a version of capitalism that does not require the separation, segregation, and making hierarchical of human groups. In practical terms, there is no capitalism that is not also racial as well as gendered.[39]

This also means that while the seeds of racial whiteness were arguably sewn in the specific context of American slavery and settler colonial expansion, the development and maintenance of white supremacist capitalism needs to be understood as having numerous agents and far-ranging expressions. It is simultaneously political, economic, social, cultural, and even psychic. For one, whiteness cannot properly be understood as *solely* a top-down strategy to divide working and poor people. Rather, across class, those eligible for whiteness have for centuries taken up the mantel of whiteness and infused it with personal and collective meaning.[40] Entire ethnic communities have labored in tandem with state and market forces in order to "become white."[41] These efforts, both personal and collective, private and structural, manifest in what George Lipsitz terms "the possessive investment in whiteness," defined not only as a powerful set of racialized logics and personal prejudices, but also institutional arrangements at every level of society with real material impacts.[42] Throughout U.S. history, whiteness itself has consistently been treated as a kind of valuable property, enshrined in legal statute,[43] subsidized by the state and market,[44] and dependent on stripping assets from other racialized groups.

It is also true, however, that in the post–civil rights era, the possessive investment in whiteness has propelled the dismantling of the welfare state and divestment from public goods. By fiercely guarding a sense of white entitlement, white majorities have repeatedly opposed policies that would improve their social, political, and economic prospects and have done so because they fear BIPOC communities would fare better as well.[45] In this, there seems a need to theorize the enduring enticements of white racism as both social and psychic. As Paula Ioanide builds upon the signature insights of Frantz Fanon, a white supremacist culture coheres around affective, libidinal, and often non-consciously held associations; people of all races socialized under white supremacy are recruited "to fear people of color and to identify with punishing, containing, and dissociating from them."[46] Such identifications fuel the rage and organized backlash that follow every advance towards multiracial democracy and economic justice.[47] Yet with a shift away from New Deal–type state investments and towards a less regulated, global economy, the fierce clinging to a sense of white entitlement may be growing more collectively destructive even for those who have the protections and privileges of whiteness.[48]

Here a number of things are true at once about the dividends and costs of racial whiteness. When compared to other racialized groups, white people are, on the aggregate, afforded better educations and socially structured health outcomes. They are given more opportunities to accrue wealth, in large part because of the enduring impacts and continuing practices of a racially unequal housing market. Their votes are weighed more heavily, and they are less likely to be disenfranchised. They are less susceptible to state violence in the forms of heightened everyday surveillance, the criminal punishment system, and exposure to direct physical violence than are their BIPOC counterparts. They are also more protected from the slow violence of environmental harms, afforded cleaner drinking water, and more breathable air.[49]

This is not the same, however, as saying that white supremacy is good for white people. Thinkers have long observed that whiteness does white people immense social and psychic harm.[50] The political alliance of whiteness is also accruing fewer material benefits today for anyone other than society's most wealthy and elite factions.[51] Still, the ability, and perhaps willingness, for most white people to perceive such indicators, and align themselves with a different vision for organizing society, seemingly remains as elusive as ever.

ANSWER FROM THE WHITE LEFT

In response to the 1960s call to white people to organize their own, a few important efforts did emerge. SNCC activists Bob and Dottie Zellner, for example, launched projects in white working-class communities, first in the South, and later in the Northeast and Midwest.[52] Other important experiments were tried in Chicago, Philadelphia, and New York City as predominantly poor and working white people organized around their immediate material interests while aligning with anticapitalist, anti-imperialist BIPOC-led efforts.[53] One of the more storied of these is the case of the Young Patriots, a group of Appalachian migrants who worked in coalition with the Black Panthers and Puerto Rican Young Lords to forge the original "Rainbow Coalition."[54]

Moreover, Students for a Democratic Society (SDS), which had a similar organizational timeline to SNCC, and emerged for a time as the largest organization among white activists of the so-called New Left,[55] would itself ultimately split around the role of the white revolutionary in anti-imperialist, anticapitalist, antiracist struggle. Some in the group aligned with an analysis articulated by many on the Black Left that white movement participants should aim to bring a broad base of poor whites into a multiracial class-based alliance. Others in SDS, however, believed that racial whiteness prevented poor whites from being a key component of any revolutionary struggle and that smaller and more militant efforts were required.[56] Such debates continue among movement participants today.

The most skeptical stance towards mass organizing of the white poor would point to instances ranging from trade union organizing to the building of community organizations, in which those raced as white have chosen the psychic and material enticements of white supremacy over the radical potential of multiracial solidarity.[57] A different perspective might suggest that organizing the white working class is not itself a doomed strategy, but has been approached in ways that have downplayed social difference, and white racism specifically, at great peril. For example, labor historian Herbert Hill documents how U.S.-based worker organizations ultimately re-instantiated racist formations and practices due to having neglected workers' "other identities which carry substantive social meaning [such as] race, religion, ethnicity, gender, skill level, and language."[58] A similar dynamic afflicted some of the community organizing projects of Saul Alinksy, who famously sought to avoid bringing "ideology," including an explicit rebuke of white racism, into local campaign efforts.[59] Research demonstrates that this tendency to avoid discussions of race continues to dog even multiracial social justice organizations, often in ways that undercut ultimate efficacy.[60] As this book will go on to examine, when and how to raise the matter of white racism when organizing white people is not a simple question, but remains a central one.

Without dismissing the important small-scale efforts by white activists to organize their own in the 1960s and 70s, no mass effort emerged. The reasons for this are myriad. Some include white activists' distaste with white communities, with whom they had experienced profound alienation and often felt disgust.[61] Many also despaired at the prospect of being distanced from the predominantly Black but racially integrated beloved community that they had found in the South.[62] There is also good reason to suggest that increasingly hostile political conditions and violent state repression pushed the Black liberation movement, as well as other anticapitalist, anti-imperialist, and anti- (settler) colonial efforts, into what might be understood as a period of movement abeyance.[63] From this perspective, it was not unreasonable for Mark Warren to observe in 2010 that one of the challenges facing whites who wished to collectively align with racial justice efforts in the aftermath of the civil rights era was that "there is no visible national movement with which to identify."[64]

THE "PRISON FIX" AND THE MOVEMENT FOR BLACK LIVES

Racism is like a Cadillac, they bring out a new model every year.
—MALCOLM X

Here it is helpful to briefly explain how powerful decision-makers attempted to resolve the capitalist crises of the early 1970s while quelling resistance efforts to imperial and white supremacist rule.[65] Such efforts shaped the evolution of the Black liberation struggle and the rise of the Movement for Black Lives, which fundamentally influences the efforts explored in this book. This part of political history also highlights how the tactics that maintain white supremacy are ever evolving. Indeed, by the end of the 1960s, sophisticated Black protest strategies in the U.S. South, as one part of a multitactic, multigenerational struggle, had won a moral consensus. No longer was it acceptable to use old-fashioned racial slurs or KKK-style tactics in polite society. Scholars thus document the rise of a new era of colorblind racism in which white majorities do not believe themselves to be racist, but racial inequalities continue to amass.[66]

In the U.S. context, a right-wing assault on the advances won by various anticapitalist liberation struggles in general, and Black liberation efforts in particular, was achieved on colorblind terms. Politicians used thinly veiled racial appeals to ignite anti-Black associations and fears across the dominant public and to secure new power alignments.[67] One of the most successful early efforts in this regard can be found in the Southern Strategy, first articulated in Nixon's 1968 campaign for president. The aims were to recruit white Democrats, both across the South and in northern cities, to change partisan allegiance by casting racialized groups and the poor—along with single women and mothers, sexual minorities, immigrants, and some youth—as an internal threat to safety and stability.[68] As one of Nixon's advisors John Ehrlichman has infamously been quoted, the strategy depended on a "subliminal appeal to the anti-black voter,"[69] articulated first in a campaign but ultimately integrated into generations of bipartisan approaches backed by massive state and corporate investments. Discursive maneuvers to construct racialized, gendered, and classed threats to society were soon codified in public policy; phrases like "law and order," "the war on drugs," and "the welfare queen" came to underwrite a decades-long build up in policing and imprisonment, coupled with state disinvestment in public welfare.

Ruth Wilson Gilmore reminds us that the "prison fix" was a response to a constellation of complex dynamics.[70] Yes, the insurgencies of the 1960s and 70s, as well as the impetus to quell Black advancement, are part of the story. At least as central, however, are efforts to resolve the capitalist crises of the early 1970s, in which profit rates began to fall while inflation rose. Akin to how state investments in public infrastructure and war-making had temporarily pulled the economy out of the Great Depression, the United States, along with allies around the world, needed a new solution. Their answer was neoliberal restructuring, in which the state divests from public goods and social wealth while investing in market welfare. By harnessing state power to market interests, neoliberalism effectively funnels wealth from the bottom up. Inequality rises, democracy is undercut, and social unrest is inevitable.[71]

Prisons and policing thus offer short-term fixes to the problems neoliberalism itself creates, while exacerbating rather than ameliorating social harms. The carceral state[72] serves to suppress popular unrest, while warehousing capitalism's growing "surplus population," a racialized designation for those whose labor has been deemed undesirable or unnecessary.[73] Investments in prisons and policing create jobs in the face of industry closures and capital flight; make use of land previously considered unusable or undesirable because of environmental harms; and give an expedient platform to unimaginative and desperate leaders who can propose few actual solutions to ongoing crises.[74] In this sense, carceral logics also serve to win consent for neoliberalism's multiplicative harms. In the face of increasing precarity and alienation for the majority, the state conjures racialized images of the criminal, terrorist, immigrant, and urban poor, and then promises a form of psychic security and gratification in their capture and punishment.[75] In turn, the structures and practices that grow dispossession and despair are cast as both necessary and inevitable, as if alternatives are unimaginable.

Yet alternatives are always being imagined, proposed, and enacted—in art, music, and literature;[76] daily forms of small-scale resistance;[77] and mass popular struggle. Such mass struggle, in the form of the contemporary Movement for Black Lives (M4BL), is one of today's most visible forms of collective refusal to neoliberal carceral expansions, undergirded as they are by anti-Black sentiment, state violence, and organized abandonment. Without attempting a movement genesis or overview,[78] it is worth lifting up some of M4BL's central emphases as these also fundamentally shape how the groups in this study have arrived at their vision, approaches, and even practical, on-the-ground partnerships.

Barbara Ransby suggests that M4BL centers (1) anticapitalist critique, (2) contemporary abolitionism, and (3) "a radical politics of intersectionality."[79] Akin to its movement predecessors, M4BL connects the pursuit of Black liberation with a thoroughgoing critique of racial capitalism and continues the unfinished work of abolition begun in the era of chattel slavery, through Jim Crow, and now positioned in response to the neoliberal carceral state. At the same time, M4BL is distinct from dominant strains of earlier Black-led mass struggle in that it centers a feminist (and queer) emphasis,[80] constituting the first time that "Black feminist politics have defined the frame for a multi-issue, Black-led mass struggle that did not primarily or exclusively focus on women."[81]

M4BL therefore enacts the analysis first articulated by the Combahee River Collective nearly half a century ago, which suggested that, "If Black women were free, it would mean that everyone else would have to be free since our freedom would necessitate the destruction of all the systems of oppression."[82] This central idea was rearticulated nearly verbatim by Alicia Garza when she, alongside queer Black feminist organizers Opal Tometi and Patrisse Cullors, explained the necessity of #Blacklivesmatter: "When Black people get free, everybody gets free."[83] Because of the singularity that gendered anti-Blackness has played in the ever-evolving operations of global racial capitalism,[84] Black queer feminist politics does not just benefit a small subset of society's most marginalized but humanity itself.

AWARENESS RAISING

Situating contemporary antiracist efforts among white people requires at least one additional discussion regarding race-conscious learning activities. A number of different and sometimes contradictory motivations led to the diffusion of such trainings. On the one hand, many activists, scholars, and educators with connections to racial justice struggles identified how confronting "the invisibility of white privilege and whiteness in American culture" could serve as an important form of political education.[85] The logics of colorblind racism mask a racially uneven playing field, while dominant socialization continues to cast whiteness as the raceless norm against which other racialized groups are negatively measured. Equipping white people to understand the role of racial whiteness under white supremacy, and the fact that silence and inaction are akin to complicity, can generate important forms of counterhegemonic consciousness.

The rise of awareness trainings can also be understood as a response to the frontal assault on affirmative action begun in the 1980s. As policy gains and legal avenues for redressing racial inequity were officially dismantled, privatized diversity initiatives were shorn up as something of a supplement, albeit a generally defanged and inadequate one, increasingly co-opted and subverted to appease white investments in the status quo.[86] Today, the proliferation of diversity trainings, consultants, and nonprofits has become a veritable industry unto itself.[87] This is not to conflate the distinct meanings, models, and aims of a contemporary workplace DEI training with those of a 1990s feminist social service agency.[88] Nevertheless, as understandings of diversity,[89] multiculturalism,[90] and now "antiracism" have been further extracted from political struggle in general and intersectional, anticapitalist, and anti-imperialist critique more specifically,[91] some commonalities do emerge.

For middle-class liberal whites in particular, antiracism is increasingly treated as a private good—an identity to be cultivated, displayed through proper modes of speech and comportment, felt as some combination of guilt and smugness, and instantiated through moral distancing from lesser, more racist whites.[92] This is not to belittle the very real epistemic, moral, and emotional challenges that arise for (a relatively small group of) white activists whose long-term commitments to racial justice include grappling with the horrors committed in the name of whiteness.[93] It is instead to argue that reducing antiracism to a matter of private mindset rather than a framework for collective struggle can lead to understandings and practices that are individualizing, moralizing, and exclusionary, with depoliticizing and demobilizing results.

Jeb Middlebrook attributes some of these troubles to the academy itself, where studies of whiteness shifted from "white supremacy in relation to capitalism, and antiracism in relation to multiracial and anti-capitalist organizing [to] an increasing interest in white privilege and white identity formation."[94] Indeed, a good deal of social scientific research has come to define white people's "antiracism" as a cognitive and moral viewpoint on the world, if one that should be coupled with at least the motivation to engage in personal and collective action. There is a significant literature exploring how white people, as the beneficiaries of white supremacy, might develop antiracist consciousness and identities, often from a social psychological lens,[95] though with somewhat unclear results. For instance, while some community-building and dialogue-based pedagogies do seem to sow the seeds of antiracist consciousness and a desire to take action among white students,[96] a good deal of evidence points to the range of discursive, cognitive, and emotional maneuvers whites use to prevent themselves from seeing racial realities as they are.[97] Moreover, scholars and educators suggest that most trainings lack sufficient attention to practical, collective, or politically impactful action. As antiracist scholar and educator Derald Wing Sue observes, "although most training programs continue to grapple with self-awareness, I submit that commitment to antiracist actions is either neglected or discussed in highly general, philosophical, and aspirational terms."[98] Consciousness-raising can be an important element of social change work, yet so too must be strategies for what to *do* with new forms of knowledge.

Other observers take a more thoroughgoing critique, suggesting that some of the central lessons and practices guiding approaches to antiracist practice for white people actually demobilize and depoliticize their audiences. In this regard, one particular text, and its accompanying learning activities, serves as an important touchstone: Peggy McIntosh's highly influential essay likening white privilege to an "invisible knapsack" of unearned advantages. While hardly the first to identify the fact that whiteness confers privileges in a society founded on white supremacy, McIntosh's work was important in its accessibility. Readers were offered tangible examples of how white privilege might shape their daily interactions, from not being surveilled when trying to shop to being able to choose a band-aid that matches their skin color.[99] As a teaching tool, a list of how white privilege can shape personal and interactional processes was an important contribution. It arguably met the moment of an ascendant form of colorblind racism,[100] raised awareness about white dominance in a number of intellectual and movement spaces, and invited a generation of white progressives into a piece of antiracist consciousness.

At the same time, scholars and activists across a number of settings have identified how, in practice, "a white privilege pedagogy" may ultimately inhibit, rather than enable, white people from moving into meaningful racial justice work. The limitations here are both analytic and practical. Some worry that the focus on white racial privilege occludes the mechanisms that uphold white supremacy, "[mistaking] the symptoms for the causes,"[101] and focusing attention away from the histories and continuing processes that perpetuate racial domination.[102] The corollary to this is that white people focus on how they might individually divest of privilege in their own lives, often to the exclusion of considering how they might collectively invest in efforts to make the social order more racially just.[103] This tendency is redoubled by McIntosh's own learning program design, adopted across educational and activist spaces, and oriented around "the privilege confessional."[104] Individuals are encouraged to publicly name the fact of their privilege, a ritual that often becomes a stand-in for other forms of more meaningful systemic analysis and political behavior.[105]

The privilege confessional is something of an exemplar for how dominant approaches to antiracist practice, particularly among whites, have in some ways missed the mark. A generous interpretation is that well-intentioned people get stuck in analysis paralysis. A more cynical reading might suggest that "feeling good about feeling bad"[106] becomes an excuse to uphold the status quo. In the context of settler colonialism, for example, Eve Tuck and K. Wayne Yang point to such maneuvers as "settler moves to innocence,"[107] a practice that replaces meaningful political activity with the performance of moral right. Tuck and Yang explain how "the cultivation of critical consciousness" often forecloses settler engagement with the kinds of redistributive actions and policies that would constitute meaningful and just remedy, such as "the more uncomfortable task of relinquishing stolen land."[108] The important work of political education, which may have originated in the service of collective action, here becomes a substitute for engaging the material bases of others' political demands.

If feminists importantly taught us that private and personal matters can also be political,[109] neoliberal logics can deceive us into believing that all politics can and should be privatized and personalized. This trickery can be witnessed as the semantics of solidarity are disseminated, diluted, and distorted across broader swaths of the public. For example, J. E. Sumerau and colleagues find that college students adopt the mantle of "ally" to marginalized groups as a "moral identity" that then excuses them from taking action to challenge systems of oppression.[110] Following more recent and visible instances of Black-led mobilization, liberal whites increasingly claim for themselves the identity of "antiracist," even when other evidence suggests their great adherence to colorblind racist ideologies.[111] Indeed, the performance of moral right through proper speech practices can be rearticulated to bolster white supremacy. Ranita Ray points to a new brand of "race-conscious racism," that "allows white people to treat race-talk as racial justice . . . positioning themselves as both morally superior and anti-racist" while excusing their own continuing complicity in racist ideologies, practices, and institutions.[112]

It is also the case that approaches that mistake antiracism for an individual moral posture are predicated on the same kinds of classed exclusion and disavowal that have always constituted racial whiteness. At a quite practical level, the learning opportunities that tend to afford white people access to refined forms of race-talk—book groups, diversity trainings, college classrooms—are often the purview of class-privileged whites. Moreover, the opportunity to cultivate pity and self-flagellation in response to others' suffering may presume a largely middle-class experience of whiteness. As Shannon Sullivan observes, "white guilt is a form of cultural capital not readily available to lower-class white people."[113] This connects to a larger argument about the meanings of whiteness in the post–civil rights era, in which proper white behavior includes being nominally offended by overt and explicit racism. "Good white people" do not engage in such conduct.[114] The hegemonic white subject—middle- or owning-class, properly gendered, and able-bodied—is positioned against the poor white, imagined as backwards, embodying moral failure and sin, and themselves at the edges of proper whiteness.[115] The poor white is today conjured as the beating heart of true racism, part of Hillary Clinton's infamous "basket of deplorables."[116] The argument here is not that poor white people cannot be racist. Rather, it suggests that a moralizing, individualizing, and ultimately power-evasive approach to antiracism actually perpetuates that which it purportedly seeks to disrupt: the power hierarchies and social boundaries quintessential of white supremacy. In this context, efforts to perform proper whiteness—whether as articulated by white nationalists or white antiracists—find unsettling commonalities. They shore up exclusionary and often essentializing meanings of racial whiteness.[117]

This may all seem quite academic, but it has real ramifications for how people approach antiracist pursuits. When practices selected under the aegis of antiracism devolve into personal identity cultivation and moral absolution, the results are ineffective, alienating, and even harmful. A strategy to move more white people into effective, enduring antiracist work needs to find ways to involve a broader base of white people in the work of multiracial collective liberation, rather than absolve individuals from their complicity in racist systems. This is because white supremacy is not centrally about good and bad people, but about relations of power. White supremacy includes the circulation of beliefs, prejudices, and storylines, which manifest in personal decisions and interpersonal interactions. Yet as racial liberation movements have long demonstrated, white supremacy is also anchored in unjust policies and institutions, procedures and material arrangements that benefit the few while harming the many. Efforts to bring more people into the work of racial justice must therefore be anchored in both an analysis of systems of power and a commitment to collective action, arguably the only form of behavior capable of adequately challenging a regime predicated on increasing economic precarity, ecological degradation, social alienation, and antidemocratic politics.[118]

KEY QUESTIONS AND CASE SELECTION

This selective history of antiracist organizing in the United States points to some of the central and enduring dilemmas that this book explores, ones that are of interest to scholars and movement participants alike. Many of these are akin to those that emerged with Black leaders' call to the white Left. For example, what are the best vehicles for organizing for racial justice in white communities, and do these differ based on which white communities are being reached? And how is racial justice defined and operationalized? What relation, if any, should it have to economic justice, for example?

Other important questions arise with the notion of a racial division of labor in movement work, proposed in the late 1960s, and encouraged by many contemporary efforts. Some of these questions are quite broad: How do movements balance the prefigurative vision of multiracial democracy, in which people of all races work together, with the need to draw in those raced as white in particular ways? And what is the appropriate role for white people, given the fact of their racial privilege, in BIPOC-led struggle? Rephrased in practical terms: Who makes decisions, about what, and in which contexts? Do white participants always defer to leaders of color? What happens, for instance, when different BIPOC leaders make competing demands?

Finally, if many efforts to develop antiracist awareness among white people have been taken up in ways that are often individualizing and depoliticizing, they emerge from a good impulse. We live in a society with few opportunities for white people to engage in antiracist learning and socialization. Moreover, political education and personal reflection are valued across many liberation traditions. In this context, how do organizations seeking to push white people into racial justice work balance the role of awareness raising with the necessity of action? As importantly, what are the most effective and durable forms of learning that can aid white people in deepening their commitment to action?

If the questions guiding this study are specific in some ways to white involvement in racial justice efforts, they also have broad applicability. Nearly all movements wrestle with how to grow their base of constituents and how to unite differently situated people towards common ends. Numerous political efforts grapple with how narrowly to define their aims. The question of how political efforts should weigh different stakeholders' perspectives and orientations is as alive as ever.[119] Many social struggles, and particularly those in the contemporary moment, navigate the affordances and drawbacks of introspection, and even personal healing, in larger political efforts.[120]

In order to explore these questions, I decided to study those who are currently grappling with them in very practical ways and have often done so over a long period of time: the leaders and groups of the federated national organization Showing Up for Racial Justice (SURJ). I selected SURJ for reasons of scale, endurance, and contemporary relevance. As measured in terms of people, resources, and geographic reach, SURJ is the largest effort to explicitly engage in antiracist organizing in white communities in U.S. history. This scale, as well as the early organizational decision to remain decentralized in some important ways, means that SURJ encompasses a diversity of groups and efforts. This allowed me to draw out central patterns in contemporary white antiracist efforts as well as identify meaningful points of contrast. As an example, while the urban and rural groups in this study share an understanding that racial and economic justice are inextricably connected, they are also quite different in terms of how membership is imagined and built as well as how issues are prioritized.

SURJ is also the most enduring contemporary effort seeking to organize in white communities at scale. This relative longevity allowed me to study efforts that have evolved significantly over time, affording a lens on what opportunities and challenges have arisen with distinct strategies and in different movement moments. This is not to discount other important antiracist efforts among white activists, many of which helped to shape both SURJ as an organization and its key personnel. These organizations, however, have often focused on learning and introspection or have remained relatively small, and often intentionally so.

I also selected SURJ as an organization that can help to illuminate what is specific and new about the terrain of struggle for racial justice. The organization has grown largely in tandem with the Movement for Black Lives, in an era of more naked forms of white racist extremism than we have seen in decades. We are no longer squarely in the era of colorblindness. Nor would it be appropriate to suggest we have returned to Jim Crow segregation and logics. Movements for justice and liberation need to respond to the way social understandings and forms of domination evolve over time. A study of SURJ allows me to do just this.

Of course, I cannot offer a comprehensive portrait of a complex and growing organization. Instead, and much like scholars working on similar projects, albeit in earlier eras,[121] I have in some sense sampled on the dependent variable—identifying the specific groups and tactics that exemplify best principles, which I elaborate in the methodological appendix. The point is not that one organization has arrived at complete and conclusive answers, but that the people and groups in this book have a depth of experience, hard won through time and experimentation. Their work and insights offer valuable lessons for scholars of race, whiteness, and movements, as well as for the growing number of us who are alarmed at the multiplying ways in which white supremacy, racial domination, and organized hate shape our society and politics.

PARAMETERS OF AN APPROACH

The first time I spoke to SURJ co-founder Carla Wallace in fall of 2021 was on Zoom; most of the interviews for this study were conducted virtually. Her smile was wide and her demeanor warm. She loved to tell stories, and she told them well. After at least an hour of me probing into her own life history, the various movements she had been a part of, and the important people and events that shaped her, Carla explained SURJ's evolution: "there are kind of these pivotal questions that faced us at each point. They are strategic questions, and they're questions of vision. Maybe they're even some spirit questions there." While these questions emerged explicitly for SURJ as it developed, they are matters that have confronted all efforts to organize in the white community for multiracial democracy. These include: *why* organize white people? *which* white people? and *how* do we organize? As Carla quipped, "because there are a lot of white people in this country [and] because there are lots of ways, all of them with their value, that people are doing work on antiracism. What is the *how* for us? What are we seeing as the need?" The following chapters of this book largely elaborate on key aspects of that *how* question. For now, I'll look at the questions of *why* and *which* white people to introduce key features of the approaches explored in this book.

Why White People?
Much of this chapter has already outlined in extended form the central reasons for organizing in white communities towards antiracist ends. It is therefore worth discussing the somewhat more contentious why of the race-based affinity model SURJ adopts: Why organize in predominantly white formations? There are certainly reasons to take pause at the prospect of white people organizing other white people towards the ends of racial justice. Doesn't a race-based organizing model reinforce racial essentialism and the politics of division? Will appealing to white people *as* white people center the white feelings and logics that have reinforced supremacy and subordination for centuries? Shouldn't we be suspect of white people's ability to assess and act on forms of violence and injustice not most directly impacting them? The answer to all of these questions is *perhaps*. Here I offer some introductory logic behind the racial affinity organizing model and its role in multiracial movement building.

The first rationale for white affinity organizing is revealed by the disputes facing movement actors at the end of the 1960s. There has been broad consensus among racial justice leaders that white people need to organize against racism.[122] Drawing large numbers of white people into movement spaces, however, can easily overwhelm organizations that wish to be run for and by BIPOC. As one example that many study participants relayed to me, when unprecedented mass mobilizations followed the murders of Breonna Taylor and George Floyd in 2020, a number of Black leaders in local sites asked SURJ organizers to "come collect the white folks and give them a political home." While there is a need to draw more white people into politically impactful racial justice work, many activists of color are seeking to build political power in their own communities. They do not have the desire, the necessity, nor the capacity to be organizing large groups of white people.

Connected to this is the idea that those who are white often benefit from spaces in which to explore dominant white socialization. This is the principle guiding some awareness-raising efforts, rooted in an insight that is not itself ill-founded. In this way, one strength of predominantly white antiracist spaces is in filling a need, often identified by people of color,[123] for white people to "[discuss] racism, their own racist behaviors, white supremacy, and their emotions,"[124] in a way that does not risk harming people of color or derailing larger movement efforts. Discussion circles may not be a sufficient way for white people to engage in antiracist struggle. Nevertheless, building relationships with similarly positioned people with whom to learn and get feedback can be a support to, rather than a substitute for, collective action.

In this regard, white affinity organizing can be viewed as following similar, if not symmetrical, principles to other forms of race-based organizing. Black Lives Matter co-founder Alicia Garza, for instance, offers the following reflections on the utility of Black affinity groups, particularly in "Black-Brown" solidarity efforts:

> Movements that bring together people of all races are vital to building the world we deserve. However, sometimes we are so concerned with coming together that we don't do the work to stay together. Like any good relationship, unity takes effort—together, and apart.[125]

Garza here underscores the important intervention that identity-based movements have long proposed, and that the Movement for Black Lives, as a queer feminist Black liberation effort, broadly espouses. In the effort to bring divergent constituencies together to challenge systems of oppression, participants benefit from building community, strategizing around certain tasks, and reflecting on process with those who are similarly positioned to themselves. For this reason, identity caucuses can be an important part of mass struggle, such as in the labor movement.[126]

There are certainly important distinctions in the logic undergirding racial affinity groups for those who have been systematically oppressed, marginalized, and violated as opposed to those who have been structurally empowered, privileged, and protected. Nevertheless, some of Garza's comments are still relevant across groups, particularly her insight that unity takes effort and that some of this work should be done apart. By honing knowledge, skills, and relationships with others who have been socialized as white, participants in white affinity groups may be engaged in useful preparation to show up more effectively in multiracial struggle.

The third argument for white affinity organizing is based on a blunter calculus regarding political efficacy and racialized risk. Building a critical mass of white people to engage in multiracial efforts for collective liberation means growing the number of people involved. This can only be achieved by proactively reaching out to new and sometimes unlikely people. The legacies of racism and residential segregation mean communities are geographically sorted by both race and class. In this confluence, there is good reason to believe that predominantly white communities are more likely to be receptive to white strangers and spokespersons than to those who appear non-white. It is also the case that white people face less risk—both from vituperative neighbors and from the prospect of residents calling in law enforcement—then would those who appear phenotypically not to be white.

Beyond its central logics, however, it is important to acknowledge that the approaches to white affinity organizing I encountered in this study are best understood as contextual, fluid, and ultimately temporary. The goal is not to develop all-white organizations but to build political power by recruiting a predominantly white base into a larger multiracial justice movement. None of the groups I studied only counted white participants, though constituencies shifted depending on location, campaign, and time frame. For example, in the case of Kentucky People's Union, a group begun in a predominantly white rural region has nevertheless become functionally multiracial in terms of its leadership and membership. Moreover, even as most participants agreed that race-based organizing has been a useful approach to date, and particularly necessary during the height of previous mobilizations in the Movement for Black Lives (2014–2020), there are emerging cross-racial discussions regarding whether race-based organizing will continue to be the best strategy moving forward.

There is an additional important element of the white affinity approach explored in this book that may be obvious to some readers but deserves explicit mention. The three urban chapters in this study, as well as the national organization and its rural projects, work in direct, interactive political partnerships with BIPOC-led organizations. These organizations share with SURJ a common political analysis, one that was described to me as broadly "anticapitalist, feminist, and abolitionist." This fact anchors my methodology and shapes my findings.

Which White People?

The second question that white antiracist efforts have to address, whether they do so intentionally or not, is which white people to target. Most have understandably started with low-hanging fruit: those already doing antiracist work or seeking ways to get involved. This was an early and obvious constituency for SURJ as well. Of course, this approach is ill-suited for growing the base of antiracist white involvement, which has been SURJ's explicit aim since its formation. As Executive Director Erin Heaney put it, "we don't have enough power, and we're not going to have enough power as a movement only by organizing the white people that have come to us. We've got to really strategically be organizing people who are not yet with us." A commitment to growth requires reaching out to those who might not seek an antiracist space for white people of their own volition.

To these ends, SURJ identifies poor and working-class white communities as those with whom they most desire to organize. In terms of regional specificity, there is also a focus on rural places, particularly in the U.S. South and Appalachia. The rationale behind these choices is multilayered. As Anne Dunlap, SURJ's director of faith organizing at the time of our interview, explained to me, while "white supremacy and racial capitalism" most directly harm "Black, Indigenous, and other people of color," these systems

> also deeply impact rural, poor, and working-class white people . . . because of the way that race has been used as a wedge to drive poor and working-class white people apart from folks of color to be able to make common cause, to challenge the power of the white wealthy.

In this way, SURJ joins with numerous thinkers from the Black liberation tradition to diagnose that, among white communities, the poor and working classes, particularly in the rural South, have the most to gain from joining in multiracial challenges to a system of white supremacy and racial capitalism.[127]

As treated in this chapter's discussion of white liberalism, many publics, including those on the political Left, have tended to overestimate the racism of poor and working-class white people in general, and rural southerners more specifically, while underestimating the racism of white people with more class privilege in other U.S. regions.[128] This has also been operationalized in movement strategy. Relatively few progressive organizations have invested resources in organizing in the rural South, particularly since the end of the civil rights era.[129]

SURJ understands this to be both an ethical as well as a political mistake. As Erin Heaney reflected of the organization's focus on poor white rural southerners,

> They deserve a better world, better lives. They deserve more, just like all of us do. Period. Point blank. And in terms of shifting power in this country, we think that those communities have a really important role to play strategically.

As a matter of sheer governing power, rural counties hold disproportionate control in their states,[130] and the Right has run a fifty-year strategy to win the white southern electorate.[131] This is combined with myriad institutions and policies that artificially augment white voting power. Some of these are built into the federalist system itself, such as the Electoral College.[132] Others are new iterations of the long tradition of racialized voter suppression, including partisan gerrymandering,[133] the criminal punishment system itself,[134] and an ever-expanding array of voter restriction policies, particularly in the U.S. South.[135]

Such voter suppression mechanisms demonstrate how white supremacy is built into, revised, and maintained by U.S. law and policy in ways that directly undermine democratic practices and principles. One could well argue that these features of the system should be the target of antiracist political struggle. Moreover, there has long been debate on the Left in general, and within the Black liberation tradition more specifically, regarding the role of electoral politics for movements seeking fundamental social change. Many regard the U.S. nation-state as illegitimate, predicated on settler colonialism, foreign wars, genocide, and a handmaiden to predatory capitalism. They argue that we imperil ourselves by confusing the selection of different players within this system with the exercise of actual political power.[136]

At the same time, we dismiss important movement histories by forgetting that access to the vote has been hard-fought and continues to be a tenuous right for many. Civil rights do not ensure human rights, but neither are they irrelevant. There is also a growing recognition among many in movements seeking intersectional justice that ceding electoral terrain to the Right over the past half century has only created conditions of ever-greater precarity and risk for the many while forcing liberation efforts to prioritize defensive maneuvers over proactive, imaginative alternatives.

One approach to this ongoing dilemma is to understand fights in the electoral arena as both necessary and insufficient, and to approach elections as one small part of a multipronged, long-term strategy. For SURJ, this strategy includes building multiracial people power by bringing in more participants from predominantly white communities, particularly those whom the state and market have left behind, and whom progressive organizations have often written off, but who have not yet been securely won by the Right.

MY ORIENTATION

Observers note that the manifold iterations of white racism have received much more scholarly attention than the possibilities for white people's antiracism.[137] This makes sense given evidence that those raced as white overwhelmingly continue to invest in a system of racial stratification, exploitation, and violence. Nevertheless, there are a number of good reasons to explore the possibilities of white people's antiracism, with all of their complexities, successes, and dilemmas. Perhaps the most important is as a usable archive and "antidote to despair,"[138] particularly for those seeking other ways of engaging with the fact of their racial whiteness.[139] Indeed, collectively forgetting that some white people have always resisted and continue to resist white supremacy only helps to maintain the status quo.

That said, writing white people's antiracist efforts into the record requires balance and nuance. At the most basic level, white supremacy shapes not only material conditions and life chances but also dominant remembrance practices. Our history textbooks, along with movies and television, often depict white leaders as morally righteous, for having purportedly freed enslaved people or advanced major civil rights legislation. Meanwhile the generations of Black political struggle that actually earned such gains, and did so in the face of violent suppression, are rendered invisible. Undue celebration of purported white heroes certainly reinscribes systems of dominance, but so too can the failure to identify the fact of white involvement in antiracist struggle, however rare and imperfect it has been.

My desire to do this research, then, cannot be separated from my investments in wanting our society to be more just, humane, and decent. As someone who is raced white, and with class privilege and security, I have long been compelled to ask what those like me can do to participate in struggles for collective liberation. I first sought to answer such questions through movement involvement, particularly in immigrant justice efforts, before finding my way to scholarly inquiry as well. My experiences in campaigns led by those exploited by the market and targeted by the state, including those without authorization to be in the United States—as well as those whose full authorization still did not protect them from great risk and harassment—were formative to my own political and intellectual development. They helped solidify my conviction, now also backed by study, that grassroots struggles are our best chance for making current and future conditions more livable. Movement involvement also provoked me to ask how participants navigate differences of privilege, protection, and social position in broad-based efforts.

I name these pieces of my biography because they explicitly shape my research approach. I understand myself as a student of those (with) whom I study: the individuals and groups that invite me in and share their time, energy, and insights with me. I build here on a methodology I first saw named by Dylan Rodriguez who suggests that struggles for liberation might be learned from and with.[140] This is a bit distinct from taking these efforts as objects of scholarly knowledge, which if an equally important methodology, is one that yields quite different results. While this does not mean I avoid integrating complexity and critique, I invite study participants themselves to be centrally involved in identifying the strengths and weaknesses of their approaches. It also means that I do not necessarily emerge with the kinds of clear storylines we often crave, particularly in complex times.

Our political conjuncture is as dark, confusing, and riddled with contradictions as it has ever been. Such moments can push us to desire final answers to vexing questions. As an example, I have at times been encouraged to write this book as a how-to, as if my research could demonstrate once and for all what white people can do to engage in collective action for racial justice. While such directives may be appealing, for the purposes of this project, they are also likely ill-founded and unwise. Conditions on the ground are always shifting and evolving. The tactics selected to achieve one set of desired outcomes can prohibit other possible futures that we may later wish to pursue. This is not necessarily a failure of any movement effort but rather the nature of what many organizers in this study aptly termed "time, place, and conditions." I therefore hope readers will take this book as part of a conversation—neither the beginning nor the end, but with important insights and provocations regarding the urgent need to bring a growing number of people, particularly those raced as white, into movement efforts for intersectional racial justice.

SCOPE AND TERMS

The scope of cross-racial solidarity efforts examined in this study is necessarily limited and deserving of mention. While it may already be obvious to readers, this book gives most of its attention to how communities constituted predominantly of those raced as white seek to align with movement efforts led predominantly by those racialized as Black. This focus is driven by the data I collected and inarguably shaped by the political moment in which the study was conducted. While the organization's origins are reviewed in greater detail in the next chapter, I note here that SURJ emerged out of the U.S. South, where founders' own political socialization had been shaped by people and institutions that were central to Black liberation efforts throughout the twentieth century. The network cohered initially as a direct response to white nationalist resurgence following the election of the first Black president. In the years since, SURJ's growth has directly corresponded with flash points in the Movement for Black Lives. For example, two of the groups in this study—in Los Angeles and Buffalo—emerged in direct response to the Ferguson uprisings of 2014.

At the same time, it is not accurate to suggest that SURJ's political commitments are solely to Black-led movement efforts. The national network was engaged early on in efforts led by non-Black Latinx immigrant communities, and the book will discuss this work in Louisville. Other efforts that I do not review include SURJ's central role in launching and maintaining the Indigenous Solidarity Network, an effort that emerged out of the 2016 protests at the Standing Rock Reservation to protest the Dakota Access Pipeline.[141] The fact that this book does not focus on this Indigenous solidarity work is certainly a limitation, if one adopted intentionally. Indigenous activists and scholars demonstrate that the specificity of demands, such as for the return of lands stolen and for the recognition of national sovereignty, do not always cohere with other racial justice efforts and so require their own forms of study.[142] For those interested in Indigenous-settler solidarity efforts, I would point readers to a rich and growing scholarship.[143] I also do not trace SURJ's efforts to contest violence and injustice directed towards Asian American and Pacific Islander communities, nor do I offer an account of solidarity with Muslim and Arab communities. With 150 active groups throughout North America, and the war crimes in Gaza commencing towards the end of data collection, such efforts were certainly underway.

Like everyone trying to choose their words in discussions of race and racism, the terminology available to me is imprecise, imperfect, and often reductive. I occasionally use "those raced as white," which reminds us of the fact that race is a social and political construct that is highly contingent and variable. Nevertheless, most readers will likely be accustomed to the more colloquial "white people" or "whites," which I often favor for simplicity and brevity. I acknowledge that the term

"BIPOC" has many detractors and is a relatively recent creation. I appreciate its specificity and inclusivity and use it in reference to concepts or literatures that include Black *and* Indigenous *and* other racialized communities that are neither Black nor Indigenous. Moreover, while some participants, particularly in SURJ's partner organizations, use terms like "Black and Brown," I seek to specify which communities are being referenced within the category of "Brown" whenever conceptually useful. I use "Latinx" in lieu of "Latino" as the gender-neutral group term used by participants themselves, though many, including myself, have come to prefer the term "Latine." "Black," of course, is its own socially, politically, and historically specific term, as well as one that varies greatly across transnational contexts. I adopt it in lieu of "African American" for two main reasons. First, it is the term used by the vast majority of study participants, particularly those who understand themselves to be Black. Second, it includes Afrodiasporic peoples living in the United States who have immigrant roots, which describes at least one of the organizers in my study sample.

Finally, if the focus on white people's efforts to align with Black-led liberation struggle in the United States is in part driven by the data, there is also political and intellectual value in adopting such an emphasis. Anti-Blackness is a central foundation upon which whiteness was constructed in the U.S. context, while also having played a unique position in the organization of global racial capitalism.[144] The notion that Black liberation portends collective freedom has been echoed by various leaders in the centuries-long Black Freedom Struggle, particularly by Black feminists, and for good reason.[145] This was an understanding that many across the groups in this study, particularly those raced as white, explained to me when articulating the ways that their group seeks to align with a vision for Black liberation.

CHAPTER OVERVIEW

Chapter 2 narrates SURJ's origins within a particular political moment while situating the organization within a longer movement lineage. I identify key decisions and developments as well as introduce the urban sites where I conducted this study. Chapter 3 then begins the exploration of *how* to move more white people into antiracist action. It examines one of the signal efforts that unites the groups in this study, that of a mutual or shared interest approach. In contrast to a white privilege analytic that can be individualizing and depoliticizing, the mutual interest approach invites white people to identify their own stake in dismantling white supremacy as a way to broaden the base, deepen commitment, and ethically engage in multiracial struggle. Chapter 4 locates mutual interest within the broader technique examined in this book, that of antiracist *organizing*. Organizing seeks to build grassroots power for long-term social structural transformation. This is done by helping participants and their groups develop important skills and relationships, experiment with institutional and extra-institutional tactics, and draw in broader constituencies. It is also within an antiracist organizing approach that electoral tactics come to play an important if delimited role.

Chapter 5 positions this organizing approach within the cross-racial and cross-organizational partnerships held by the urban chapters in this book. There is no single recipe for establishing and maintaining productive partnerships. Instead, the groups under study demonstrate flexibility in the face of ever-evolving political and relational contexts and continue to experiment with various strategies. Chapter 6 examines efforts to shift a culture of self- and collective flagellation that has often accompanied the efforts of white people seeking to engage in antiracist work through an examination of the urban groups in this study. It pays special attention to the work of "calling people in," originally pioneered by Black feminists, as well as some of the strengths and vexations of group approaches to prefigurative politics, conflict resolution, and restorative justice. Chapter 7 synthesizes key lessons taken from the groups in this study and considers how these might be more broadly applied.

Movements for racial justice have long suggested that dismantling white supremacy requires a level of collective resistance capable of challenging a political, economic, and social regime. This is because white supremacy is not merely a set of beliefs, prejudices, and storylines but also a system of policies, institutions, and material arrangements that benefit the few while harming the many. We know some about the key features that can motivate and sustain individual whites in their antiracist commitments.[146] We also know a fair amount about how white people's attempts at antiracism can go wrong.[147] There is a good deal more to learn, however, about how movement efforts might recruit, mobilize, and sustain growing numbers of those raced as white towards the ends of multiracial liberation.

The stakes of such inquiry have never been higher, and the misconception that antiracism is primarily about combatting personal bias and bad behavior misses the urgent task we face. Our current conjuncture sees consolidating forms of nativism, authoritarianism, and fascism the world over, bolstered by growing economic immiseration.[148] Investments in policing, prisons, and militarism continue to funnel wealth from the many to the few. Majorities lack access to basic rights and care, while the likelihood of climate catastrophe continues to amass. The groups in this study identify such conditions as indecent and untenable and show us the day-to-day work of helping more white people to understand and act on the fact of our profound, enduring, and unquestionable interdependence. The efforts of those in this study are not without complexities and dilemmas. Yet they understand their mission quite clearly: recruiting and preparing predominantly white communities to be active participants and partners in the pursuit of multiracial democracy.

2 WE STEPPED INTO A LONG HISTORY

THE NETWORK THAT WOULD ULTIMATELY become SURJ began with a phone call convened by SURJ co-founder Pam McMichael on September 11, 2009. Pam remembers the political moment viscerally, the immediate, organized, and ruthless white racial backlash following the election of President Obama.[1] Serious political commentators had suggested that the election of the first Black president portended a more equitable and just U.S. racial order, a prediction that seems quite naïve in hindsight.[2] Instead, from her position, Pam remembers hearing about "Black children being excited on the school bus the day after the election [of Obama] being told by white bus drivers not to talk about that." Regarding this particular anecdote, Pam continued, "These are tip of the iceberg kind of things, but they're really indicative of the larger tactics and strategies around attacking him." In terms of the energy that ultimately spurred the birth of SURJ, Pam was clear: "our work was not about him [Obama], but it was about what that backlash meant."

In what follows, I lay out the immediate political context as well as the deeper movement lineage from which SURJ emerged. This includes exploring various movement groups that were important to the network's formation. I also trace key elements of the organization's evolution over its first fifteen years, exploring the group's earliest actions and

MOVEMENT ROOTS

A few months before convening the network's first phone call, Pam had participated in a strategy session, "with a small group of multiracial thinkers [talking] about the moment." It had long been apparent that some coordinated response was necessary, but Pam recalls that strategy call as a turning point: "it was clear to me that we needed a new formation, or at least a way to amp up, scale up, and coordinate work among antiracist whites." In other words, there needed to be new structures, whether an organization or some other mechanism, that could bring many more white people into fighting racist political backlash. After consulting with a few other movement colleagues, including long-time friend Carla Wallace, Pam sent out the email invitation.

The group's first call counted twenty-two participants, including racial justice educators, organizers, writers, and non-profit staff, predominantly hailing from the U.S. South but also from California, Oregon, Kansas, Chicago, and New York City. Their stated meeting agenda included developing strategies and tactics among "white antiracist activists to counter racism fueling the tactics of the Right." Examples of such tactics, listed for participant review, included racist attacks, by Fox News anchors and the Tea Party, against President Obama as well as his recently appointed environmental advisor to the White House, Van Jones. Also listed on the call's agenda, and perhaps today most salient in the organization's collective memory, was the role of the healthcare debates. As Erin Heaney, SURJ's executive director, writes of SURJ's origins, "SURJ was founded in 2009 after the Tea Party turned large swaths of working white people against the Affordable Care Act through strategic racism."[3]

Carla Wallace, a key SURJ co-founder alongside Pam, explained how these healthcare debates provided clear evidence of the need to recruit white people away from racist assumptions and into politically impactful, antiracist action. She recalled,

White people were getting up saying, "We can't let the immigrants have healthcare. We can't let those people who don't work as hard as we do,"— i.e. Black women, you know, "have healthcare." And it undermined healthcare for everybody.

The way that white racism was wielded against a social good that would benefit the vast majority exemplifies the larger case SURJ continues to make. Everyone loses, including white people, when white supremacy reigns.

Pam was well positioned to convene the call, in part because of her role as the executive director of the Highlander Center. Located in the Appalachian region of eastern Tennessee, Highlander was co-founded in 1932 by popular educator Myles Horton during the height of the depression era and Jim Crow segregation. The vision was to bring Appalachian workers together across racial lines in order to agitate for better labor conditions and a more equitable society. If there was some early caution among Black organizers about working with the center, in part because it was often under surveillance and had been smeared as a "communist" organization,[4] by the 1950s it would become a central hub for the Black liberation struggle. In his study of the key organizations and influences in the civil rights movement, Aldon Morris terms Highlander a "movement halfway house," defined as an organization that does not have its own membership base but can offer "social change resources such as skilled activists, tactical knowledge, media contacts, workshops, knowledge of past movements, and a vision for a future society."[5] For close to a century, the Highlander Center has been equipping social change efforts much like SURJ: groups that are often born in the South, that prioritize organizing among poor and working-class people, and that work towards racial and economic justice.

Highlander's presence in the network's formation also speaks to a larger history into which SURJ enters. As Pam put it, "being able to have Highlander in the yeast of this is also a critical part of that story."[6] The organization understands itself as a continuation in a lineage of white people attempting to defect from white supremacy and to align with racial justice, if always "too few and imperfectly," as the organization often quips during training calls and published materials. Pam emphasized, "we didn't invent this. We stepped into a long history of white people, particularly white southerners . . . doing this work." Thus, even if the email Pam sent to participants to join a phone call in September of 2009 was a first invitation in the strictest sense, it was also a continuation of the long summons issued out of BIPOC-led struggle; "the invitation was really people of color saying [to white people], 'we need you to do your work.'"

The lineage of white southern resistance out of which SURJ emerges is also deeply shaped by Anne Braden, both in an instrumental sense as well as a cultural one. Braden directly mentored SURJ's co-founders Pam McMichael and Carla Wallace for decades while serving as a towering figure in the legacy of white involvement in racial justice work more generally. Braden was quite rare for her generation: a white woman born in the 1920s South to a wealthy and deeply segregationist family, who would go on to organize for racial justice, often at great risk to herself and her family, and would continue this work until her death. Braden continues to serve as an important model for whites seeking to divest from white supremacy, who often face a dearth of visible examples.[7]

College was an important intellectual awakening for Anne, but her more significant political transformation arguably began upon meeting her husband, journalist and organizer Carl Braden, when she returned to Louisville to pursue a career in journalism. Anne and Carl were relentless in their commitments to social change, and they would become close to and struggle alongside major leaders in the civil rights movement, including Dr. Martin Luther King Jr.[8] One of the Bradens' most storied acts of dissent was an effort in 1954 to surreptitiously aid Black war veteran Andrew Wade in acquiring a home in a white suburb after Wade had been repeatedly denied the opportunity to make this purchase. The transaction led to a period of white racist terror rained down upon both the Wades and the Bradens, and the Bradens were ultimately jailed and charged with sedition.[9]

During her national tour seeking support during Carl's sedition trial, Anne would meet Ella Baker in Harlem, who was quickly sympathetic to the couple's plight. Baker is often described as one of the most talented and visionary community organizers of both the civil rights movement and the twentieth century;[10] Ella Baker became an important mentor to Anne Braden as well as a lifelong friend with the couple. Despite their innumerable differences, historian Barbara Ransby describes Anne Braden and Ella Baker as midwives, of a kind, to a generation:

> Both served as powerful alternative role models for young women who came of age politically during the early 1960s. Bold, confident, and intellectually sophisticated, they were tireless organizers and generous mentors.[11]

Baker was clear in her conviction that strong movements do not need charismatic leaders so much as mechanisms for skills and leadership development among everyday people,[12] a perspective that she and Anne shared. Both were committed to the importance of organizing rural people and meeting them on their own terms. In the Highlander tradition, they taught some by way of direct instruction but even more so by modeling what was to be done.[13] These emphases shape the way the groups in this study understand and approach their efforts.

The Bradens' influence on organizing for racial and economic justice and against militarism and imperialism continues to be felt in the city of Louisville. Central to their legacy was an effort, inspired in large part by Ella Baker, that began by seeking to free Angela Davis following her 1971 arrest on spurious charges. Ransby describes Davis, an abolitionist feminist and scholar, as both "a legendary figure in Black liberation movement history" as well as a formative influence on today's Movement for Black Lives.[14] The Bradens, alongside Davis following her release in 1972, would continue the work to free political prisoners of color, founding the National Alliance Against Racist & Political Repression, and its state chapter, which Louisville activists today shorthand as the Kentucky Alliance. After Carl passed away in 1975, Anne continued her tireless commitments to organizing, often with the Kentucky Alliance, as well as writing, often working eighteen-hour days, until her own death in 2006.[15]

Carla Wallace explains that the Bradens were in her life from the beginning. Carla's mother came from a working-class resistance to the

Nazi occupation of Holland, while her father, who worked as a journalist in Louisville, came from inherited wealth. After learning about the sedition charges against Carl, Carla's father would contribute to the Bradens' bail fund, a story that Carla grew up with even if it preceded her birth. Carla laughs about Anne's reaction to her father's generosity around the sedition trial, "Anne Braden was like, 'Who on earth is this white man sending us money?'" Carla was a teenager when the Kentucky Alliance was founded, and notes that she quickly got involved in their efforts, which were "anti-prison, anti-KKK, anti-police violence, but also worked around political prisoners." From a young age, then, both Anne Braden and Angela Davis would play an influential role in Carla's political development.

Pam McMichael, born to a working-class family in a more rural part of Kentucky, moved to Louisville to attend graduate school in 1978, where she would ultimately meet Carla. Pam was part of lesbian separatist and women's liberation spaces, and Carla was involved in a number of movement efforts, ranging from international solidarity work to economic and racial justice campaigns. Through their relationship, Pam asked that Carla bring her to a meeting of the Kentucky Alliance, where Carla was on the board. Here Pam was introduced to Anne Braden as well.

Carla and Pam went on to help found and lead several movement efforts, including Louisville's Fairness Campaign, which became a national model for centering racial justice in the struggle for LGBTQ equity, and Southerners On New Ground (SONG), which focuses on multiracial and intersectional organizing with LGBTQ communities living in the U.S. South. Daniel Martinez HoSang specifically names SONG and the Highlander Center as important organizations that have "trained tens of thousands of people in . . . the traditions and practices . . . of group-centered leadership, popular consciousness-raising, and direct action" espoused by Ella Baker and the many she mentored, particularly Black women.[16]

Anne Braden, who maintained the insight and commitments of Baker long after Baker's death in 1986, supported both Carla and Pam throughout their social change work. Pam recalls asking Anne Braden for a recommendation in 2005 when Pam was being considered for the executive director position at the Highlander Center. Anne was only begrudgingly willing to offer it, she told Pam, because Louisville would sorely miss Pam's organizing talents. Through their mentor and friend in Anne Braden, their shared as well as individual movement work in Louisville, and Pam's tenure of more than a decade at Highlander, both Pam and Carla brought to SURJ lifelong political partnerships and friendships with a number of influential Black organizers throughout the South. Many of these individuals have gone on to become SURJ's important organizational partners, both in the Louisville chapter as well as nationally.

OTHER MOVEMENT FORMATIONS

Pam McMichael had convened a call of twenty-two participants, a group whose numbers doubled by the next phone meeting and continued to grow. Some of those who would join came from white antiracist groups formed in the early 2000s that were already doing work with local communities, as well as making efforts to connect with each other. Akin to the way that the Highlander Center is central to SURJ's story, many leaders in these other white antiracist collectives were directly or tangentially shaped by two additional community organizing and racial justice training institutes. These were the People's Institute for Survival and Beyond in New Orleans, formed in the 1980s by Black veterans of the civil rights movement, and its white-led offspring, the Challenging White Supremacy (CWS) workshop in the San Francisco Bay Area. CWS was formed in 1993 by white civil rights veterans Sharon Martinas and Mickey Ellinger, who had participated in the People's Institute and decided a meaningful direction for their work would be creating a training for white organizers in becoming more principled and effective in their antiracist commitments.[17] To understand how these training efforts, in addition to Highlander, would also help facilitate the growth of SURJ, I begin with the launch of Catalyst Project.

CATALYST PROJECT

Based in the San Francisco Bay Area, this collective counts a number of important influences, including the call by Black leaders in the civil rights movement for white people to organize their own. Catalyst formed in response to a specific political context, however: the unprecedented activist efforts to shut down the meetings of the World Trade Organization (WTO) in Seattle in 1999. A pivotal moment in the global justice movement, the WTO protests nevertheless drew feedback from leaders of color that these efforts were troublingly white dominated. Famous among such critiques was Elizabeth ("Betita") Martinez's 2000 essay, "Where Was the Color in Seattle?"[18] Martinez, a lifelong Chicana organizer, educator, and writer, as well as former staff member of the Student Nonviolent Coordinating Committee (SNCC), was among many asking WTO protest organizers to consider the way that white supremacy was continuing to structure their approaches. Catalyst co-founder Clare Bayard recalls that many global justice activists around the United States took the critique quite seriously, having study circles and considering how to best respond.

Catalyst was officially launched in 2000 as a project of the Challenging White Supremacy (CWS) workshops. Because of Martinas and Ellinger's deep movement connections and longtime commitments to internationalist struggles, including in the Central America solidarity movement, they were well positioned to respond to the important critiques BIPOC organizers and thinkers were bringing to the U.S.-based constituency of the global justice movement. Nevertheless, Clare Bayard notes that Martinas understood she was not herself deeply embedded in the global justice work of this new generation of activists. It would ultimately make more sense for her to mentor younger organizers in launching their own formation. Catalyst Project would thus become its own entity, birthed by but independent of CWS.

Catalyst Project followed in the model of the aforementioned movement halfway houses, conducting political education, organizational support, and leadership development with the aims, as member Elisabeth Long explained it, of "[supporting] white people to effectively contribute to building multiracial movements for justice across many fronts of struggle." One of the ways this strategy was realized is by going to sites of mobilization when invited by BIPOC partners. Catalyst conducted trainings and offered direct support so that those white activists already on the ground could participate in the most effective and principled ways possible. The group had significant involvement in the aftermath of Hurricane Katrina in New Orleans beginning in 2005, and then a decade later at the Standing Rock protests in 2016. Catalyst also hosted ongoing political education and leadership development through their Anne Braden Antiracist Organizer Training Program, begun in 2008. This four-month intensive was designed to help white organizers, generally those with a depth of organizing experience and often from poor and working-class backgrounds, to become more intentional, accountable, and principled in their commitments to racial justice.

Catalyst members were formative to the early SURJ network, and the two organizations understand themselves as playing distinct, if complementary, roles in what participants often term the "movement ecosystem." As Clare Bayard distinguished between the two efforts,

> Catalyst is not the "how do we take white people and convince them that racism is a problem" but "how do we work with people who already have some sphere of influence, there's already some kind of base that they're working with, something they're passionate about, and support them to figure out how is antiracism part of that? How do they make their work more effective and accountable?"

Whereas SURJ seeks to recruit new and sometimes unlikely white people into antiracist campaigns, Catalyst supports white people who are already politicized and mobilized.

GROUNDWORK AND CARW

Other predominantly white antiracist groups deeply involved in SURJ's formation also traced their roots to the early 2000s. Kristen Brock-Petroshius, whom I spoke to in 2021 because of her leadership role in deep canvassing efforts with White People for Black Lives in Los Angeles, credited her own activist history to involvement in one of these groups: Groundwork in Madison, Wisconsin. Kristen explained how Groundwork was one of multiple formations in which

> a crew of people who typically came out of the Challenging White Supremacy Workshop out of the Bay Area, and the People's Institute for Survival and Beyond out of New Orleans, then lived in different parts of the country [and started] white antiracist collectives.

Z! Haukness, SURJ's national organizing co-director at the time of our interview, who had also been centrally involved with SURJ since its formation and was a graduate of Catalyst's Anne Braden program, credited Groundwork for providing them an important opportunity for political development. Groundwork, an active SURJ chapter for over a decade, exemplified many of the features pursued later by SURJ, which Z! described as being focused on base building and "connecting with other people of color–led organizations in building partnerships" to win campaigns ranging from housing insecurity to immigrant justice.

Another local organization akin to Groundwork was the Coalition of Anti-Racist Whites (CARW) in Seattle. Not dissimilar from Catalyst, CARW co-founder Scott Winn described being part of the "activist WTO folks" in the late 1990s and traced CARW's formation to the critique of white dominance in the WTO protests in Seattle. Scott attended a CWS training with Sharon Martinas around the time of CARW's formation. The People's Institute was already doing work in the Northwest at the time, which Scott identified as helpful in bringing people to CARW in the group's first years. From his position as a leader in CARW as well as a long-term antiracist trainer and college educator, Scott joined SURJ's leadership team in its first years, ultimately stepping back in 2013. CARW was one of SURJ's first local affiliates and continued as a SURJ chapter at the time of writing.

AWARE-LA

The Alliance of White Anti-Racists Everywhere in Los Angeles (AWARE-LA) also formed in the early 2000s, though group founders do not trace their origins to the global justice movement per se. I provide greater detail here on AWARE-LA than the previous organizations discussed because it is the organizational bedrock for one of the central groups in this study: White People for Black Lives (WP4BL). AWARE-LA is also more organizationally complex than many antiracist white collectives in that it maintained a multipart structure. This included a decades-old set of spaces for dialogue, political education, and other introspective practices, and the more recently formed WP4BL, a SURJ chapter that focuses on organizing and action.

The entity that would become AWARE was initially launched by an experienced community organizer and antiracist educator, Cameron Levin, alongside then-college student Jason David, and a third high school–aged participant. The three had met through their involvement in a Los Angeles summer camp promoting cross-racial dialogue and antibias education. The camp also counted among its participants Patrisse Cullors, who would go on to be a co-founder of Black Lives Matter (BLM) and co-leader of BLM Los Angeles (BLM LA). Jason maintains a friendship with Cullors, a relationship that would become politically important when he went on to be part of WP4BL's launch in 2014.

Cameron, later joined by Jason, helped co-facilitate the white affinity space when the camp would divide participants along racial lines during its caucus activities.[19] While both Cameron and Jason saw some value in this practice, they also came to share Cameron's critique that "it was effective to a point, but it was predicated on the pain of the people of color to extract the guilt from the white folk." Cameron also believed that while BIPOC youth were finding political motivation and empowerment through their own histories of resistance, no such option was offered to white youth. When the camp closed in 2003 for financial reasons, Cameron was eager to build a different model for white antiracist introspection.

Those involved in AWARE's first years identify their group's approach as being quite different from other ways of doing antiracist education for white people at the time. The focus was on being welcoming and compassionate to white participants with a view to keeping people involved for the long haul. Shelly Tochluk, an antiracist educator, writer, and leader active with AWARE since its first meeting, reflected:

> The thing that made AWARE-LA very different than anything I saw out in the world, and what made me able to stay involved in AWARE-LA, and what I believe has made AWARE-LA so sustainable and powerful—and I would like to believe influential, [if] not nearly as influential as I want us to be—is that there is an absolute dedication to loving one another.

Jason concurred that this ethos was central to the group's origins, "there's a lot of programs that kind of hammer white folks, right? The whole point is just to get really good at naming how much privilege you have and how fucked up that is." AWARE understood its role as going beyond building awareness around white privilege, particularly as those who gravitated towards the formation were already trying to be both active and principled in their commitments to racial justice. In lieu of a dominant model in which white antiracists "check" each other for mistakes made, Jason described AWARE's intention "to create more room for complexity around this, to practice trusting and loving each other through this work."

If AWARE's first years included gaining clarity about their visions and model, choosing a name, and developing an organizational presence, the group also met its share of criticisms. In 2006, for example, AWARE sent a cohort to the White Privilege Conference, an annual, multiracial convening. Jason recalls:

> There was so much suspicion and skepticism of what we were doing, most of it from white folks, who were just like, "No, you can't do that, that's unaccountable. We can't be trusted. There need to be people of color in the space making sure we're not letting each other off the hook."

AWARE participants did not necessarily agree with every criticism they fielded, but they too were committed to being accountable to BIPOC organizers. They decided to create a Racial Justice Accountability (RJA) Board by approaching the people of color social justice leaders with whom they held long-term relationships. The idea was that the board would oversee and approve the group's activities. Yet those approached did not want to participate in this way. As Jason recalls, they responded by saying, "'We're not here to be your rubber stamp. That's not interesting to us.'" This was not a rejection of what AWARE was doing, however. Instead, these partners were genuinely interested in AWARE's project. Jason paraphrased them:

> "We don't know anyone else who's doing this. We're really glad you're doing this, and we actually think you should trust yourselves. We're happy to be in partnership, but we don't want to advise you. We don't want to approve your stuff. So, why don't we create like an alliance, space where we can be in conversation, but you keep doing your work?"

AWARE understood that its first task was to give white antiracists a different understanding of their stake in dismantling white supremacy. They thus created the model of a "radical white identity," later turned into a published essay, which introduces many of the central ideas that SURJ promotes today.[20] The essay identifies racism as a tool of a greater system in which white supremacy upholds the interests of a small elite. The majority of white people might enjoy racial privilege, but they also have much to gain from joining with BIPOC to challenge the system.

AWARE would go on to generate a number of documents to outline their models for white antiracist practice. These include a list of seven reasons why AWARE believes in a white racial affinity model, termed "Why a White Space." Perhaps their most circulated document, "Powerful Partnerships,"[21] documents the experiences of AWARE in building its RJA board and suggests that "transformative alliances" are ones in which white allies become full collaborators, willing to make mistakes, rather than pursue forms of "one-sided accountability" or overly deferential relationships.

AWARE engaged in important moments of political action during its first years—such as in the immigrant rights uprisings of 2006 and in housing justice work with a BIPOC-led group, with whom they continue to partner. AWARE's theory of change at its formation was nevertheless somewhat distinct from the one SURJ broadly adopts today. As Jason reflected, the idea was to "do personal transformation, consciousness raising, start there, develop people over a number of years." Then, when the political moment arises, the thinking went, there would be a cohort of white people ready to work in collaboration and solidarity with BIPOC-led struggle. Ideally, they would have forged strong cross-racial relationships over years and would be equipped to show up in more healed and healthy ways to the exigencies of the movement. The reason this is somewhat different from the approach traced in this book is that it understands introspection and identity work as a first step in building a base of antiracist white people ready to take action. It is also the case, however, that during these early years, there was no unified racial justice movement nationally or in Los Angeles with which white people could easily align in the way that the Movement for Black Lives would later become.[22]

AWARE's story is vital to understanding SURJ as both organizations have indelibly shaped each other. AWARE contributed people and expertise to the early SURJ network, including supporting the articulation of why white affinity organizing is valuable to multiracial struggle. Through trial and error, AWARE developed a model for white involvement in cross-racial antiracist partnerships. They were one of the earliest formations seeking to practice compassion and care in white antiracist organizing, a stance that was deeply important to SURJ from its inception. SURJ has also shaped organizing in Los Angeles. White People for Black Lives, AWARE's now full-fledged action arm, came into being following SURJ's 2014 call for white people to actively align with the newest iteration of the centuries-long Black Freedom Struggle, the Movement for Black Lives.

FIRST ACTIONS

During the months that followed their first convening call in September 2009, the network that would become SURJ continued to have monthly conversations, forged a loose organizational structure, and began to draft a statement of their purpose, aims, and framework. In April 2010, the passage of SB1070 in Arizona, colloquially known as the anti-immigrant "show me your papers" law, became a movement flashpoint to which the group could concretely respond. SB1070 was understood as the most sweeping and draconian anti-immigrant legislation the United States had seen in generations.[23] Among its myriad regulations, the policy made it an Arizona state crime to be in the country without immigration authorization; to not carry proof of one's immigration papers at all times; and to hire, transport, or otherwise aid anyone who did not have proper immigration authorization. Likely most objectionable to activists and legal experts, the law required Arizona law enforcement to detain anyone whom they suspected of being undocumented, a policy that all but ensured racial profiling.[24]

The activist response to the law was led by Latinx, Indigenous, and immigrant organizations in Arizona, who launched direct action and civil disobedience as well as education of and defense for migrant communities. That first summer, in what would ultimately turn into years of resistance, became an important opportunity for the nascent SURJ. Clare Bayard of Catalyst recalled, "where [early SURJ] first started to really get traction, as a network versus as a conversation between people involved in a bunch of different projects, was really 2010 Arizona." Z! agreed, "this was the first time where we were like, 'okay, we have people who we can bring together to have an impact along with other national partners.'" Clare added that the movement response to SB1070 provided a first opportunity in "starting to direct resources [and to] focus attention and energy towards a particular people of color-led campaign on the ground." A number of people involved in the SURJ network spent time in Arizona that summer, including participants from all of the aforementioned groups: AWARE, CARW, Groundwork, and Catalyst. The movement moment also saw the growth of SURJ's first chapter formation in Arizona, led by a resident in Tucson who had graduated from Catalyst's Anne Braden program.

SURJ's involvement in the response to SB1070 was also an important early opportunity in receiving feedback from partners. Particularly in conversations with Black leaders in Louisville, Carla and Pam heard both support for combatting anti-immigrant policies along with a warning not to lose sight of the importance of fighting the anti-Black racism that in many ways animated SURJ's initial formation and is an enduring, unique, and central feature of white supremacy. Pam reflected,

> In that moment, because the attacks on immigrants were so virulent and present, we needed to be working on immigration issues . . . but that couldn't be the sole manifestation of our work . . . we also had to address the centuries old, and still current, critical anti-blackness that's so prevalent and key in this country.

Of course, there are immigrant communities that are racialized as Black who face the nexus of these issues. Arizona's SB1070, however, was largely an attack on generally non-Black Latinx communities.

SURJ has certainly integrated this feedback. I was actually more than a year into conducting interviews before I learned of the network's early participation in immigrant justice work. This is likely informed by the rise of the Movement for Black Lives and extant political context during the course of this study. The way that SURJ publicly narrated its history was much more about combatting the anti-Blackness that accompanied the healthcare policy debates under Obama than about contesting anti-immigrant policies in Arizona.[25]

As participants engaged in their first political actions in Arizona, and attended the global justice movement's United States Social Forum later that summer in Detroit, the question of the network's name became increasingly important for defining an organizational identity. Pam McMichael had convened the first call under the title "White People Stepping Up" as a temporary placeholder. By spring of 2010, soon before many would travel to Arizona, the group adopted the mantle of "U.S. for All of US," situated within a larger statement of "Let's Build a U.S. for All of Us: No Room for Racism." Some reflect on this name with uneasiness, seeing it as a quaint appeal to an idealized multicultural nationalism, and one that masks central forms of settler colonialism and racialized violence that have always undergirded the U.S. national project. Nevertheless, it is useful to identify some of the political crosscurrents from which such a name emerged.

In 2010, the immigrant rights movement was arguably the strongest U.S.-based racial justice struggle when measured by number of adherents, organizations, and resources as well as the size and frequency of visible protest events.[26] This movement thus had a considerable influence on the Left at large. Scholars demonstrate that between 2000 and 2014, a major strand of immigrant rights messaging adopted a "liberal nationalism," in which "advocates [adhered] to core national principles while also advocating for a more inclusive political community."[27] While neither a universally adopted nor permanent messaging strategy, appeals to immigrant inclusion as a core American value often minimized the specificity of settler colonialism and anti-Black racism. Take, for instance, the popular slogan of being "a nation of immigrants," which erases both the Indigenous peoples of North America and the kidnapped African peoples brought across the Atlantic as chattel.[28] Moreover, the discourse of multicultural inclusion might be situated in the aftermath of the election of a first Black president, which some progressives sought to leverage. Their argument to the U.S. citizenry was, insofar as it had chosen a Black man to hold the highest office, there was evidence that the ideal of a racially just and equitable society was within reach.

Pam reflected that in this context, "[U.S. for All of Us] was about reclaiming the kind of country we want to live in, a country that was fair, that was just, that included all people, took care of its people." Clare concurred that the name emerged out of the question of "how do we talk about the importance of claiming our commitment to this being a multiracial democracy, which is not the direction that our enemies want to take it." Yet the network received critical feedback about the name nearly from the onset.

Some of this criticism came from those in the Black liberation tradition. Reflecting on the lessons of the civil rights movement, they were quite clear that the U.S. nation-state was no guarantor of equal rights.

The loudest voice of opposition, however, came from Indigenous leaders and their allies. As Carla recalled, "folks who were much more deeply in Indigenous solidarity work than I have been brought up the very right thing of like 'U.S. for all?'—Okay, who's the all of us? And wait, whose land was this?"

Pam added:

> That phrase [U.S. for all of US] was obviously problematic in terms of country-hood so to speak, and we shifted from that language later as we continued to sharpen our politics and our messaging and our vision.

Here, Pam referred to the fact that what is understood as the United States itself occupies the territory of various other Indigenous nations who continue to fight for the protection of land, water, and other natural resources as well as the acknowledgment of their political sovereignty.

The process of renaming happened with surprising ease during a group retreat at the Highlander Center soon after the summer of 2010. Someone proposed "Standing Up for Racial Justice," which those in attendance liked. While memories of what happened next differ, the name was ultimately modified to "*Showing* Up for Racial Justice" in order to signal an attentiveness to disability justice.

ORGANIZATIONAL STRUCTURE

One of SURJ's central emphases from its inception has been a focus on what many in movement work term "base building." This is a political organizing strategy that seeks to reach new audiences in order to grow the pool of constituents while simultaneously developing the skills, capacities, and analyses of those already involved. Indeed, both the national organization and some local groups, such as the Los Angeles White People for Black Lives, are quite numerically specific in these aims. They have adapted the principle, established by political scientists, that when 3.5 percent of a population opposes a regime, that is enough to drive its collapse.[29] SURJ therefore endeavors to recruit 3.5 percent of the white population into active resistance to racist policies and institutions. This book focuses largely on the practices by which SURJ pursues its base-building aims. Here I offer some key aspects of the organizational structure it has adopted to do so.

THE TWO-PRONGED MODEL

One of the first parts of the organization to emerge was that of a chapter network, in which local groups across the country choose to affiliate with SURJ. One of the decisions the organization's leaders had to consider early on, then, was the criteria they would require of their chapters. After careful consideration, they decided to, as Pam put it, "lean towards openness, if someone wanted to start a chapter, there was a bar, but the bar wasn't that high. It was not cadre level." A number of SURJ leaders juxtaposed their chapter network to this idea of a "cadre" organization, a term that comes out of a Marxist organizing tradition and generally requires that members espouse a high level of political alignment.[30]

Allowing interested groups around the country to become chapters as long as they agreed with SURJ's basic principles had the benefit of drawing in as many people as possible. Pam continued, "It connected us to new people, it built new relationships, it spread the work across the country." At the same time, the openness also meant that different SURJ chapters could be quite different in their orientations:

> In some places, there was more focus on education than action. In some places, there was action without the education. In some places, people wouldn't take a step without a person of color telling them it was okay, and that's not how we interpreted accountability at SURJ.

Carla added that as chapters began to develop, some were not "in accountability with communities of color" at all, "they had no relationships there." Another pitfall of this unevenness was an issue of reputation. Those who interacted with a local chapter that was not operating as intentionally, robustly, and actively as the organization would wish might come to negative conclusions about the network as a whole and be wary of any further collaboration.

While national leadership was aware that the chapter model held pitfalls, it was also clear that, as Pam put it:

> Chapters were in motion and a lot of chapters were doing good work. So, how do you take the strengths of that, nurture that, help deal with some of the complications and the challenges of that model, keep resourcing that?

Over time, SURJ developed a few mechanisms to harness the strengths, limit the pitfalls, and fill in the gaps. One of these has been both requiring and supporting chapters to adopt an action focus that puts clear demands on those in power. Chapter coach Linnea Brett in Buffalo explained that in order for groups to operate as SURJ chapters today, they need to be working on a "campaign," defined as "a plan to get your folks and your friends to force a decision-maker to give you the thing that you want." Having just facilitated a chapter training on campaigns, Linnea continued:

> [A campaign] is focused on an issue. You're mobilizing your base. You're working in relationship with people of color, your partners, and other allies. You have an escalating plan to get there that involves bringing new people in, cultivating leadership, and leading towards ideally winning.

In addition to offering trainings and other coaching support to individual chapters, SURJ also encourages groups to learn from each other. For example, when the Los Angeles group was working to pass an abolitionist ballot initiative in the first months of 2020, the national organization brought in members from seven other chapters around the country to participate in and learn from the campaign and then bring lessons back to their own groups.

Erin Heaney acknowledged that refining the criteria for groups to formalize their chapter status has also required effort. "There's been a couple places where we said goodbye because it turns out, [those chapters] just weren't aligned." She described how such a conversation might go:

It's great for you to want to do a book club and to really focus on self-study. And that's not what we're doing. That's not what SURJ is about and that's okay. There's many lanes people need to be in, but making a commitment to being a chapter means that you're committing to action and to moving more of your people into action.

Facilitating chapters in becoming more action-oriented is important, but it does not address another limitation of the chapter model that became more apparent over time. Most SURJ chapters form in cities and large towns, and these often draw participants who are already interested in "antiracism" and who tend to have class privilege. Chapters are therefore not the most effective mechanism for drawing in the poor and working-class white people, particularly in the rural South, who have been a priority organizing bloc for the organization since its inception.

SURJ spent a number of years strategizing around the question of how to better reach such communities and ultimately adopted what Pam termed a "two-pronged strategy." The organization would support existing chapters in their development as well as intentionally seed new organizing formations in the rural South. One example of such a formation is Kentucky People's Union, which opened this book. As is detailed further in the chapters to come, these groups generally begin as listening projects, in which SURJ staff go door to door, talking to residents about the changes they might wish to see in their community. Through multiple conversations, people are brought into organizations in which members develop leadership skills, conduct issue-based research, choose campaigns, and often secure policy changes that improve their lives. These groups generally have their own names and do not hold a primary identity as being a SURJ project, though funding and resources do come through the national organization.

With its two-pronged strategy of largely, if never exclusively, class-privileged urban chapters and working and poor people led rural organizations, SURJ has made the calculated decision to eschew what organizational theorists might term a "tightly coupled system" in favor of a more decentralized model. All groups are expected to align with basic principles and to pursue collective action in the form of a campaign, but there is a great deal of flexibility in how such aims look in practice. Though staff are directly involved in the rural groups, national leadership is not in the business of policing the work of SURJ chapters. The result of this level of decentralization is not without drawbacks. The most obvious is that groups with the greatest autonomy are generally also all-volunteer and with limited resources, which can hamper collective capacities. Moreover, people's encounters with different local groups can leave vastly different impressions of what the national organization is trying to do, a fact made apparent to me as I presented this research to audiences familiar with SURJ groups operating in different parts of the country.

There are some important strengths of this organizational model, however. Decentralization means that decision-making can be guided by group membership, political conditions, and local organizing partners. In turn, members feel ownership over their local work, which brings a sense of empowerment, satisfaction and dignity. Different groups can quickly respond to changing conditions without needing to seek extensive approval procedures. They can prioritize local relevance over national brand. What one group in one location does, or fails to do, has less impact on the fortunes of other organizing efforts than it otherwise might.

There are also newer features of SURJ's work that are more centralized and can serve as a safeguard for decentralization's weaknesses. Take, for example, SURJ's national membership program, which emerged following the height of movement interest during summer of 2020. This program is able to draw in individuals wherever they might be located and connect them to concrete political action as well as collective opportunities for training and reflection, often facilitated by digital technologies.

Linnea gave an example of how the national membership model can be useful when a chapter formation is not feasible. She told the story of a group "in a very rural part of New York state, where everyone kind of lived a few hours apart from each other and were like, 'we can't make this work' after a few years, especially with COVID." Linnea continued:

Now several of those folks are part of the national membership ... maybe [they] can re-form in a local context again at some point. [They] just don't have the capacity to do that right now. That's been a really good way to keep people in the movement and not necessarily at a local chapter.

Building organizations, however small and local, is challenging work, requiring collective time, energy, and stamina. Sometimes such requirements pose too high a bar for those who might otherwise wish to engage.

The national membership program evolved quite dramatically over the course of research. When I began the study in 2021, ongoing national work included one monthly online "abolitionist action hour." These typically drew around ten participants to take actions in support of BIPOC partners' campaigns—calling legislators, tweeting at corporate executives, and writing messages to state officials, for example. By 2023, SURJ had formalized the process of becoming a national member. One committed to take a number of regular actions and to pay dues on a sliding scale. By 2024, national organizing was bringing together thousands of members to engage in almost daily actions. These included phone banks to reach potential SURJ members and undecided voters, as well as nationwide door-knocking efforts, to defend a slate of progressive candidates that SURJ and its partners supported.

COLLECTING RESOURCES, HIRING STAFF

Such a shift in scale has required SURJ to collect resources in order to pursue its aims. The decision in 2014 to move in this direction was not made lightly. Leadership understood that their impact would remain limited as a solely volunteer operation, but many were hesitant about a predominantly white organization raising funds. In a movement field populated by already under-resourced organizations, it is well-documented that funding is racially stratified.[31] Moreover, competition for scarce resources can lead to intra-movement conflict and derail social change coalitions.[32] The network thus engaged in a discernment process, compiling a racially and geographically diverse list of movement participants with whom to consult. Pam described these as "one-on-one conversations about [these activists'] reflections, their thoughts, their feedback on what it meant for SURJ, as an organization designed to work with white people, to raise this kind of money." Some did express concern about the potential that SURJ might gain resources that would otherwise go to BIPOC-led groups. Most, however, believed that SURJ needed to begin to raise money.

Like many of their formative conversations, the deciding one on this matter took place at the Highlander Center, which would also serve as SURJ's initial fiscal sponsor. Pam recalled the group sitting in a circle of rocking chairs and making the decision "that in order to scale up and have the impact that we were being called to have and the impact that was needed to move people, we needed to have dedicated hands working on it." The group did not ignore the fact that their own fundraising might inadvertently pull resources from BIPOC-led groups and so decided to pursue a technique that participants alternately have come to term "solidarity," "collaborative," and "companion" fundraising. The basic premise, as Pam described it, is that "we would raise money for people of color organizations, while raising money to do this work." The multiple, creative, and impactful ways that SURJ has put this fundraising model into practice are detailed in Chapter 5.

By the end of 2014, SURJ was able to raise enough money to hire its first staff member to coordinate the organization's work around the country. Over the next five years, the organization grew steadily, adding one or two full-time staff annually, with many more working in various part-time capacities, often in order to help train and support chapters or to work intensively on specific campaigns. The summer of 2020 uprisings, a watershed moment for racial justice efforts generally, brought thousands of people as well as unprecedented resources to the national organization and local groups alike.[33] The majority of funds raised once again went to paying staff. At this point, SURJ was able to transition many of its part-time employees into twenty new full-time positions. Between 2021 and 2023, SURJ would grow to over forty staff members, with a majority serving in a full-time capacity. Most come from organizing backgrounds, with many having worked as volunteers with a local SURJ group. Others have transitioned from other movement organizations. Those engaged in the rural southern organizing work tend to come from the communities in which they organize or similar ones.

Akin to many worker organizations and other grassroots organizing projects, SURJ has endeavored to raise funds predominantly from its own membership base. As of 2024, 85 percent of the group's revenue came from individual donors, supplemented by foundation support. Compared to other nonprofit organizations, which often rely primarily on foundation monies or earned income,[34] being funded primarily by members allows SURJ to have greater flexibility regarding organizational mission and activities. In theory, and as many participants affirmed, this ensures the organization is responsive to the expressed desires of membership while allowing for experimentation, reflection, and adjustments in response to a shifting political context.

Some of the leaders I interviewed who had enough context to comment on SURJ's growth over time agreed that the organization's expansion was simultaneously exciting and something to monitor with care. As one of SURJ's early and influential leaders reflected, "there's an ongoing, understandable tension. 'Wow, should really this much money be going into white people?' Well, [that] depends on what they're doing with it."

Clare Bayard, co-founder of Catalyst Project, agreed that such a tension is an important one to continually navigate, pointing to the fine line between "vigilant" observation and unduly destructive criticism:

> It is right and necessary to stay vigilant about a white people organization the size of SURJ. Like we actually have to stay vigilant. And I think we have to be careful where that overlaps with the tendency to tear down leadership.

Grace Aheron, SURJ's communications director, was sympathetic to those who might be skeptical of the size of the organization's staff and amassed resources. Yet in line with the original conversations SURJ leaders had about whether to hire employees, Grace believed that a dedicated staff was the best way for the organization to meaningfully contribute to political change. She reflected, "Tactically people might disagree with the big nonprofit that SURJ is now. And I feel so clear on this work needing to be done at scale. And how urgent it is."

CROSS-RACIAL PARTNERSHIPS

A final important feature of SURJ's work that is structural, strategic, and foundational to the organization is its commitment to working in partnership with BIPOC-led movement groups. As Pam reflected of the group's original vision:

> It was not about going off by ourselves as white people and just doing this work. It was about white people stepping up with responsibility and accountability for our part in dismantling racism and building a more fair and racially just society.

This is not to say that cross-racial partnership dynamics are simple or straightforward, as Chapter 5 explores. Here I introduce some central considerations for the organization.

Erin Heaney remarked that SURJ's deep engagement with BIPOC-led organizations is often the most misunderstood aspect of the organization, explaining, "we don't think white people should just go off and do work on their own, even though that's sometimes what's projected on to us." Erin added that, among left-leaning groups throughout the country, "there's actually plenty of white organizations that aren't deeply connected to BIPOC-led work that are doing things off by their own," though generally in ways that fail to name this fact or reckon with white dominance.

In their efforts to build cross-racial and cross-organizational political power, SURJ acknowledges that BIPOC organizations run the gamut of priorities and political visions. The organization is not just seeking BIPOC partners wherever they might find them. Instead, the groups that SURJ counts among its "strategic" or "accountability" partners are politically aligned, which Anne Dunlap described as follows: "We may not agree on all the things, but we're generally abolitionist, anticapitalist, and feminist."

Nana Gyamfi, the executive director of Black Alliance for Just Immigration, agreed that productive accountability partnerships require multiple nodes of affinity across organizational and racial lines. As a Black organizer, strategist, and movement lawyer for over twenty-five years, Nana has worked with BLM Los Angeles and White People for Black Lives. Using the example of this partnership, she offered some basic queries that SURJ groups more broadly might consider:

> If you're saying it's White People for Black Lives, then you need to be accountable to Black people. Who are the Black people you're accountable to, though, right? There needs to be some grounding. What's the purpose? What's the interest? And then how are you accountable?

Under these multiple considerations, SURJ does hold a number of national-level partnerships with BIPOC-led organizations, which they make public. Such partnerships tend to be more formalized than the myriad constellations that exist at the local level. For example, now that SURJ has a large enough staff, different SURJ employees are often designated as the specific liaison with a given partner organization. This means regularly communicating with that partner in order to help facilitate SURJ's work to support BIPOC-led projects at both the national and local level. There are also regular feedback mechanisms by which SURJ's partner organizations evaluate these partnerships as well as individual staff members. For instance, as one portion of each SURJ employee's annual performance review, the employee receives feedback from the person at the partner organization with whom they work most closely.

Local chapters are encouraged, though not required, to work in partnership with at least one BIPOC-led group in their region. The particular SURJ groups I focus on in this study have built and maintain deep levels of trust and coordination with their partners. Nevertheless, a dilemma that a number of participants raised was what to do when a SURJ chapter does not have a local BIPOC-led group with whom they share political alignment. My data do not allow me to determine what percentage of local SURJ groups find themselves in this situation. It does seem that this issue rarely impacts SURJ groups that have existed for more than five years. Whether or not this is because groups without local partners tend to disband more swiftly is an open and interesting question.

Some SURJ leaders with whom I spoke in 2021 were actively considering the dilemma of SURJ groups without local partners. Liz Sutton, a longtime organizer of the Los Angeles group, who had also worked on projects with SURJ national, explained her belief that "the relationship with the accountability partners is *the* thing. It is the number one most important thing, and it is the thing that makes or breaks SURJ chapters." Even with this strong of an assessment, Liz did not believe that this should prevent a SURJ group without a local partner from forming in the first place. Instead, Liz framed the quandary as

> trying to create paths to accountability for chapters that don't have BIPOC-led groups to work with, like an area where it's very white. So, it *is* organizing in isolation and not in direct accountability, which is problematic. But does that mean that those people shouldn't do that? No, we need everyone to do it. And so that's an ongoing thing.

Here, "that" and "it" can be assumed to mean bringing more white people into racial justice organizing.

The primary structural solution to this is the creation of the national membership system, by which individuals join SURJ-coordinated efforts at the local, state, and national level, always in collaboration with partners. Still, the organization does not want to dissuade local groups from forming if there is momentum, even in the absence of a partner. To this end, the organization does believe it possible to align with a Black liberation vision without the presence of Black-led partners. Many leaders referenced the public platform of the Movement for Black Lives in this regard. Grace Aheron, for example, explained:

> [The] Movement for Black Lives is so clear on what's supposed to happen right now. They've already told us. They've already told the world. There's multiple robust ideas for legislation, [for] work in your local community, study stuff. We've been told what to do, by them, and that's bring more and more people into alignment around the

model to divest money from police and the carceral state and invest it in community infrastructure.

Anne Dunlap corroborated this approach, while acknowledging its vexations: "it is possible to move in alignment with [our partners'] political vision, even if there's not really anybody to be in relationship with on the ground, which is tricky." Anne went on to delineate between two kinds of accountability, which are in many ways interconnected. The first is being accountable to a vision and set of policy aims in the abstract. This is the way that SURJ hopes groups that do not have cross-racial partnerships might nevertheless proceed. The second part of this accountability, however, is anchored in actual relationships across race, relationships that many activists and scholars agree are crucial in supporting white people in seeking to align with a vision of racial justice.[35] Anne continued:

> You can be accountable to this vision, but who are you actually in relationship with who will be able to tell you like you're actually not leading towards this vision in these particular ways? [Who] can actually hold you accountable for when we make mistakes, because we will? How will you know if you're actually moving in a good way if you're not in some kind of relationship somehow that can help with course correction, if you will?

Of course, if having no local partnerships "is tricky," such trickiness is not eliminated when a group appears to have all of the "right" ingredients, such as at least one healthy and functioning cross-racial partnership with an aligned organization. Anne continued, "It's still tricky 'cause: (a) humans and (b) white supremacy." Put otherwise, SURJ does not believe in a magic recipe for moving in accountability with BIPOC-led struggle, even if it does have a sense of some optimal conditions for doing so. Moreover, as a guiding principle, SURJ generally avoids allowing the pursuit of perfection to prevent it from moving people into action. In this instance, SURJ has concluded that for the time being, as Anne put it, "the lack of [BIPOC] people to partner with is not reason enough to feel like you can't be aligned in the work."

It is also helpful here to understand SURJ's larger vision of accountability to BIPOC-led struggle, which is anchored in building a critical mass of white people to join in racial justice struggles. As Carla Wallace put it:

> If we're going to be accountable to Black, Brown, and Indigenous people, if we're going to be accountable to antiracist struggle, we have to grow [the white base]. There is no accountability when there's three of us. We can't challenge power. We can't challenge oppression. We aren't bringing enough to the table. We have to bring a whole lot more if we are going to be genuinely in solidarity and accountability with communities of color, with poor people, with people who are disabled.

The organization thus assesses that only by bringing many more white people into movement, and leading strategy in predominantly white communities, can actual accountability to a BIPOC-led liberation strategy be realized. I now turn to introduce the three urban chapters selected for this study.

LOUISVILLE SURJ (LSURJ)

Louisville SURJ officially formed in 2012. I selected LSURJ because of Louisville's rich movement history and the important individuals involved in this group. Louisville is Carla Wallace's hometown, a city that Pam McMichael also calls home, and the place in which important influences—from the Bradens to Ella Baker and Angela Davis—did a good deal, and in the Bradens' case, the majority, of their organizing. While not a central reason for its selection in this study, it is noteworthy that Louisville was the location of the high-profile police murder of Breonna Taylor in the spring of 2020, which ignited months of intense protest activity. This movement context is obviously an important one. Many interviews, particularly with Black partners, emphasized LSURJ's central role in supporting Black-led protest during the year following Taylor's murder.

LSURJ's first coordinated action in 2012 was to show up at a KKK rally in the Kentucky state capital of Frankfort with signs that read "Another White Person for Racial Justice." Other early efforts included fighting for the rights of Walmart workers and, later, joining an ultimately successful environmental justice campaign led by Black women living in the California neighborhood of Louisville.[36] Early LSURJ leaders had also been active in countering ICE attacks on Latinx immigrants in the city. Beginning during the first Trump presidency, LSURJ would play an important role in coalition work to fight ever-more draconian immigrant enforcement efforts.

LSURJ also took part in various efforts around prisons and policing as part of their abolitionist commitments. In 2016 and 2017, the group worked with Black Lives Matter and allies to fight two Kentucky-wide policies. The first delineated the police as a protected class who warranted protection from "hate crimes."[37] The second enhanced penalties for purported gang members.[38] Beginning in 2018, and working with the local affiliate of the Bail Project, LSURJ began their long-term campaign to end cash bail, which continued at the time of this writing. That work was expanding to include the fight against a new jail, in collaboration with a number of Black-led organizations in the city. LSURJ held a number of other partnerships, both with local Black and Latinx organizations, as well as individual organizers who have changed affiliation over time.

WHITE PEOPLE FOR BLACK LIVES, LOS ANGELES

This chapter has already dedicated a good deal of discussion to the AWARE network, from which White People for Black Lives (WP4BL) in Los Angeles emerged in 2014. WP4BL continued as the action arm of the larger AWARE organization, and during the years of this research, held its primary partnership with the local affiliate of the global Black Lives Matter network: BLM Los Angeles. I selected WP4BL primarily for its size and significance as a local SURJ chapter as well as the group's embeddedness within AWARE-LA. WP4BL was at the forefront of not just responding to Black-led organizing initiatives, but also in mounting its own broadly abolitionist campaigns in predominantly white communities. Important among these was the group's development and testing of the technique of deep canvassing, a door-knocking tactic that has been demonstrated to shift people's enduring attitudes and belief structures.[39]

Investigating WP4BL also allowed me to trace the development of white antiracist organizing approaches over two decades, as AWARE predates and deeply influences the national SURJ organization. As has been explored, AWARE was among the first to push for a more welcoming and nonjudgmental approach to white antiracist culture. The group was also early to experiment with and assess a more reciprocal approach to cross-racial partnership. Finally, WP4BL gave me the opportunity to investigate a unique chapter-level structure, as AWARE maintained distinct if overlapping spaces for various antiracist practices. These ranged from dialogue spaces (Saturday Dialogues) to intensive training institutes (Unmasking Whiteness) to the action and campaign space of White People for Black Lives. I participated in all of these during the course of research.

SURJ BUFFALO

I introduce SURJ Buffalo by telling a bit more about Erin Heaney, who was instrumental to the formation of the Buffalo chapter before she would also help shape the trajectory of the national organization. Erin grew up in Buffalo in a political household. Her Irish American grandfather, whom she never met but was often told she resembled, was involved in the Irish freedom struggle in the 1960s. Her father was an investigative reporter and a lead negotiator in his union. Erin was further politicized in college at Swarthmore, doing human rights organizing and working on Obama's campaign in some of the swing counties in Pennsylvania that would prove pivotal to the 2008 election.

After college, a family friend introduced Erin to a group of people in the western New York town in which her father had been raised. Erin described them as

> mostly white working folks, who were really sick. They lived in a very, very industrialized community. There were like 50 industrial

plants within a two-mile radius and a lot of people living there; so very high rates of asthma and cancer.[40]

The group had raised some money to hire a community organizer, and, as Erin explained, "I met with them and really fell in love with them and really was moved by the organizing they were doing: very, very scrappy organizing." While returning to Buffalo had not been her initial plan, Erin agreed to work for the group, which ultimately won important campaigns, forcing a number of companies to pay remedies to the community for their unscrupulous practices. This group would later formalize itself as a nonprofit that continues to fight for environmental and economic justice issues throughout the region.

Erin's organizing experiences also taught her about the political impacts of white racism. By her analysis, racism was the reason that the group lost the campaigns it did lose. Particularly as the group became more multiracial, white racism would "blow up the coalitions that were required for us to actually win, if it went unaddressed." Erin also witnessed how the group's "opposition would use racist divide and conquer tactics to peel white people away from the coalitions that were required for us to win really big things." Erin thus became more and more obsessed, as she put it, with how "to bring and keep white people in the multiracial coalitions we need so that we actually have enough power to win."[41]

Around this time, in 2014, the Ferguson uprisings were drawing national coverage, to which Erin, as part of a multiracial group of activists, was paying attention. SURJ Buffalo would form in tandem with the Black and Latinx-led group Just Resisting (later Black Love Resists in the Rust), both groups wanting to organize for racial justice in the Buffalo area and ultimately becoming long-term strategic partners. SURJ Buffalo was supported by the national network, not so much in terms of resources—SURJ was still what Erin described as "a very bare-bones kind of all-volunteer effort at the time"—but in terms of "helping us understand ourselves as part of and connected to a much broader lineage" of white people involved in Black-led liberation struggle.[42]

The group had its first meeting in the same church basement where

I would go on to meet them seven years later. Erin explained that SURJ Buffalo's first participants were generally committed activists working in a number of issue areas, who had been in the streets in solidarity with the young Black activists in Ferguson, but they wanted to do more. The group's first action was thus to raise money for the bail fund of Ferguson activists who had been arrested.

Soon after, they began door knocking in predominantly white neighborhoods, as Erin recalled, "to try to see if we could build some sort of more visible support for racial justice work in the city." While visiting the homes of strangers certainly requires guts, and a few of their neighbors were "wild people who were against us," the group actually found a number of white people "hungry to talk about race and to be invited into something different and bigger."[43] As the organization grew its base of volunteers, they joined with Just Resisting to help "disband . . . the most ruthless and violent parts of the Buffalo Police Department [and] won some big cuts to the sheriff's budget." These campaigns were selected and led by Black organizers. Erin suggested that SURJ Buffalo was nevertheless "playing a really important role in terms of demonstrating visible white support for these changes. And I think that that was a really critical part of having the power to win." Bringing white people into multiracial, Black-led struggle is, as Erin explained, "the work of SURJ." While SURJ Buffalo has engaged in other campaign efforts during its tenure, it continued to work with the same strategic partner, Black Love Resists in the Rust, at the time of writing and had ultimately come to focus its efforts on the county-level Erie Sheriff's Department as part of its broader abolitionist commitments.

In terms of the national organization, Erin became SURJ's executive director during a time when those who came out of poor and working-class organizing were still in the minority. Many were also uncertain of how to take their efforts to scale, and whether or not they even should. Carla emphasized that Erin's influence on these matters was pivotal:

> Heaney came out of work in majority white working-class neighborhoods and knew the rigor it took to develop vision that is actionable, to build a base, to grow leaders among people who had never been

engaged in social justice work, to create the on-ramps so people get involved instead of fading away.

Any individual's capacity for leadership is shaped by the many from and with whom they learn and organize. Yet Carla assessed that Erin's influence on the organization had indelibly impacted the ability to grow its membership and strategic capacities, particularly beyond the usual cohort of those white people being brought into social justice work: liberal-leaning, middle-class, and wealthy people, often residing in urban and suburban places. The terminology of "on-ramps," used by many study participants, indicates creating a range of clear, specific, and accessible ways that people from all walks of life can find a role in movement work.

I selected SURJ Buffalo for a few reasons. First, it was a group recommended to me by early contacts because of the working-class makeup of the city and region, a place that has been shaped by the state and market transitions of deindustrialization and welfare cuts begun in the 1970s. These transitions, which have had their most significant impact on BIPOC communities, also deeply impact the poor and working-class white communities that SURJ wishes to reach. Second, at a very practical level, Buffalo was a city that I could drive to in a matter of hours. While in early 2021 I saw most events happening virtually across the groups I studied due to pandemic conditions, by later that year I was able to join in on-the-ground campaign activities with the Buffalo group. Third, a number of SURJ staff, including Erin Heaney, were based in Buffalo during my research. The next chapter begins the more sustained exploration of *how* the groups in this study seek to build a critical mass of white people to take action for racial justice.

3 WHITE PRIVILEGE IS NOT AN ORGANIZING STRATEGY

IN OCTOBER OF 2017, RESIDENTS in and around the town of Shelbyville, Tennessee, learned that white nationalists were planning two local rallies to oppose resident immigrant and refugee populations from Central America and Somalia, whom they claimed threatened their pursuit of a "white ethnostate."[1] It had been less than a year since the violent white nationalist Unite the Right rally in Charlottesville, Virginia, which injured many and left one counter-protester dead, a context fresh in people's minds.[2]

Kelly Sue Waller, who lived a few miles outside of Shelbyville at the time, joined with some local friends to oppose the hate rally. They asked Shelbyville businesses to put up "Boo to Hate" signs in the windows, as Halloween was coming. They knocked on neighbors' doors, including a mixed-race, low-income housing project adjacent to where the White Lives Matter rally was planned. Kelly Sue recalls, "Most people didn't want it. The city council didn't want it, but also didn't want to condemn it. A group of churches did condemn it."

On the day of the rally, the Latinx community had organized a huge pozole potluck a street away, which drew many more people than the rally. At this potluck, one of SURJ's then co-directors met Kelly Sue and asked to be taken door knocking to meet local people. The potlucks would become a monthly occurrence, though with a small group of predominantly white, poor, and working-class women. Kelly Sue recalled how the conversations began to evolve, with people asking, "Why did [right-wing extremists] come here? Why did they think our town? What are the problems?" Kelly Sue would ultimately be hired by SURJ to try to figure this out and to help build a response.

For ten months, Kelly Sue and the community leaders she identified and recruited into action went door-to-door, having conversations with more than 230 renters in Shelbyville, a town whose population is 56 percent white, 26 percent Latinx, and 12 percent Black.[3] If the threat of a white nationalist protest had given those in Shelbyville an urgent motivation to get organized, the group identified a widespread and enduring economic struggle and injustice: a handful of unscrupulous landlords who held a monopoly in a city of mostly low-income renters. What would ultimately emerge as the Bedford County Listening Project (BCLP), a group that I will continue to analyze later in this chapter, exemplifies how SURJ seeks to enact a mutual interest framework in their organizing.

The mutual or shared interest approach invites those from predominantly white communities to identify how they hold common cause with Black, Indigenous, and people of color (BIPOC) in dismantling key features of the current social order. It centers an analysis of white supremacy as intersecting with, and serving to uphold, a number of systems that do harm to nearly everyone, whites included. Mutual interest organizing seeks to demonstrate to white communities how racism operates as a political wedge. Those with less power are enticed to direct their fear and resentment towards each other rather than at powerful decision-makers. This approach stands in stark contrast to the more singular focus on white privilege that has become dominant in many white antiracist spaces, often in ways that become individualizing and demobilizing. Centering white peoples' shared stake with BIPOC acknowledges that white people have racial privilege, but this is not the same as saying they have individualized power within the larger social system.

There is certainly no foolproof approach to antiracist organizing, particularly among white communities. Nevertheless, a shared interest lens is adopted within a set of overarching principles: that movements for racial justice require many more white adherents and that effective political work does not require that whites acquire erudite analysis or moral perfection before they act. Instead, collective action is understood as both necessary for changing social systems as well as itself a site of important forms of learning and personal transformation.

In what follows, I lay out the rationale for making a shift from the white privilege analytic to a shared interest approach. I then turn to how shared stake organizing can look in practice, focusing on the Bedford County Listening Project in particular, and SURJ's rural organizing infrastructure more generally. I also explore how mutual interest organizing can operate in this study's urban groups, where the focus is generally on campaigns for prison and police abolition. Throughout the chapter, I consider potential challenges with the approach as well as how organizers assess and seek to confront these.

THE WHITE PRIVILEGE ANALYTIC

SURJ leaders suggested that when the network began to cohere, a significant number of white people who were engaged with antiracism were guided by the framework of white privilege. SURJ co-founder Carla Wallace explained:

> [For] a lot of the white folks who were already in motion, [the white privilege frame] was kind of their starting place. We have workshops to tell white people they have white privilege . . . and those are all legitimate, important conversations.

In line with the scholarly critiques discussed in Chapter 1, many participants discussed how the analysis of white privilege was often taken up in a manner that focused on white people's personal growth without an eye to political organizing and action.[4] Grace, a self-described multiracial Asian American southerner who works for SURJ, explained how her initial encounters with white antiracism included "learning about white privilege and doing classes, and not as much about campaigning and building power." SURJ organizers suggested that the white privilege analytic has tended to send white people in the direction of seeking to correct for their individual shortcomings without the context of a larger, collective vision for action.

Jason, who has been involved in antiracist work in Los Angeles for over two decades, reflected that "Peggy McIntosh's work ... becomes the confessional form of antiracism. It's like, 'how good can I be at naming all my privileges.'" Through this framework, Jason saw people "get really good at unpacking their stuff" but continue to lack "the frames that move people to see themselves as like actors and having agency in a different way."

Carla Wallace continued:

[It] left white people very internally focused on "I'm going to personally make myself a better white person." And it was totally disconnected from base building, growing something that could join with Black and other people of color to challenge power, challenge the system. Folks were getting stuck there.

Activist projects require both individual and collective transformation, but this subject work needs to be tied to the forging of new social and political systems as well.

A number of white participants also suggested that the emphasis on racial privilege alone failed to provide the kind of intersectional analysis that had drawn them into their own antiracist commitments. Elisabeth Long of Catalyst Project recalled that in her attempts to join white antiracist groups in earlier years, she often found they were dominated by middle- and owning-class whites, who were "equating their very classed experience of whiteness with the experience of being white in the world." Elisabeth had been raised working class and was ultimately "politicized through women of color feminism." By reading the work of Black feminists in particular, Elisabeth was able to envision a world in which the police would not have exacerbated her own experiences of sexual violence as a young person. Her mother's mental health issues would have been addressed with care and dignity rather than putting the family in financial duress. Her father, uncles, and cousins would not have spent years in jails and prisons. Elisabeth found that she often entered white antiracist groups as the sole white person who had not grown up with class privilege, and that others were "talking about white privilege . . . as if white people never experience any harm from the criminal punishment system." That experience felt like it erased Elisabeth's close and regular interaction with policing and prisons.

Despite being part of the upper middle class, Rebecca traced a similar experience. As a former community organizer, Rebecca recounted "really wanting to be part of this organization" when she joined the Los Angeles group in 2017. She was eager to have a place to struggle for prison abolition and racial justice as a white woman. Still, after eighteen months of finding her group "so focused on privilege, I started to feel really alienated." Rebecca explained that she had come to Los Angeles after many years of living "in a really unsafe situation, domestic violence relationship," and that her own stake in antiracism and abolition had been forged in large part by "living in a society that only trained me to call the police when I needed help [that] didn't serve me at all, when I actually needed help." Instead, calling the police made things worse. Rebecca never contested the idea that white people have been given certain privileges under white supremacy, but she believed a more complex, intersectional assessment of white people's stake in the work was needed.

On a much broader scale, SURJ organizers have found that approaching many working-class white communities with an analysis predicated on their privilege often conflicts with people's subjective sense of their social and economic status. Erin Heaney, SURJ's executive director, explained that

> as the primary organizing invitation [white privilege] just doesn't resonate for like lots and lots of poor and working-class white people. Even though I would say poor and working-class white people still do have white privilege. It is not an invitation into the work, and it doesn't speak to people's real lived experience.

Erin here captures the fact that many poor and working-class people do not assess themselves as living with privilege as they struggle to make ends meet.

Beth Howard, SURJ's Appalachian organizer, explained how the framing of white privilege has long kept white majorities from wanting to join groups like SURJ. She offered a hypothetical from her own upbringing:

> So you're talking to a poor white person in my community, for example, who grew up in a trailer park, who had a single mother trying to raise three kids, worked two jobs, didn't have a reliable car, didn't always have school clothes, had to walk to work, on and on, and you tell them they're privileged. Like, that shuts the conversation down immediately, right?

While organizers understand that white people enjoy racial privilege even if they lack class privilege, they find that the language of white privilege does not work as an initial invitation in their efforts to grow a larger base of white antiracists. A declaration of this lesson that organizers have come to repeat is, "white privilege is real, but it is not an organizing strategy."

Deciding not to lead with the discourse of white privilege is a tactical choice and must be justified in this way. It is not true, of course, that white privilege does not speak to poor white people's real lived experience, so much as it contrasts with their subjective understanding of that experience. As many have shown, it is precisely the fact of being white, with its privileges and sense of entitlement, that leads many white people across class status to reject an assessment that they have privilege in the first place. Indeed, white people have been consistently and actively recruited to see their misery as an insult to their whiteness, and often their maleness, and as a result of unfair preferences being given to people of color.[5]

White privilege certainly works differently by class and location. For example, in urban environments we know that poor white children go to school with more middle-class children than do poor Black children. Poor whites find it easier to get housing in well-resourced neighborhoods and are less susceptible to living near polluting facilities than are middle-class Blacks. While such findings have less to say about how white privilege operates in the rural South, where SURJ has prioritized much of its organizing, we do know that one form of unearned privilege enjoyed by white southerners and whites living in rural areas is the artificial augmentation of their voting power should they choose to vote in the first place. Indeed, the direct political power of the white southern electorate is one of the strategic reasons SURJ has for organizing with these communities.[6]

Moving away from the discourse of "white privilege" does not mean SURJ organizers do not discuss race, or that they resist naming white racism, when seeking to reach out to new members. They actively do both, through a process that is slow, sustained, and rooted in building relationships, as this chapter will explore. In so doing, however, organizers also seek to meet people where they are, which means honoring subjective experiences as well as objective circumstances. Here, organizers prioritize making antiracist action seem sensible and appealing to a wider white audience, believing that it is through struggle itself that antiracist consciousness and commitment can most effectively be forged.

This approach is very much in line with the tactical flexibility espoused by Anne Braden, a longtime mentor to the SURJ co-founders: Carla Wallace and Pam McMichael. Braden issued a statement to fellow white activists in 1966 soon after the Student Nonviolent Coordinating Committee had asked white people to leave the organization. In it, she described the need for white organizers to center the goal of racial justice even when approaching poor and working-class white people in the U.S. South. Braden was very clear, however, that it would be "stupidity" to suggest "organizers ringing doorbells in white communities and opening the conversation by saying, 'I'm here to talk about white supremacy and Negro-white unity and what you can do about it.'"[7]

THE MUTUAL INTEREST FRAME

SURJ organizers ultimately assessed that conversations around white privilege were neither motivating and sustaining collective action nor drawing in the white communities that SURJ most wants to reach. Carla recalled, "This was the place where we started realizing, okay, if not the white privilege frame, what is our frame? We have to have one. And that's where mutual interest came out." All social movements must work to move potential adherents (the many people who may be sympathetic to a cause) to become actual constituents (those willing to take political action). One way that movements do this is through the deployment of collective action frames, which help diverse peoples to forge a common understanding of both the social problem at hand and the steps necessary to achieve a social systemic solution. Successful collective action frames need to be compelling enough to transition potential movement adherents into constituents, to mobilize people into action.[8] SURJ sees the mutual interest approach as holding the potential to accomplish this task in ways that the white privilege analytic could not.

The frame of mutual interest is premised on the idea that the vast majority of white people also have something to gain over the long term from ending a social order predicated on white supremacy. Erin explained:

> The mutual interest approach to this work says that we all have a stake in ending white supremacy. Not the same. It's not to minimize or flatten the very different ways that racism [works]. It's not to say that white privilege doesn't exist.

A mutual interest approach does not require that differently positioned people have identical experiences in order to find points of meaningful political affinity.

Grace added that the mutual interest frame pushes against dominant ways of thinking and acting around race in U.S. society: "white people have been politicized around race effectively to believe that they don't have anything in common with people of color struggles." For as long as whiteness has existed, white people have been recruited to oppose, abuse, resent, and extract from communities of color. Today, most whites believe that political struggles for racial justice will result in their own losses.[9] A shared interest approach seeks to demonstrate to white majorities, particularly those who are poor and working class, how multiracial alignment can build a social order that betters conditions for all. This framework also pushes against neoliberal logics more generally. Instead of seeking individualized solutions to systemic problems, a shared interest lens posits a social structural critique and emphasizes our collective interdependence.

Beth reflected on how an understanding of her shared stake with BIPOC, and the political education that followed, led her to "see the world differently" in a way that she could not unsee:

> Like growing up working class, growing up a girl and later a woman in Appalachia, you know, a lot of pain and suffering I have experienced kind of fell into this whole systemic view: the majority of us will struggle, suffer, and die so a handful can be billionaires.

Of the particular struggles she saw her community face, Beth named some of the common ravages of poverty: insecure housing, poor working conditions, low-paying jobs and joblessness, addiction and overdose. She explained how the lens of mutual interest had the potential to show white working people their own stake in dismantling white supremacy. She continued:

> Racism has systematically been used to divide my people—poor and working-class white people—away from Black and Brown people so that we can have collective power to protect ourselves, fight for each other, and win the world that we desperately need.

Alicia Hurle—a longtime Black organizer in Louisville, partner to various SURJ efforts in Kentucky, and executive director of the Commonwealth Alliance Voter Engagement at the time of our interview—similarly observed, "especially when you're talking to poor and working- class people, you can't just say, 'Hey, did you know those people over there are suffering?'" By way of contrast, she suggested that the mutual interest approach begins by really grounding people in what [poor and working-class whites] are experiencing, and then how that's tied to other people that they wouldn't normally consider as perhaps sharing struggle, right? And then how do we actually come together to push back against the people who are actually oppressing us?

In this context, mutual interest is understood as the most strategic way to invite white people into an effort strong enough to meaningfully challenge the current social order. Like many movement efforts, SURJ understands the need to bring people together across difference, in this case with a particular focus on race, in order to force concessions from those who hold outsized social, economic, and political power.

In line with this, Attica Scott—a longtime Black organizer in Louisville, partner of LSURJ, and Kentucky state senator at the time of our interview—emphasized the need to focus working and poor people of all races on their clear and urgent need to unite. Commenting on "low and moderate income" communities in the racially segregated city of Louisville, she remarked:

> We're being pitted against one another, being told that there's a scarcity of resources that we got to compete for, versus realizing, acknowledging and working on the fact that we have so much more in common than we do that's different. And if we can build from there, we can build some collective power and really change some things.

The mutual interest frame has clear potential for organizing poor and working-class people across race. It also resists the common tendency for white people to see themselves as mere helpers in racial justice struggles or, worse, to act as heroic saviors. Such a pattern has emerged throughout history, creating power struggles and conflicts that have derailed multiracial action.[10] Alicia Hurle continued:

> In my previous organizing with a lot of white folks, it always kind of felt like a little bit of charity-based work, right? Like they were there to help or to assist, not so much like, what's your stake in this, right?

Alicia recalled her profound frustration with this orientation, wanting to tell white people in movement work that, "You're not just being altruistic; you actually are working for a better world for yourself, too!"

Providing a pathway for white people to come to know and feel their own vested interest in fighting for racial justice may also have practical implications for activists' endurance. Scholars and organizers have long been interested in what sustains movement participation, a question that gains complexity in the case of those who struggle against systems that do not most directly impact them and from which they may even benefit. Some research finds that these activists tend to be more risk-averse and less committed when compared to a movement's "core constituents."[11] Orienting white people to the ways in which struggles for racial justice might also enhance their own lives holds the potential to deepen white people's commitment to antiracist action.

Alicia called SURJ's shift from a focus on white privilege to a mutual interest organizing approach to be "a game changer" both in terms of the way white people talked about antiracism as well as their practical impacts. Where the discussion of racial justice efforts among white-led groups used to be "that work over there that Black and Brown people do," she found SURJ's shared interest approach diffusing across activist spaces. White people seemed more and more to be engaging in what Alicia termed, "this collective project ... white supremacy is a disease that affects us all. [It] is about solidarity and mutual interest and that it is a responsibility of all people, and especially white people to dismantle white supremacy." Just as importantly, Alicia saw this shift as enabling SURJ to both "broaden and deepen" what she called "grassroots organizing base-building work" across the state of Kentucky and, in so doing, bring many other groups along with them.

There are nevertheless important challenges that SURJ must confront in its choice to pursue a mutual interest framework. For one, even if white people are presented with overwhelming evidence of how racism prevents them from making common cause with communities of color to fight for better conditions for *all* people, mutual interest does require a sense of solidarity and long-term investment. Elisabeth of Catalyst acknowledged that while it "is not strategic in the long run" for white communities to invest in white supremacy, "on a material level, white people do get shit if they are racist." She continued, "if you're like, 'I want to have more money for my family' . . . you can make racist decisions that support that." Particularly in urban and suburban areas, such decisions might include choosing to purchase a home in a predominantly white neighborhood, where multiple stages of the home buying and selling process have been shown to materially benefit whites.[12]

White supremacy has also been repeatedly mobilized to offer white people social and psychic rewards in order to incentivize them to break ranks with those racialized as non-white who share their material interests.[13] Building on this knowledge, Elisabeth explained her disagreement with a common refrain on the Left that poor and working-class white people "are always voting against their interests," as if those interests were solely economic. Rather, she acknowledged how powerful the psychic rewards of white supremacy can be: "plenty of people genuinely want to feel above other groups of people." This is one of the powerful and historically proven ways that white supremacy has won the loyalty of those raced as white.

A keen observer might also note that the shared interest approach sounds somewhat akin to Derrick Bell's crucial insight regarding interest convergence, which has come to stand as one of the fundaments of critical race theory. Bell observed that, when it comes to political change, "the interest of blacks in achieving racial equality will be accommodated only when it converges with the interests of whites."[14] This is a form of interest convergence that upholds white supremacy: Black people are afforded freedoms and inclusion only when it suits those raced as white. It is nevertheless important that Bell specified this "interest convergence" as motivating key decision-makers within the dominant racial state and market. SURJ's shared interest approach pursues a different vision, that of abolitionist and anticapitalist critique, and manner of implementation, that of grassroots organizing towards the ends of multiracial democracy. This is not to say that this appeal to white peoples' mutual interest with BIPOC does not risk devolving into Bell's conception of interest convergence, but that it intends to be something quite different.

BEYOND SELF-INTEREST

In order to anticipate such dilemmas, organizers understand that their approach must ultimately move white people beyond a narrow sense of self-interest. While efforts may begin by appealing to peoples' immediate, material needs, this is done so as to invite people into political struggle. The theory, anchored in participants' experiences and building on various organizing traditions, is that through movement involvement, people's understandings of the world, and of their own interests, can evolve and transform.[15]

Kelly Sue, whose organizing in Shelbyville, Tennessee, opened this chapter, understood this as precisely what happened with her. Growing up "below the poverty level" in "small towns all across the South," Kelly Sue would tell those with whom she organizes, "I am of and from here. And I have transformed my belief systems of the world without leaving home, without going off to college, without getting exposed to some other world, right here in Tennessee." Kelly Sue credited her transformation to finding a worker's center when she was in her early twenties after organizers left flyers in the hotel where she was cleaning rooms. Kelly Sue continued:

> I was transformed by the movement here, by the relationships that I built, and by becoming a part of a group that was not just identified by my family or the color of my skin but was around the identity of being a worker.

Here Kelly Sue identifies an important feature of a shared interest approach, which appeals to the other subject positions white people hold in common with BIPOC—for example, as tenants, as those vulnerable to mental health challenges and drug addiction, or, in Kelly Sue's case, as workers.

By coming together with other workers in shared struggle, Kelly Sue "was introduced to the idea of multiracial solidarity" and came to understand her racial privilege, working alongside hotel crews who were largely Latinx. She reflected, "I already knew that there were many ways that bosses would use to keep us separated." This included assigning people to certain more or less desirable hotel floors based on their race and spoken language, or putting someone from one group in charge of people from another. It was not until the conversations at the worker's center, however, that Kelly Sue understood just how intentional these tactics were: "literally some people were paid more than other people for doing the same job in the same hotel on the same floor."

Kelly Sue thus came to see the complex inheritance of her whiteness, how she was both harmed as a worker but protected because of her race, which bosses used to pit her against fellow workers:

> I was white and this was a predominantly Latino worker's center. I saw that I was also being screwed over. But what I didn't have happen is bosses trying to use my documentation as a way to take advantage of me. I was monolingual, but most of the people in charge were monolingual the way I was. They spoke the language that I spoke.

During worker-initiated negotiations, "the bosses" would grant Kelly Sue a higher respect, attempting to speak with her instead of her Latinx colleagues when she was not the designated spokesperson. The worker's center had prepared its members for this, and Kelly Sue knew to refuse the effort at ingratiation.

Reflecting on this process, Kelly Sue was clear that her learning had to occur in the context of fighting for better immediate working conditions, coupled with the worker's center's framing and analysis: "that worker's center never once told me, 'Kelly, you have white privilege,' because they didn't have to, because we were in struggle together, and everything we did was built upon 'let's reflect on what happened.'" Kelly Sue juxtaposed this to being "sat down in a room" and offered new and rarefied vocabulary, such as the term "white privilege": "I just wouldn't have known what they were talking about. And it wouldn't have applied to my life the way that it did to move through wage theft cases with people."

Research affirms that appealing to people's most immediate self-interest, such as Kelly Sue's desire for better working conditions, can serve as an effective first step to building a movement constituency. Studies also suggest, however, that in order to sustain continued involvement, a sense of collectivism has to develop. This is in part because long-term political struggle requires participants make personal sacrifices for something beyond individualized or short-term rewards.[16] Sometimes group meetings are boring. Many tactics include some risk. For Kelly Sue, developing a sense of mutual interest across race, nationality, and language required building relationships with other workers in struggle.

As another example, SURJ co-founder Carla referenced her organizing work for gay and lesbian rights during the 1990s in Louisville, which informs SURJ strategy, as a way of explaining the trajectory that a shared interest approach can take. Many self-identified gay and lesbian activists, predominantly white, perceived their fight for recognition and access as separable from racial justice, though Carla and a few other leaders were convinced of the need to approach these efforts in tandem. She recalled how the gay and lesbian activists came to "[stand] with [the] Black community on an issue based on [the assumption that] if we stand with people that stand with us," it would be good strategy. In this instance, even if the initial motivation to make common cause was quite transactional, the point was to bring people together in practical struggle across their social differences:

> We always had the idea that getting people there, they would fall in love with each other, and care about each other and not want each other to be hurt. And that is exactly the experience we had when we can get people up in it with each other and really [believing] that our liberation is connected, even though our experience of oppression may be very, very different. It's never about saying it's all the same.

The mutual interest approach may seek to recruit adherents through short-term campaign efforts but ultimately intends to forge meaningful relationships between differently situated people. It seeks to transmute material incentives into solidary and purposive ones.[17] These include the rewards of political camaraderie as well as the satisfaction of having attached oneself to a larger collective vision. In this way, and as distinct from Derrick Bell's insights about interest convergence, SURJ works across "an expanded and more nuanced view of 'interest'" so as to reveal "the ways in which racism both benefits and disenfranchises whites."[18] The organization hedges its bets that, through sites and practices of struggle, white people will find that white supremacy is founded as much on moral and psychosocial poverty as it is on extractive and exploitative material conditions.

Michael Williams of BLM LA offered a final consideration of how participants' initial motivations to join movement work might be transformed through political engagement itself. Michael began by explaining his belief that "our basic altruism . . . is based off self-interest at some level," and so it likely makes sense for movements to recognize this in their recruitment efforts. He went on to clarify that his own involvement in BLM was "not because I was necessarily Black, but because where I live, I had a young man killed right up the street from me," an incident that "hit home finally, made me realize that this stuff can happen to me." Michael continued that, as someone who has now been deeply involved in political struggle for years, he doesn't "have the luxury" of deciding what pulls other people into the work. He discussed this both in terms of his Black family and neighbors as well as white participants, explaining, "I don't really care if you're doing this because you think you're going to benefit from it. The work still just needs to be done because everybody needs to do the work."

Drawing on his own experience, Michael also observed that one's perceived interests often shift during the course of political struggle. Considering the role of white people in Black-led efforts, Michael referenced his own involvement as a "cisgender straight man" in "women's spaces or LGBTQ spaces," where he had ultimately come to contextualize his own role within a shared interest approach. Michael concluded:

> I have a stake in their [women's and LGBTQ] freedom because it makes me more free, right? . . . It's the same thing with white folks coming into Black spaces, where it's like, you are becoming a better version of yourself the more you interact and fight for justice for Black folks.

Through his movement work, Michael has come to understand his own relationship to patriarchy a bit differently than he did initially. No longer does the terminology of "allyship" capture his orientation, he observed. Rather, he identifies his shared stake in this work. This offers a distinct example to the discussions of moving from self-interest to collective interest, as Michael's transition is one that goes from perceiving himself as a helper to understanding his own stake. His testimony nevertheless demonstrates how political struggle itself can reshape participant perceptions and motivations.

BEDFORD COUNTY LISTENING PROJECT

The Bedford County Listening Project (BCLP), which opened this chapter, demonstrates how a mutual interest approach can be transformative not only to its participants but also to larger political structures. I pick up the story where organizer Kelly Sue was joined by other residents in going door-to-door to gather testimonies around unlivable housing conditions, landlord intimidation, and mendacious leases. The group compiled this data and ultimately came up with a shared set of demands to bring to policymakers. They also engaged in a range of learning activities, conducting regular workshops to inform local tenants of their rights. They helped with crisis mitigation through mutual aid, working to consolidate resources among those who have been exploited by the market and neglected by the state. They engaged in actions to draw media attention and community support, holding satirically titled events, such as homeless warming parties and missing person events for absent property managers. Through this range of tactics, the group began to establish itself as a local presence. Meanwhile, participants deepened their understanding of how anti-immigrant sentiment and anti-Black racism are harmful to everyone. What residents really needed was the ability to join forces across race to fight for access to quality affordable housing.

In terms of bringing poor and working-class white people into a struggle premised on mutual interest, one journalist explained how this effort worked to unite "cash-poor white folks and immigrants, traditionally pitted against one another."[19] What at first coalesced as a group pushing for better housing for themselves and community, however, would ultimately become quite broadly responsive to racist attacks in the community. One of the first important moments in this evolution came in December of 2019. BCLP had planned a press event before the regular meeting of the Bedford County commissioners. The group would be releasing its housing report, demonstrating the failure of local government to protect renters. The morning of the event, Kelly Sue received a call from an organizer in Nashville who informed her that one of the commissioners, who had been unresponsive to the group's housing concerns, was planning to introduce an antirefugee ordinance at that evening's meeting. While the ordinance would do little in practice, it was symbolically hateful.

Kelly Sue took this information to members of the BCLP. She did not tell them what to do, simply what this commissioner was planning. The group of predominantly white single mothers immediately decided they wanted to rewrite their press statement to include the fact that the commissioner was now trying to villainize their refugee neighbors. Kelly Sue explained that the group also decided "to make different signs to hold up [at the event] that said, 'less slumlords, more refugees.'"[20] The decision was made "last minute, people decided that's what they wanted to do." Kelly was clear about who was in the BCLP: "none of them were activists prior to this. And nobody was Democrat." If "some of them voted for Trump" in the 2016 election, before the BCLP was formed, most had not voted at all. These were people whom Kelly Sue had met through door knocking, with whom she had built relationships and done leadership development. They were "kind, nice people [and] smart and strategic. They knew that two issues against that guy [commissioner] is better than one."

BCLP members were certainly offended by an ordinance that said, "'they don't want your neighbors here, who live in the house next to you.'" Many in the group had also become quite politically astute, understanding the ordinance as a distraction. One BCLP member was clear:

> That refugee thing was doing nothing. It was just another dumb tactic of someone trying to talk about something that wasn't gonna

put food on [her] table, wasn't gonna get her a better job, wasn't gonna give her kid a better school, and wasn't gonna give her a better rental house.

The group's decision to unite against the antirefugee proposal, which they ultimately helped to defeat, offers some proof of concept. Through a mutual interest approach, BCLP members came to have great clarity that improving local housing conditions also means refusing xenophobic racism.

By September of 2020, as the presidential campaign was heating up alongside down-ballot races, an organizer with BCLP, Stephanie Isaacs, announced her run for city council.[21] This was a decision made after months of frustration with how the group was being received in council meetings. Kelly Sue recalled:

> I remember the day [in February 2020] we went to talk to city council, and they wouldn't listen to us. They rejected us. I remember [Stephanie Isaacs] looked at all them and was like, "Well, if you're not going to help, we'll just vote you out."

Isaacs's time with the BCLP was formative to her electoral campaign. Kelly Sue continued:

> She took what she had learned being a part of the Bedford County Listening Project, and she knocked every door in her neighborhood, talked to everybody in her ward. Everybody. Wore her shoes out. They all knocked doors, renters who she had built relationships with in the campaign work [with BCLP].

Isaacs's pro-renter platform would ultimately become an anti-Klan one as well. This is because in early October, many Shelbyville residents, particularly those expressing support for the Biden campaign, found their yards littered with business cards, explaining that they had been "paid a social visit" by the KKK and threatening that the next visit could be "a business call."[22] The group immediately organized an anti-Klan rally, and in November Isaacs unseated a decades-long incumbent, a feat that is particularly difficult in rural and small-town America. Following Isaacs's win, the BCLP continued to organize. They would finally win basic legal protections for low-income renters nearly three years later.[23]

The point here is not that Isaacs's election ended KKK agitation in Shelbyville. Nor does a city council vote mark the definitive end to unscrupulous landlords. Indeed, Isaacs faced fairly intensive harassment once seated, though she remained in office at the time of writing. Rather, this account demonstrates some ways in which the mutual interest approach can find success. By bringing poor and working-class white people into struggles intended to better the tangible and practical conditions of their lives in the short-term, participants also discover the social and psychic possibilities of building multiracial solidarity. In this instance, poor and working-class whites were even at the forefront of resisting those white nationalist networks that have been so eager, and sometimes successful, in recruiting them.[24]

Yet it is also important not to conceptualize poor and working-class whites, particularly in the rural South, as somehow more difficult to organize than any other group of people raced as white. As Carla emphasized:

> We can sit there wringing our hands about how the other side is coming for rural white people, or we can actually listen to rural white people and smaller town white folks about what they're going through and what their struggles are.

This is one of the many reasons why SURJ has created an entire dimension of its organizational structure to engage poor and working-class white people, particularly in rural regions and in the South.

RURAL PROJECTS

The term "redneck" was first used as derogatory slang in the nineteenth century to describe the sunburned necks of poor southern farmers. By the 1920s, however, the same term was reappropriated by union coal miners and made physically manifest in the form of a red bandanna worn about the neck as an expression of worker solidarity.[25] This latter meaning of redneck is what Beth Howard called upon when she penned a public letter to fellow Appalachians in the summer of 2020, called "Rednecks for Black Lives." In the letter Beth writes about the Battle of Blair Mountain in West Virginia in 1921.

Blair Mountain was an infamous moment in the history of labor organizing. Eight thousand coal miners—white, Black, and other people of color—tried to form a union against the will of company owners and operators. They wore red bandannas around their necks to indicate their solidarity with one another as workers. Evidently, the unity of so many workers against their bosses was threatening enough that the coal company called in thousands of officers from the U.S. Army and the West Virginia National Guard. Estimates are that at least sixteen people were killed, with hundreds wounded and many more arrested.[26] Beth wrote in her letter:

> Even though the miners did not get their union at the end of that battle, it laid the foundation for a much bigger labor movement in years to come, exposed the dangers miners faced in the West Virginia coalfields, and maybe more than anything created power in the multiracial solidarity of poor and working people.[27]

The story of Blair Mountain is often told at Kentucky People's Union events. In fact, members of the group all have red bandannas with the story literally written on them.[28] For KPU members, Blair Mountain represents the promise of mutual interest organizing to anchor powerful forms of multiracial solidarity, even when the fruits of struggle are far from immediate and may in fact require the ultimate sacrifice. As KPU leader Amelia put it, herself "a mixed woman, African American, and white":

> We've taken that [symbol of the red bandanna] to show our solidarity, and to say "regardless of where you come from, what you look like, you [can be] a member of Kentucky People's Union. We are going to keep showing up and fighting for what we all deserve, what we all know is right."

Like the Bedford County Listening Project, Kentucky People's Union is one of SURJ's rural formations. These are what Erin Heaney described as "other kinds of projects that are not called SURJ that hold this organizing work."

The name Kentucky People's Union, for example, was selected so to appeal to poor and working rural people. The nomenclature of a *people*'s union, explained Beth Howard, "called on our union history, but also made it clear that [the group] was for everyday working-class people." This included the many who might not hold "traditional jobs," and might be "disabled, homemakers, students, etc." Leaders then took the name along with other options to people's doors, where it was clear that Kentucky People's Union resonated: "we noted how quickly [local people] understood the concept of a union even if they were new to organizing. They got that we were a group of working-class people fighting for something."

SURJ Assistant Director Julia Daniel explained why the rural projects bear their own names, "with any kind of organizing, if you're gonna start a conversation with people, they're going to want to understand what is their role in the work, and do they have a belonging in the work." Many in the organization believed that, in the predominantly white, poor, and working-class rural communities where SURJ seeks to organize, "if we showed up on some doors with racial justice in our name, it might not signal to people that this was about them." Much like the decision not to lead with a discussion of white privilege, choosing not to use the term "racial justice" when first speaking to predominantly white residents is a tactical choice. With that said, it is also intended as a temporary one. All KPU leaders I interacted with had come to understand SURJ as "KPU's mother organization."

In addition to bearing different names, SURJ's rural projects are distinct from the chapter network in their origins as listening projects, what Carla Wallace described as "a very intentional way to make sure that local people and most impacted people are at the core of whatever is going to happen." Listening projects generally entail organizers spending a significant amount of time in a community in order to identify what it is that residents experience as well as what core values motivate them. The organization that emerges is anchored in the expressed priorities of the community itself. The kind of canvassing that happens in a listening project is therefore quite distinct from that which is undertaken during a campaign. People are not being approached in order to take specific action towards a predetermined political effort. Instead, organizers are working to identify where predominantly white community members might hold potential forms of mutual interest with a Black-led liberation agenda.[29]

A central goal in these listening projects includes the cultivation of local leaders.[30] As Kelly Sue explained, "if we're doing our work right, someone who lives there and is of that community eventually will take on that work." This has happened in both of the rural formations in this study, which have brought on staff organizers from their membership base. It is also how Kelly Sue herself was hired into the organization.

Carla recalled SURJ's conversations when they learned that white hate groups planned to target Shelbyville, Tennessee, in 2017. Leaders knew that "we can't just have people come from Nashville and other places go in and say 'bad KKK, bad far right.'" Instead, the question was, "what does it mean to support local people to decide how they want to react?" A SURJ staff member went to Shelbyville to spend time in the community and to understand what organizing efforts were underway. Soon after finding Kelly Sue, SURJ offered her a paid position so that she could give her full attention to going to people's doors in "low income, majority white" neighborhoods, "listening to see: What are folks struggling with? What are people having a hard time with?"

The fact that rural projects are rooted in the expressed interests and needs of predominantly white communities, if always also multiracial ones, is distinct from the urban groups in this study, where priorities are generally set in direct consultation with Black organizational partners. As Erin Heaney explained, "the work [in rural projects] looks pretty different [than chapter work] even though it's all leading to the same impact. But we're asking people about the issues that impact *their* lives." This "same impact" means pulling an increasing number of those raced as white into multiracial efforts to advance racial and economic justice.

The work of rural projects demonstrates what Carla described as "the hunger of rural and small-town white folks for coming together to make changes in their communities that are deeply also connected to the issue of racial justice." In other words, these efforts may not be explicitly pitched as seeking to dismantle white privilege. By fighting for economic justice, housing security, and accessible healthcare, however, these groups identify issue areas that are both antiracist and intersectional.

Carla continued by discussing how this work has a good deal to teach "liberal white folks in urban areas, who blame rural people, who blame small-town people." Among the over 150 groups that make up the national organization, rural efforts are often drawing larger numbers to their meetings than are groups in highly populous urban areas. Through what Carla termed "a mix of organic and intentional" organizing processes, they also seem to face less of a "learning curve" in understanding that forms of marginalization are interlocking. Carla explained this in a way that contrasted the organization's rural work to more class-privileged leftist efforts, poking gentle fun at the latter, "because of who people are, and because of what they're going through, there's not suddenly three meetings needed to talk about why we're going to stand up for trans lives. It's like, 'yes, these are our people.'" This may also be part of why, in practice, some of SURJ's rural groups, such as KPU, have quickly become racially mixed and include more people with visible disabilities than do the urban groups in this study.[31] In this regard, rural projects do not fit neatly into the white affinity organizing model often associated with SURJ. If urban chapters tend to understand themselves within a local ecosystem, working in cross-racial and cross-organizational coalition with local BIPOC-led groups, rural projects are often the only major organizing formation in their region.

Even so, SURJ still collaborates with partners at the state and national level when choosing where to launch a rural project. As Carla put it:

> We don't just [announce] "okay, we're here, we're doing this!" We do a lot of conferring with POC-led work on the ground, making sure, "Is this helpful? Can we bring something? Do you want us to bring something?"

Jerome Scott, a longtime Black organizer and founder of Project South, who serves as a SURJ advisor, explained his thoughts when he first learned about this rural work:

> They [SURJ] were filling a gap that we had felt for a long time in terms of organizing. The fact that they were concentrating on organizing white people in rural areas around the South, that to me could not be a bad thing, given their ideological position. I was down. Yes, do more of this!

Here, Jerome was naming SURJ's "ideological position" as pursuing intersectional racial justice, undergirded by an anticapitalist critique. Jerome's enthusiasm was not unequivocal, however. He understood that organizing poor and working-class white people, particularly if approached primarily "as white people," can and has gone wrong throughout history. Jerome encouraged the SURJ organizers he mentors to consistently "take a break and do an evaluation" to ensure they are staying on track. This, he added, is something that all organizers need to do, but is particularly important given SURJ's intended base. At the same time, Jerome was clear in understanding the organization's rural work, undergirded by the framework of mutual interest, as integral to collective liberation:

> If we're gonna do anything significant in terms of transforming the political and economic dynamics of this country ... we gotta have an ability to unite the active, struggling section of the working class, no matter what their color is. And you can't do that unless you do work in the white rural community. It's just not possible.

Paige Ingram, a leader in the Movement for Black Lives national organization, agreed about the importance of rural organizing. She also understood SURJ's efforts as contributing to an important division of labor. Much like the race-based organizing model, "we're each doing our part ... that's just so much more realistic and doable." More precisely, Paige understood SURJ's work in rural spaces as fairly unique among movement groups, acknowledging that for M4BL, "we don't really do a lot of stuff with rural folks in general, Black folks or otherwise." In this context, "folks in SURJ who've been focusing on remote communities" can help hone movement strategy. Paige gave the example of receiving feedback from SURJ partners about what kind of messaging might be appropriate in rural, southern communities. This, for Paige, was a way that SURJ "helps us to sharpen our approach to the work as well, like a steel sharpening steel kind of thing."

"IF WE DO NOT TALK ABOUT RACE..."

Participants within and outside the organization agreed that focusing organizing efforts on poor and working-class communities, and approaching white people based on their shared stake with BIPOC, constitute both significant and strategic shifts in the movement. At the same time, many were frank about the need to remain clear-sighted in their efforts. The contention that the main problem with racism is that it divides the working class is not new, and it is an argument that can have blind spots. These include ignoring the other injuries and forms of dehumanization that racism authorizes; downplaying the psychic and material benefits of whiteness; and ignoring a long history of cross-racial class-based alliances that have won victories for white members of the coalition who then left others behind.[32] Furthermore, even if poor white people are not racism's most powerful perpetrators, there is a risk, as Elisabeth put it, that "the expression of racism by poor and working-class white people can sometimes be erased or minimized."[33]

These are considerations that many SURJ organizers are aware of and with which they actively grapple. Against the romance of somehow mobilizing a majority of poor and working white people, the organization clarifies that its aims are humbler. As Beth Howard put it, "we just have to get a large enough number of white people—not all of them—but a large enough number to defect from whiteness and white supremacy to go towards solidarity." Elisabeth added, "There is no magical block of white people, period." Moreover, as distinct from efforts, both past and present, that seek to recruit white people into multiracial, working-class struggles but avoid addressing white racism, SURJ consistently centers a discussion of white racism in their organizing projects.[34]

Carla Wallace regularly cited mentor Anne Braden's lessons about centering an analysis of race and racism when organizing poor, white southern communities, and applied this lesson to current conditions:

> Anne Braden has this famous saying that, "if we do not talk about race in the struggle for change, what monster organizations will we create?" Because if we're organizing white folks, and we're not talking about race, and the other side comes and says, "it's the immigrants," we have just opened the door to say, "Come on, and blame the immigrant people." And then who bears the brunt of that suffering because of our bad strategy is immigrant people, especially poor immigrant and undocumented people.[35]

Explicitly addressing racism during shared stake organizing is perhaps as much art as it is science. Beth observed that when people learn about her work, they often want to be told how to talk to white people about race and racism, as if "there's a formula," which, she believes, there is not. The organization does pursue some best practices that they have developed by studying history as well as through trial and error. These tend to center on relationship building and leading with curiosity.

Beth told a story of how one of these conversations might look based on her time before the 2020 election in rural North Georgia—a largely neglected, white area that Black and Brown leaders in the state had asked for SURJ to prioritize. This was a region in which residences are often miles apart from each other. Organizers have pictures of trying to drive up a one-lane gravel road where the water was so high, due to inadequate drainage, that they had to turn their vehicles around. Beth recalled "driving up to places where people are like, 'no one ever comes out here. I cannot believe you're out here.'" To the degree that any political literature was being handed out, it was from the Republican Party. The Democratic Party had not even tried to do outreach in the region.

One organizer ended up at the residence of an older white woman, who expressed confusion that her town was renaming the local school away from that of a Confederate soldier. By leading with curiosity and validating the woman's sense of confusion, the organizer was able to open up a discussion about what a school's name might signify. The organizer began by asking whom the woman might name a school after, to which the woman replied that she would choose her mother-in-law and proceeded to name a number of admirable qualities. Beth reflected:

> And [the organizer] was like, "Well, it sounds like your mother-in-law would be an amazing person to name a school after. But I think a lot of people feel like this Confederate soldier didn't have the qualities that your mother-in-law had, and that the Black and Brown people that live here, go to the school, don't feel welcome in it." And so that opened up that conversation, right?

Beth continued, "transformation happens over time. It's like multiple conversations with people. When we talk to someone, we're gonna have to visit them again and again, you know. And asking so many questions, right, continue to be curious and ask questions." This too is very much in line with Anne Braden's insights regarding antiracist organizing in white communities: "Any organizer worth his salt listens a long time before he talks much, and he learns to adapt his approach to the people he is working with and to their life situations."[36]

Beth concluded that approaching white communities through a mutual interest framework that centrally addresses white racism is best done by white people with white people as preparatory work for building multiracial projects:

> I think there's a lot of wisdom in white people organizing white people . . . [not] going in and just putting that burden on Black and Brown people, coming into the coalition before [white people]'re ready, before they're politically there.

In this sense, SURJ's model of organizing white people is conceptualized as an early stage of multiracial movement formation, a stance that was reiterated by partners as well. For instance, Paige of M4BL reflected:

> There's still utility for Black organizing and power building and for white organizing and power building. But all the work that we're doing in preparation, in building our own power and getting ourselves together, should be in service of something even larger, get-

ting together across those identity [categories] to help our people to feel effective, to feel a part of something bigger.

Building political analysis and organizing capacity in race-based formations is not the end goal, but an important step towards generating more effective forms of multiracial solidarity. I now consider how the mutual interest approach can work in more urban groups.

ABOLITIONIST ACTION

While knocking doors with SURJ Buffalo's 2021 sheriff campaign, three conversations, all with white-presenting residents, were particularly impactful to me. The first was with a man in his thirties, dressed in a sweatshirt and jeans. He stood in a dark alcove, so that I could barely make out his features. I introduced myself nervously, following the walk script. I began by asking his thoughts on conditions in the Erie County Holding Center, the local jail. His response was immediate and defensive. Was I there because I knew he had himself been jailed? Quickly off script, I scrambled to reassure him that, no, I was there with a group concerned about local jail conditions and the sheriff in charge. I returned to the script to read how the sheriff's office had been "cited by the state for dozens of violations, including abusive conditions that have resulted in thirty-one people dying inside." The man stepped forward, opening the storm door so I could see his face. As he learned more about SURJ Buffalo, and I more about him, he admitted to being dubious that a local group could impact jail conditions. He was not completely apathetic about the political process, revealing that he planned to vote for Kim Beaty, the candidate SURJ Buffalo endorsed. Yet he expressed doubt it would make much difference. I had been trained to ask if he wanted a yard sign, which he did not. He was noncommittal about joining SURJ but shared his contact information nonetheless.

The second conversation took place two weeks later. A small woman, likely in her fifties, was locking the side door when I approached to introduce myself, immediately asking for her thoughts about the Erie County Holding Center. To my surprise, her response was swift and decisive;

she was very concerned by the jail's conditions. She was a corrections officer, she explained, though employed at a different facility. She had friends unhappily employed at the jail. I asked if she planned to vote for Kim Beaty. She deflected, "I like the fact that Beaty is a woman, women just run things better." I continued to press, as I had been trained, asking what might convince her to commit to support Beaty. She paused, considered, and then admitted with a chuckle that she had actually just convinced herself. She agreed to take a lawn sign and was eager to learn more about SURJ. I took her contact information.

The third conversation was at the very next house. I began the rehearsed introduction, asking about the person's feelings about the local jail, only to realize the woman I was speaking with was on the verge of tears. She explained being "vaguely aware of conditions in the holding center, yes," but admitted that she tried to ignore what she heard. Her son had been in the jail because of his own struggles around mental health and addiction, though at the time of our conversation, she explained, "he is doing much better." She planned to vote for Beaty but made it clear that she could not tolerate continuing our conversation. I thanked her and left without asking for further commitments.

In only two stints of door knocking with SURJ Buffalo, as part of an electoral effort situated within a larger abolitionist approach, the reach of our current policing and prison systems was clear. I spoke to someone who had themselves been in jail, another who worked in the system, a third who had temporarily lost her son to it. My canvassing experience was not particularly unique. In the neighborhoods of Buffalo where SURJ knocked for Kim Beaty and in the other abolitionist campaigns undertaken by the urban groups in this study, it was evident that many white communities, especially poor and working-class, are impacted by the systems of policing and imprisonment that most dramatically and disproportionately target BIPOC. As one participant in Louisville SURJ's campaign to end cash bail reported after knocking doors in the predominantly white working-class neighborhoods of southern Louisville, "almost everyone I talked to knew someone who had been involved in the system," and a number of people "had family members who were correctional officers."[37]

The three urban groups in this study pursue issue campaigns that align with an abolitionist vision, whose definition they draw from the organization Critical Resistance, as having the ultimate aims of "eliminating imprisonment, policing, and surveillance and creating lasting alternatives to punishment and imprisonment." There are certainly important questions about how to operationalize such a vision in practice.[38] The groups in this study make decisions about how to pursue their abolitionist aims through both internal assessment as well as collaboration with local and national partners. Over the past several years, SURJ Buffalo has set its sights on the Erie County Sheriff's office; Louisville SURJ has largely focused its efforts on ending cash bail in the county; and WP4BL has worked on various initiatives to reroute investments away from LA jails and prisons and into community responder models. These efforts all aim to shrink the infrastructure of policing and imprisonment, both through defensive maneuvers and supporting community-based alternatives. They also endeavor to broaden the base of white support for intersectional racial and economic justice. Through abolitionist campaigns, SURJ groups reach out to those white communities who are themselves impacted by prisons and policing and demonstrate the far-reaching harms of the criminal punishment system to a broader swath of the public. This is how organizing out of mutual interest, and in partnership with BIPOC organizations, can be translated into strategic practice.

A number of WP4BL participants recalled that their work on the Measure R ballot campaign was a particularly resonant demonstration of the mutual interest approach. Rebecca, who had helped to move her organization away from a focus on white privilege and guilt, said that "as [WP4BL] and key leaders became more steeped in their personal stake, we just became more ambitious as an organization, and I think that led to the Measure R campaign." Kristen agreed that the Measure R campaign marked an important moment in the LA group's evolution:

> I don't think we had ever organized in that way, like setting a really big ambitious goal [for] doing work that was supporting Black-led organizing, but . . . leading a vision for what we could do. We weren't

just doing a specific thing that was being asked of us. We suggested like, "We want to be bold and get this many signatures, what do you think?"

Measure R was a 2020 ballot initiative proposed and supported by a coalition of abolitionist groups in Los Angeles, with Patrisse Cullors, BLM co-founder, taking central leadership. The measure, which came up for a vote mere weeks before the onset of COVID-19, would reallocate funds away from jail expansion and instead direct them into community resources. It also provided greater oversight powers to the civilian committee that oversaw the Los Angeles Sheriff's Office.[39] Passing Measure R required two major mobilizations—the first to secure signatures to get the initiative on the ballot; the second to get enough votes to pass it. In both instances, WP4BL markedly increased its contributions to the coalition in terms of leadership and scale, approaching the Black organizers leading the campaign with a proposal for what WP4BL could contribute rather than waiting to be asked. Of the 150,000 signatures required, WP4BL ended up collecting 26,000.[40]

While collecting signatures marked the largest volunteer effort WP4BL had yet undertaken, it was the group's outreach to voters once the initiative was on the ballot that many understood to be transformational. Liz explained WP4BL's particular role: "We were deep canvassing the white people so that we weren't putting the labor of having these conversations with white people on Black and Indigenous and people of color." Moreover, rather than conduct a more typical electoral canvass, WP4BL decided to engage in the somewhat novel organizing technique known as deep canvassing. Distinct from most electoral pushes, which seek to maximize votes, deep canvassing has been shown to shift voters' more enduring attitudes.[41] The technique depends on a much more extensive and emotionally vulnerable conversation between the volunteer and the stranger who answers the door. Somewhat akin to SURJ's listening projects in rural communities, deep canvassing also includes asking questions, sharing stories, and building personal connection. WP4BL recruited hundreds of volunteers to pursue this tactic, one that requires more time and training while potentially reaching fewer voters. The group believed in the payoff, however, that working to shift white voters' attitudes and build support for abolitionist policies was worth the extra investment and short-term trade-offs.

In their efforts around the Measure R campaign, WP4BL was appealing to its own participants' personal stake in abolitionist work while reaching out to white communities with a message of mutual interest. As Rebecca observed, "Personal stake was like the cornerstone of our deep canvassing." Not only did WP4BL require its members to give more of their time, resources, and emotional vulnerability than they had to previous efforts, deep canvassing required reaching out to white communities in Los Angeles County with a message of how policing and prisons do damage across communities, and not only to people of color. Liz explained how the white canvassers "had conversations with [white voters] about alternatives to incarceration, and how all people are impacted by incarceration. All people are impacted when we criminalize substance abuse and mental health and poverty." Rebecca added that Measure R was "really good abolitionist policy that was about . . . diverting people from jail by utilizing alternatives . . . and our whole strategy was around what's at stake for white people . . . making the idea of abolition something that white people want for themselves."

A COMPLEX FRAMEWORK

Adopting a shared interest approach makes sense in a strategy that seeks to grow a broader base of white support for racial and economic justice and deepen the commitment of those involved. It is nevertheless worth acknowledging that mutual interest is a complex framework. In this sense, it is not wholly dissimilar from the white privilege analytic. Both can be oversimplified and distorted in ways that are individualizing and therefore not conducive to movement building. As Elisabeth of Catalyst observed, "in working on getting [white] people to understand their stake, it's not like, 'I'm only involved in this work because of the sexual violence I experienced, and because I don't want to experience it again.'" Any individual's experience of socially structured injustice is necessarily partial, unable to make the important connections that a more collective vision can achieve. Participants in this study were also clear that racial justice efforts should be led by the insights, visions, and strategies of those most directly harmed: BIPOC movement participants.

Elisabeth continued that her own political analysis was guided by the Black feminists who helped her to first envision a different social order. She observed that for white people involved in racial justice efforts, "you should have a larger sense of your political compass being what's guiding you, and your relationships and principles." White people certainly need to identify their shared stake in dismantling white supremacy. This stake must, nevertheless, be connected to a broader analysis and theory of change. Coming to see white supremacy as structural and systemic rather than merely personal and private is key to building this larger theory.

Black organizer, strategist, and movement lawyer Nana Gyamfi, who had supported the partnership between WP4BL and BLM LA since 2014, shared this assessment. Affirming her belief that helping white people to understand their personal stake in antiracist efforts "makes sense," she continued, "I think the general problem—or not problem—*challenge* is how you balance the conversation about individual and structural." She was clear that all participants need to understand their own stake in movement work because, "if you feel like you have no skin in the game, we already know you are not gonna do anything." On the flip side, Nana believed that "too many people" make decisions about how to involve themselves in collective projects guided by a narrow sense of their own self-interest. Using her background as an educator, Nana reiterated the metaphor of white people being part of "a group assignment on multiracial democracy." She situated the role of a shared stake approach within this analogy:

> This is why, group assignments, people don't like them. Because it's very hard for people to do that balance. Either they're into it, they care, they want a good grade. They're gonna put their whole heart into it because they want a good grade. Sometimes people don't give a damn. And they're like, "I don't care what the grade turns out to

be." But if you don't care about the *group's* grade, we're gonna have a problem.

For white people, not caring at all about racism is a primary pitfall. Only caring about one's own stake (one's own grade), however, also poses trouble. The group grade, or social outcome, is what is of ultimate consequence.

At the level of practice, some participants clarified that the concept of mutual interest has not been intuitive to all of SURJ's desired constituents. This is particularly the case for chapter members, who disproportionately tend to have class privilege and have often already been taught to focus on their white privilege. Speaking as a chapter coach, Linnea explained, "lots of chapters just inherently are structured with middle-class people in leadership based on who has the time and resources to start a volunteer organization." She continued by explaining her sense that the mutual interest frame has been more of a stretch for these groups:

> I think lots of folks with class privilege who've always had class privilege, there's a learning curve in terms of more deeply understanding . . . where systems are failing and harming them and their loved ones . . . moving from, "I think racism is bad because it hurts other people," to like, "white supremacy and capitalism are like killing us." Right? Those are just different understandings.

Some participants also recalled how a shared stake approach has faced resistance from some group members, who feared that new participants would be put off. During Rebecca's early efforts to center her group around their mutual interest with BIPOC, she recalled receiving a phone call from another group member who worried

> [new] people are going to really freak out. They're at their first meeting, and they showed up here in order to help people of color. They're gonna feel like this is really selfish, like this is centering whiteness in a way that's going to make people not wanna come back to our organization.

Referencing equally hypothetical evidence, Kate of Louisville surmised that the move to mutual interest might be off-putting to some would-be members, "I think maybe some people roll up to LSURJ and maybe expect or want more of the white privilege [conversation], like doing your personal work, to unpack your stuff." Kate acknowledged the value of these approaches but concluded that that was not LSURJ's emphasis: "we really focus more on organizing, political change, working collectively." Assessing these concerns empirically is beyond the scope of this study as I did not sample would-be participants who had been dissuaded by the mutual interest approach. Nevertheless, such anxieties point to how the mutual interest approach could be (mis)understood.

It is worth emphasizing here that appealing to white people's shared stake with BIPOC is not intended to evade the fact of white privilege. Integrating an acknowledgment of white privilege within the mutual interest approach, however, is not simple or straightforward. Erin Heaney described this integration as requiring a kind of "political maturity," which she elaborated as the ability "to sit in discomfort, to live in the contradiction of *both* having been given privileges by whiteness and also being clear of what you've lost." While such a stance is in line with many Black liberation thinkers who identify white supremacy as a kind of poison that everyone imbibes, whites included, Erin was clear that mutual interest is "not a simple idea that someone can go to a workshop and come out with total clarity about."[42]

Others suggested that it might be useful and even predictable for white participants to move from one emphasis to another, and that perhaps there is a developmental arc, particularly for white audiences with class privilege. Jason, for instance, had been doing antiracist work with white people through the AWARE network for two decades at the time of our interview. Many participants with whom he had worked hold some class privilege, and Jason had a depth of experience in supporting them through the challenging feelings that often accompany early encounters with the realities of white complicity. He therefore saw political potential in the fact of white guilt, particularly for middle-class people who may "[struggle] to find those places where they truly have mutual interest" with people of color based on common class interests. Jason agreed that "[personal stake and mutual interest] are the models I want to run with more than guilt and shame-based privilege models," but continued, "I've become more and more convinced that guilt probably is baked into the very first stages" for some white people in learning about racism. He believed such guilt might be "good fuel for diving into the deep end."

Jason's insights are supported by research that identifies moral shocks, often among those with privilege, as being catalyzing for many activists, particularly those who are materially secure. In the case of white people, such shocks often include being confronted with proximate evidence of the enduring force of racism. What scholars have termed "seminal" or "approximating experiences" often entail feeling guilt or sadness for one's complicity in a system that is doing people harm.[43] These emotion-laden experiences can motivate white people to learn more and take action. The key question for movements, then, becomes how to bring motivated people into strategic forms of collective action and sustain their involvement. This is where a movement organization can become important for ensuring that guilt, as Jason put it, can "be channeled into threads of personal stake [to] create really beautiful long-term commitment."

It is therefore important that the mutual interest approach be situated within multifaceted efforts to organize in predominantly white communities. Among other things, organizing includes showing up at people's doors, developing relationships, and inviting people into forms of action where they can learn important skills and hone their political analysis. Organizers often term such efforts "base building," which includes both broadening a movements' constituency as well as developing the competencies of those involved. These efforts to engage in white antiracist base building are the subject of the next chapter.

4 THE THING THAT WILL GET US FREE

WHEN I FIRST SPOKE TO Beth Howard, SURJ's Appalachian organizer, in February of 2022, the process of building the group that would become Kentucky People's Union had just begun. Three SURJ organizers went to the doors of poor and working-class people in the predominantly white Appalachian town of Ashland. Beth explained how that first day included five hours of "knocking on doors and deeply listening to people about what they're telling us." As they spoke to residents, Beth, Taryn, and Alex focused on the central questions that organizers often do: "What are the issues that are deeply and widely felt here that people are talking about, that they feel that they would move on?" Given SURJ's emphasis on mutual interest, their approach had some framing, seeking "opportunities to bring [predominantly white residents] together to see their mutual stake with Black and Brown people."

That first day on the doors confirmed what had begun as "a hunch," when Beth, a Kentucky native, helped identify Ashland as "a potentially opportune place to launch an organizing project." This was due to Ashland's location in Central Appalachia, its proud union history, and its economic struggles in the wake of capital flight and state abandonment.[1] The organizers found that Ashland residents were hungry for the opportunity to better their lives and community. As Beth reflected, "we hit the right turf because people are fired up, and no one's talking to them. They are just ready to talk, ready to tell you things, ready to introduce you to their neighbors."

As a listening project, those first months of door knocking were about meeting local residents and listening to what people had to say. As Beth put it at the time, "it's still to be determined what's the action . . . but I would love to see a statewide working people's movement." Within the year, KPU had identified eight leaders, counted sixty people regularly taking action with the group, and selected their first campaign around housing justice.

If KPU's story is one of strong initial success, I introduce it here to indicate the central orientation that all of the groups in this study adopt: that of antiracist *organizing*. There are myriad ways to try to move predominantly white communities into antiracist collective action. Organizing is sometimes juxtaposed to other social change practices, such as political advocacy and mass mobilization, though it can and often does co-exist with these.[2] Indeed, recent years have demonstrated mass mobilization as a deeply important means for movements to exercise grassroots power. At the same time, large protest waves rarely arise as spontaneously as they might appear.[3] Moreover, while mass mobilization certainly has important impacts on the political context as well as activists themselves, street protest alone is rarely sufficient for generating and maintaining fundamental societal and political change. Such change requires broad-based, enduring social movements, generally those forged through grassroots organizing. Without offering an exhaustive account of organizing's various influences and distinct approaches, I lift up a few key features that I identify as important to SURJ's approach.[4]

Grassroots organizing, or base building, intends to bring people into formations where they can develop relationships, skills, and analyses; mount tactics that reveal social conditions as they are to themselves, diverse publics, and key decision-makers; experiment, fail, learn, and reassess. These are the resources necessary to amass grassroots power and win practical aims.[5] Given the focus of the last chapter, it is perhaps unsurprising that various organizing traditions work to develop and hone participants' sense of shared interest as a foundation for taking collective action. This is often begun by helping individuals identify and refine an understanding of self-interest so as to motivate, inspire, and ultimately engage in collectively defined aims. It is also the case that organizing can be personally and collectively transformational. By acting together to alter relations of power and the social systems that do people harm, organizing transforms those involved.[6]

Political theorist Deva Woodly puts this eloquently when analyzing political organizing in the Movement for Black Lives as "fundamentally about socializing people into a new kind of subjectivity—one in which they think of themselves as efficacious political actors who are both capable of acting and responsible to act in concert for political change."[7] Woodly's insights refer to efforts to organize Black communities, which have been marginalized, brutalized, and structurally divested from in ways that are both specific and, in many instances, counterposed to the structural forces that elevate and protect those raced as white. Yet under late capitalism, all communities, if in different ways, have been collectively recruited to understand meritocratic individualism as the common sense, and to exist in social and political conditions that breed competition, fear, atomization, polarization, and despair. Whiteness offers little remedy for such afflictions.[8] Helping ordinary people of any race to understand themselves as capable of, and indeed responsible for, acting together to better collective conditions is thus both a counterhegemonic project and a necessary one.

Grassroots organizing is not an inherently liberatory practice, having at different times bolstered internal group dynamics of racism, sexism, and xenophobia. This is true in many examples from the labor movement and other forms of community organizing.[9] There are also longstanding and important debates on the political Left about whether growing mass organizations actually curtails, rather than enhances, the disruptive potential of collective grievance, particularly among the poor and marginalized.[10] Even so, antiracist organizing in white communities holds the potential to bring more white people into alignment with the aims of multiracial liberation, and to do so in a manner and at a scale that begins to shift the balance of power. Those raced as white, albeit in diverse ways, need new competencies, analyses, experiences, and incentives so that they might fight against rather than for the maintenance of white supremacy. SURJ's organizing efforts demonstrate some of the ways this can be done. It is also the case that some form of political organizing among white people is inevitable; what is contingent is the direction it takes. As leaders in this study often repeat, "if we aren't organizing white people around their suffering, someone else is." The social, psychic, spiritual and material voids in white people's lives prime them for political capture by antidemocratic, hateful, and violent forces if a countervailing effort does not exist.

Exploring what organizing means for the groups in this study provides a lesson that took me some time to understand. It is not quite right to understand SURJ as an issue organization but rather as a grassroots power-building effort. Drawing white communities away from consolidating forms of authoritarianism, nativism, and fascism and into a multiracial movement for collective dignity and justice requires an approach that is both practical and transformational. It must include pursuing specific political aims aligned with an intersectional liberation agenda. At the same time, participants engage in a range of processes by which they build relationships, while collectively learning, applying, and honing new political analyses and competencies. These are the resources required to build towards long-term struggle.

In what follows, I begin with an exploration of what many understand to be the central vehicle of grassroots organizing: the issue campaign. I consider the multiple forms that a campaign win can take and investigate how participants make sense of the role of electoral work in their organizing approach. I then turn more explicitly to organizing as a project of collective learning and (re)socialization. I trace how groups situate the acquisition of knowledge and skills in the service of political action, examining a range of sites from formal training opportunities to the quintessential organizing practice of door knocking. I conclude by considering what it means to organize in "movement times," which requires being responsive to time-bound moments of mass mobilization, some of which have brought unprecedented numbers to these groups.

ISSUE CAMPAIGNS

On April 15, 2023, fifty members of KPU came together in Ashland's Central Park for an auspicious meeting. The group had been in existence for about a year. That day they would choose their first campaign. KPU's paid organizer, Celina, a white woman likely in her early thirties, explained that an issue campaign is designed to improve people's lives in very practical ways while drawing in more participants. This meant that KPU would build its people power to win on even more of the group's chosen priorities.

The first portion of the meeting gave us a chance to get acquainted. By a show of hands, we learned that about a quarter of those present first heard of KPU when someone came to their door. A few participants offered testimony in front of the group, explaining why they joined KPU. We were then invited to share our own stories in groups of three or four. Next, a member of the research team, Miles, a Black man in his twenties, stood to introduce us to the campaign portion of the meeting. Raised in Ashland, Miles explained that he left to attend college, returning after graduation. Miles soon realized he would be moving back in with his parents. Local rentals were either unaffordable or ridden by pests or mold. "I have asthma," Miles explained, "There's no way I'm living in a place with mold."

Miles and Celina proceeded to walk around the pavilion, introducing us to three proposals the group would be deciding between, depicted on butcher paper. The proposals included: making the registry of landlords that the city of Ashland already maintains more robust and publicly available; passing an antidiscrimination ordinance; and pushing Ashland to activate URLTA, a policy that clarifies both landlords' and tenants' rights and responsibilities. While URLTA was passed by the state of Kentucky in 2016, it requires that cities proactively adopt it.

We broke into small groups and were encouraged to spend fifteen minutes discussing our thoughts on each proposal. I was paired with two women, both of whom appeared phenotypically white, one likely in her forties, another in her sixties. As the conversation proceeded, the younger of the two shared her support for an antidiscrimination policy. She explained that she would not want the time she had spent in prison for a drug problem to be held against her. The other nodded affirmatively and admitted she was struggling to choose among the options. She had just visited a friend whose trailer park residence was beset by a sewage leak. The friend did not want to complain for fear that the authorities would shut the entire place down, leaving residents homeless. The back and forth between the two women accelerated. They discussed friends and family living in all manner of unsuitable housing: foundations rotting, mold, pests. All were afraid to complain to their landlords or the city for fear of losing their housing completely.

Our group was far from a decision when we were invited back to a full group discussion in which each person received three different colored sticky notes. Celina explained that as we discussed each proposal, members should hold up blue to express enthusiasm, yellow if they had questions, and red if they had serious reservations. While we would ultimately vote, this first-round procedure was to encourage conversation. KPU is a union, Celina reminded us, and people were not just voting for themselves. They should also be conscious of and informed by what those around them were thinking.

A good deal of conversation ensued. People asked hard questions. Many were skeptical of the political process as a whole. Some expressed concern about whether any proposal was winnable. Others wondered if a given proposal would actually have an impact. Celina along with Beth Howard, SURJ's Appalachian organizer, validated these concerns. It was Miles, the KPU leader from the research team, who ultimately intervened. He reiterated that the three proposals were the product of careful consultation with experts and advocates throughout the state and region. These were the policies that they had suggested were "practical and winnable and would have an impact." He added, "I do believe that they are all winnable."

KPU members ultimately cast their official, anonymous ballots and moved on to share in food and conversation. I took the group photo. Once the ballots were counted, we were told that the group had opted to advocate for both the public housing registry and local adoption of URLTA, a tenant's bill of rights.

If organizing includes "the practices of meeting, sharing stories, mutual education, and on-going agitation,"[11] the first campaign meeting of KPU demonstrates some of these dynamics in process. Members share stories, often across socially structured differences, in order to build and deepen relationships. They identify and refine points of affinity, positioning what might originate as immediate, individualized needs and desires within the context of their mutual interest. We are a union, Celina explains; people are not just voting for themselves as individuals. Participants are also guided through deliberative exchange. As Kelly Sue had told me about her work with Bedford County Listening Project, "One of the things that we want to create in organizing, if it's done well, is the ability to make decisions together. Fair decisions together."

Sociologist Francesca Polletta argues that such processes can lead to a number of socially and politically important transformations for movement participants and their groups. The practice of deliberation itself exposes those new to the political process to important forms of knowledge and information. Participants develop an understanding of the root causes of social problems and come to imagine a wider range of possible remedies. They also refine self and collective perceptions while becoming more savvy political actors. As Polletta describes, "reasoning together about options and solutions led to new conceptions of self-interest and new perceptions of strategy."[12]

This meeting thus demonstrated a number of sophisticated forms of learning and knowledge work that happen in grassroots organizing. Miles had been involved in a collaborative research process, which translated months of inquiry into accessible language, lessons, and proposals presented to fellow members for consideration. We saw how

SURJ staff organizers, Celina and Beth, held space for participants to ask questions and express doubt, validating the expertise that ordinary people derive from their lived experience.[13]

This meeting, of course, was focused on planning KPU's first issue campaign. In various organizing traditions, campaigns serve as time-bound efforts focused on winning practical gains, situated within the longer-term strategy of building grassroots power. Sociologist and movement veteran Marshall Ganz describes issue campaigns as "strategic and motivational."[14] Each small win, whether a new petition signature or the actual passage of a policy, offers people a sense of their personal and collective efficacy, deepening commitment and making larger objectives seem closer in reach. Campaigns can also multiply key community resources and apply these towards winning social change by recruiting new people, deepening relationships, and providing venues for participants to learn, practice, and refine important skills and knowledge. Celina explained some of this to the group when introducing how a campaign has both the short-term aims of winning concrete policy goals as well as the longer-term vision of growing the group's people power.

During interviews, participants also suggested that campaigns do a kind of necessary translation work, turning broad commitments into actionable objectives. Kelly Sue observed that the concept of racial justice can be unintelligible and hard to pin down: "I think it's hard to bring people into a fight if you say we're here to fight for racial justice." She followed this observation with a litany of questions that point to how vague a concept racial justice might first appear: "How do you fight for racial justice? Which issues? Who are you pointing people against? What's the end goal?" Issue campaigns therefore can help translate a broader vision into tangible and immediate options, which Kelly Sue understood as key for "moving people into action."

Attica Scott, a longtime organizer, partner to LSURJ, and member of the Kentucky House of Representatives when we spoke, agreed. Particularly when it comes to organizing busy and overextended people, and those with limited money and time:

> We can't make it abstract, because we're talking about people who have two or three jobs and, you know, may not have a car and they're relying on the bus. "Don't throw a whole bunch at me, tell me something we can work on together. And let's work on that."

At the same time, the campaigns that the groups in this study select are not meant to keep collective aims narrow or modest. Grace Aheron, SURJ's communications director, described how the organization understands the role of campaigns as situated within a very ambitious strategy, which includes

> organizing to break the power of the Right by peeling off white people from their base and bringing them into *campaigns* where they can understand their mutual interest in the racial and economic justice work being led by people of color. (emphasis added)

In this sense, campaigns provide the practical steps by which the groups in this study believe they can move many more white people into alignment with a Black liberation agenda.

KPU leader Elliot, self-described as white, working class, and a "trans-masculine nonbinary person," explained how they had come to understand the role of an issue campaign within an organizing approach. Even as Elliot described how they personally "very much enjoy activism and doing big impactful actions," they understood organizing as a more sustained and therefore impactful social change technique. To Elliot, organizing included "building a base of people who are going to fight with you for the long term" and "really getting into the foundation of what needs change in a more sound and structural way." Within this strategy, KPU's campaign for housing justice was an effort to win specific outcomes, which was selected because of its potential to grow and fortify multiracial solidarity and build lasting grassroots power. Elliot continued:

> Housing affects everyone across race, like all working class and poor people. We build solidarity by saying "I know you're affected by this issue, and so are we, and we want to do something about it. Can you join us?" And it brings people in.

Indeed, after a year of running its housing campaign, KPU had acquired close to a thousand signatures from Ashland residents. In a town of 20,000, that is not a small showing of popular support. KPU participants had also knocked on over a thousand doors, recruiting tens of new members to take regular action with the group. In addition to their monthly membership meetings, and regular canvasses and phone banks, the group was organizing a series of well-attended, public events. One of these was a summer cookout on the river with live music and story sharing about the personal and collective impacts of unaffordable and substandard housing. Another was a breakfast with community leaders, who were then invited to visit one of the apartment complexes where KPU had been organizing in order to see the substandard conditions for themselves. The group also had a regular presence at monthly board of commissioner meetings, and one KPU member was preparing to run for commissioner himself.

While KPU, much like SURJ's other rural projects, identified housing insecurity as a first priority issue, Amelia explained that the group was ready to confront other economic justice concerns as well:

> Right now [housing is] our main focus, but we're not just a housing organization. We're an organization for creating change throughout the community. There's tons of issues—the opioid crisis, job security, healthcare. What's being so deeply felt right now is the housing crisis here in Ashland. But whatever the main issue is, that's what we're going to be fighting for.

Amelia lays out a range of economic justice issues afflicting poor and working-class rural people: the desire for secure and fairly remunerated work, accessible and affordable healthcare, and relief in the face of the opioid addiction and overdose crisis. These are matters that SURJ's rural projects tend to center. Amelia also highlights the organizing tradition upon which KPU is built, as an effort to grow grassroots power to fight for dignity and justice for poor and working-class people regardless of the group's particular policy demands.

Erin Heaney explained that the strategy in SURJ's rural sites is rooted in "good community organizing" that "is really intentional about political education, helping people both fight for the things they need, but also get really, really clear about who their true enemies are, and understanding it's the rich landlord, it's not my immigrant neighbors." Carla Wallace added that "campaigns are a way to center directly impacted people, to build really clearly around a vision set by our strategic partners, our accountability partners, and to bring in a lot of people." Through this process, rural groups ultimately come to mobilize around a number of seemingly disparate issues that are nevertheless intersectional in nature. Bedford County leaders have engaged in racial justice organizing in defense of refugees and against local Klan agitation. KPU has likewise fought against the Right's efforts to curtail the rights of women, trans, and nonbinary people. KPU joined SURJ-coordinated efforts to help defeat Kentucky policies curtailing reproductive freedoms in 2022 and has been at the leading edge of fighting statewide anti-trans legislation in rural Appalachia.[15]

The groups in this study pursue issue campaigns in order to win policies that can tangibly improve people's lives. The struggle itself draws in a broader base of participants, while allowing ordinary people to develop and refine their political skills and analysis. Participants discover a deeper sense of shared stake across race and other socially structured divides while working to shift the public narrative around key economic and racial justice issues. If rural groups tend to focus on economic justice issues that emerge out of the expressed needs of local community members, the urban sites in this study have broadly directed their energies towards police and prison abolition in line with the priorities of BIPOC partners.

"WINNING IS NOT A BINARY"

On a cold and drizzly Saturday in early October 2021, I found my way to the church basement where I would first meet the SURJ Buffalo group in person. A woman, likely in her mid-sixties, head covered in a scarf, eagerly welcomed me from behind a table and indicated where I should put my contact information. I explained why I had just driven three and a half hours to participate in the day's campaign activities. She expressed excitement that I had made the journey, and the fact that I had done so as a researcher only seemed to increase her enthusiasm.

The room was well-worn and appeared to be a regular forum for community gatherings. A handful of folding tables and accompanying chairs were set up for use, while tens more had been stored against a back wall. I saw the usual paraphernalia that accompanies a neighborhood canvass: clipboards piled with walk scripts and campaign literature; an oversized wicker basket with shelf-stable snacks; a cooler filled with disposable water bottles.

As more people arrived, about ten of us were directed to the back of the room to begin our training. We spent ninety minutes being introduced to the basics of door-to-door canvassing and this particular campaign script, including time to role play and ask questions. Our conversations were meant to elicit strangers' core beliefs and values with a focus on the infamously poor conditions in the local jail. I was paired with a more seasoned volunteer, and we drove to a predominantly white neighborhood in Buffalo. Most people were not home, but a few came to their door to speak with me. Some of them were genuinely interested in our conversation and provided the time and space for me to arrive at an ultimate set of requests: that they commit to vote for Kim Beaty, the more progressive of that year's candidates for sheriff; that they put up a lawn sign that communicated as much; and that they get involved with SURJ Buffalo.

For most of its existence, SURJ Buffalo had focused its energies on the county sheriff's office as part of its abolitionist commitments. The group regularly monitored and fought proposals to grow the county's investments in new and expanded jails and prisons as well as greater police presence. SURJ Buffalo's focus on the sheriff's office had also led to two major electoral pushes, in 2017 and again in 2021. The first of these was a campaign to unseat an incumbent, the infamous Sheriff Tim Howard, who oversaw rampant abuse, neglect, and deaths in the local jail and expressed support for a far-right militia group.[16] In that campaign, SURJ Buffalo did not mention Howard's opponent. In 2021 their approach changed as they ran a proactive campaign *for* Kim Beaty, the more progressive of the two viable candidates in the race. The decision to campaign for Beaty, as opposed to merely against her opponent, responded to the direct request of the group's partner, Black Love Resists in the Rust, along with the group's own assessment of effective strategy.

In neither case did SURJ Buffalo see electoral victory. Yet participants were not so convinced that these campaigns were simple defeats. As longtime participant Josie put it, these electoral losses included "a lot of big wins" and "reveal how winning isn't just a binary of a win or lose." Sheriff Howard was "reelected by a razor-thin margin" with the Beaty versus Garcia contest four years later at least as competitive.[17] Josie continued that, "we are the reason there was such a close race to begin with . . . our work so dramatically changed the narrative." SURJ Buffalo member, Linnea Brett, also a SURJ chapter coach, concurred, explaining the campaign's impacts on a few levels. Particularly in 2017, many of the people that the group reached at their doors "might not know that the sheriff was an elected position, wouldn't have heard of Howard." Canvassing thus served as a basic form of civic education. As the 2017 campaign ensued, canvassers began to find that, as Josie put it, "people from all walks of life were like, 'Oh, Tim Howard. He's a racist, right?'" By the 2021 campaign season, many households were aware of conditions at the jail and understood they were again voting for sheriff.

As importantly, the campaigns served the group's longer-term aims, broadening the base of local support while equipping participants with new skills and analysis. Josie continued, "a really rigorous, robust, and well-led campaign pulled a lot of people into the work . . . when it comes to our base, there was a lot of development and a lot of engagement." Without discounting the real disappointment that followed both electoral losses, an organizing approach privileges more enduring objectives of member recruitment and skill development over short-term successes. This is in part because such capacity building portends important future impacts.

As just one example, by late 2023, SURJ Buffalo secured an important nonelectoral victory. Working with their partner organization and other allies, the group brought tens of members to give testimony on the proposed sheriff's budget, successfully convincing the county legislature to shift some of the allocated funds towards other social services. This included investments in a community responder project, which offers mental health and social work professionals as an alternative to police response. As a group facilitator declared about this budget reallocation at the general membership meeting in February 2024, "that was a victory for us."

This pattern of facing a loss, or a series of losses, before accomplishing a win occurred across many of the groups in this study. Recalling the unsuccessful first tenants' rights campaign of the Bedford County Listening Project (BCLP), Kelly Sue recalled:

> We did lose that campaign, but we built a group around it. We established ourselves in the city as a group that they had to reckon with, like they did have to talk to us. Then later, in 2020, one of our members became a city council member.

Such a trajectory certainly speaks to the practical politics of an organizing orientation; even when immediate demands are not met, campaigns build power for subsequent struggles.

There is also transformational potential in the forms of collective action that undergird both SURJ Buffalo and BCLP's initial losses. Building on an Arendtian theory of action, Deva Woodly highlights that in an organizing tradition, "when an individual or group takes action, they are bringing the reality of the world into focus by delineating their place in it and underlining their human capacity to change it by beginning something new."[18] While the campaign efforts mounted in both Buffalo and Shelbyville may not have initially won their demands, they helped to cohere their groups as political actors with whom city decision-makers had to "reckon," as Kelly Sue put it. These diverse campaigns for economic justice and abolition exposed systems of dominance to their participants, various publics, and potentially elected officials themselves. They also turned ordinary people into political actors who showed up at people's doors, and in arenas of state governance, in ways that highlighted their collective capacity to imagine, and act to secure, new and more dignified ways of living in common.

This is not to overlook some of the vexations these groups must navigate as their organizing efforts evolve and begin to secure more concrete wins. As outlined in Chapter 2, SURJ has grown tremendously in its first fifteen years, which includes increased financial capacities and a much larger staff. This has come with the ability to pay local organizers, which has been pivotal to growing rural projects and winning various campaigns. One organizer gave the example of rural listening projects in order to illustrate the necessity of having sufficient resources. Before 2018, SURJ had made at least four other unsuccessful attempts to seed listening projects. All were overseen by a single staff person. The collective assessment was clear: "we needed more staff. Having one person to do five [listening] campaigns was not adequate." The Bedford County Listening Project was the first one that "stuck," in no small part because of the ability to hire talented local organizer Kelly Sue.

At the same time, with the benefit of being able to pay local organizers, new dilemmas arise. Having some local people be paid while others are not can generate forms of hierarchy and complicate different participants' relationships to each other and their groups. Moreover, when some organizers work for a larger entity, local forms of collective imagination, innovation, and self-determination can be stifled. As one group member, herself a movement veteran, reflected:

> I've seen it with any organization as they get bigger. The work is done easier when you have a staff person who is in charge of all the little pieces. But the danger is losing a more collective kind of decision and input. We can have a discussion about something, but ultimately, the decision has already been made.

Such an insight aligns with Frances Piven and Richard Cloward's foundational work on how accruing resources and organizational standing can ultimately weaken the political efforts of the marginalized.[19] These dilemmas are therefore hardly unique to the groups in this study. They do, however, warrant careful consideration so as not to distort or dilute the very power grassroots organizing seeks to grow.

It is also the case that in selecting a campaign's ultimate aims as well as emphases, all groups have important considerations to balance. For instance, prioritizing tangible wins can ultimately distract from developing crucial relationships and leadership capacities or, worse, cause regression rather than progress.[20] Groups that never force concessions from decision-makers, on the other hand, are likely to be written off as ineffectual and will struggle to maintain and grow their base of constituents, a central aim for any movement. The complexities and contradictions of campaign work are perhaps nowhere more exposed than in the context of electoral organizing.

ELECTORAL ORGANIZING

A number of SURJ's campaigns were, at the time of writing, electoral ones. This raises important questions about the role of electoral politics in an organizing approach that seeks to be enduring and ultimately transformational. Debates regarding the role of voting and elections are nothing new to leftist movements in general and racial justice efforts specifically.[21] The groups in this study tended to approach electoral organizing as an important, if highly limited, terrain of struggle. Dahlia Ferlito of WP4BL in Los Angeles had a particularly pithy way of synthesizing this perspective in meetings and presentations: "our liberation is not coming from electoral politics, but our oppression sure is." A similar sentiment was shared by many leaders in group trainings, campaign activities, and personal interviews.

In our conversations, Erin Heaney explained to me that SURJ had done minimal electoral work in its first years. While partially due to limited capacity, the network was also reticent to put its energies into supporting candidates. As part of an organizing approach, Erin explained, "we are interested in building power beyond just one election cycle, and we have an assessment that candidates aren't going to save us . . . candidates disappoint people and have to work within the confines of a system." Yet over time, and often in response to requests from partners, the organization had engaged in much more electoral work, which included endorsing candidates, as in the case of Kim Beaty. This aligns with a growing acknowledgment that, as Erin put it, "we need to elect people so that our movement has the best conditions possible to be able to advance the things we want to win."

During one of its phone banks ahead of the 2022 mid-term elections, the national organization was joined by Alicia Garza, a co-founder of Black Lives Matter and outspoken advocate for electoral organizing. Garza was clear that "I am not here to tell you that electoral organizing is like the end all be all; it's not." Nevertheless, she offered a cogent analysis for why elections should matter to the Left, even if there "has been a longstanding debate about the utility of electoral politics in our movement." She continued, "the people and the interests that want to make decisions about us without us have a vested interest in keeping their power. And the primary way that they do that, besides money and force, is through voting and electoral politics." Incorporating electoral organizing within a multipronged strategy was framed as the only way to stand up to an "opposition," which has for the past several decades been quite strategic in "[putting] people in decision-making roles that share their agenda."

SURJ thus seeks to balance the imperative to engage in elections with the equal conviction that, as Erin explained, "we need to connect with people deeply around their values and their own lives and the things that they care about. And we don't think that we do that, get that kind of deeper connection, if we're only talking about candidates."[22] The groups in this study pursued a few common practices to productively meet this ambivalence. As with the example of guest speaker Alicia Garza, trainings and campaign activities regularly introduced elections by acknowledging their limitations as well as their importance. Moreover, the groups in this study prioritized long-term aims over short-term outcomes in all of their campaigns, including electoral ones. This is perhaps most obvious in the design of campaign scripts.

In practical terms, scripts for canvassing and phone banks help volunteers know what to say when talking to someone about a campaign. At a deeper level, the design of such scripts helps communicate a political methodology both to volunteers and their audiences. For instance, SURJ Buffalo's script to elect Kim Beaty was designed to elicit a fairly lengthy conversation rooted in curiosity and shared values, working towards deepening political education and engagement. Volunteers began by asking how residents felt about conditions in the local jail. They posed questions to encourage their neighbors to critically engage with their assumptions about the carceral system. Sometimes they educated people about the fact that the sheriff is an elected position and delineated the responsibilities of the office.

Many in the Beaty door-knocking training commented with some surprise that the script did not mention the candidate earlier. Our trainer, Steph, an experienced labor union organizer, confirmed that while most electoral efforts seek to maximize the number of voters reached, this was "a totally different model." It became clear that electing Beaty was not the only campaign aim, a lesson reiterated by the metrics we were asked to track. In our collective debriefs, we celebrated the total number of conversations had at peoples' doors and the number of stories shared alongside more typically valued outcomes, such as committed votes. This practice reiterated important campaign goals beyond the election, including political education, public engagement, and relationship building.

In the Los Angeles effort to pass Measure R, WP4BL took the emphasis on political education through relationship building even further with their deep-canvassing approach. Not dissimilar from the Beaty script in Buffalo, deep canvassing requires a lengthy conversation in which volunteers share personal experiences with a stranger, ask questions, and seek to reach a place of shared vulnerability and connection. Liz described WP4BL's deep canvassing as "actually kind of depoliticizing," with a script that began with, "'What do you actually care about, like what matters to you?' . . . instead of, 'Is this how you want to vote? Yes or no,' let me try to salesman you into this." Certainly, the conversation would ultimately arrive at why the person should support Measure R, which Liz explained as "still getting to the political piece but not having that be the point." Moreover, for several years after the Measure R ballot initiative successfully passed, WP4BL continued deep canvassing LA's predominantly white communities in an effort to shift carceral attitudes.[23]

Allen, who was a "newish father" of two young children when he found W4BL in 2016, described how some of the phone-banking efforts for Measure R were also quite different than previous voter engagement work he had done, "where we were just calling voters, being like, 'do you have terrible politics? No? Great!'" and then asking people to vote a certain way. As one example, WP4BL used the campaign as an opportunity to reengage those who had at some point attended an event with the group, asking questions such as, "'What were you feeling in that moment that got you to a place where you were like, 'I need to do more?'" Allen described the Measure R phone calls as, "really taking the time to connect with folks in a way that felt useful, but it was also authentically relationship building." For Allen, these conversations were his turning point in terms of understanding an organizing approach to social change. In the effort to build relationships and explore common values, Allen explained, "I recognized myself really clicking as a quote unquote organizer."

SURJ's rural projects also take a nuanced approach to electoral politics, though the partisan terrain in which they organize is quite distinct from the urban chapters in this study.[24] Julia Daniel explained SURJ's analysis for why rural America has become a stronghold of the Right, naming the intertwined dynamics of globalization, capital flight, and attacks on organized labor having led to "less union density" and, hence, very little "progressive organizing presence." Coupled with this, following the Republican Party's Southern Strategy first inaugurated in 1968, Julia explained how "the Democratic establishment has decided those [rural and southern] communities are essentially throwaways and has not been engaged, has not been on the doors, has kind of abandoned [them]."[25] It thus makes little sense to begin organizing in SURJ's rural sites by asking that residents support the very candidates who have neglected their communities for generations.

At the same time, formal governing power is not irrelevant to people's lives. Giving the example of the Bedford County Listening Project (BCLP), Julia explained, "we are very conscious that living in a Republican trifecta state, such as Tennessee, really constrains what kind of wins a group like the BCLP can have or the statewide work can have." In line with its overarching approach to electoral politics, Julia explained how SURJ's rural organizing seeks to balance the "need for a more progressive governing power at the state level" with an emphasis on "being engaged in sustained and transformative organizing relationships," which SURJ assesses neither begin nor end with electing better candidates.

What this means in practice depends on context and emergent conditions. It often begins with supporting more local candidates, and often leaders within a group. This is sometimes coupled with eschewing higher profile, partisan endorsements. For instance, in Shelbyville, Tennessee, in 2020, Bedford County Listening Project member Stephanie Isaacs ultimately decided to run for city council herself, a position that is not party affiliated.[26] In 2024, Kentucky People's Union also planned to get involved in nonpartisan local elections, running one of their own members for the Ashland Board of Commissioners and endorsing other candidates. At the same time, KPU collectively decided not to formally endorse incumbent Kentucky Governor Andy Beshear in his 2023 bid for reelection.[27] Amelia explained that the group's decision was predicated on a few factors. These included a lack of unanimous support for the governor's policies as well as members wanting to "keep the focus on us and our current campaigns." Amelia noted that the main concern for the group, however, was actually the stickiness of partisan politics, "we didn't want to alienate potential supporters [of KPU]," who might not themselves support a well-known candidate, or a Democratic one, for myriad reasons.

It should also be mentioned that, just as in any organization, individual participants are not always in agreement with the tactical or strategic decisions made at the group level. As one example, Dahlia of WP4BL explained of Measure R that "people within our collective didn't all agree that they wanted to throw down for a ballot initiative. Even to this day, not everybody agrees in using the electoral system for anything." While none of the participants I interviewed espoused this hard line against all electoral work, many spoke about the complexities of seeking to take action within the system, particularly to promote abolitionist aims. The Beaty campaign was an exemplar in this regard as volunteers were asked to proactively advocate for a career law enforcement officer, far from an abolitionist herself. Tiffany of SURJ Buffalo explained that "when we decided to endorse Beaty, that was obviously difficult for some people as abolitionists," recalling how one participant decided not to be part of the campaign itself even as she remained in the group. Many Buffalo volunteers I spoke to while canvassing confirmed their sense that the campaign was ridden with contradiction even as they committed their evenings and weekends to the challenging work of door knocking.

From across the country, Allen of WP4BL admitted his surprise upon learning that the Buffalo group was proactively working to elect a sheriff. Allen connected this to the ambivalences he too had faced doing electoral work:

> I think it's a good lesson in the messiness of working within an electoral system that obviously has its own limits and contradictions, being strategic in the moment in time that you're living in and organizing in to make the best decision that you can.

The lessons learned through organizing abound. I now turn more explicitly to the matter of learning in an organizing approach.

"TRAIN PEOPLE, ALWAYS TRAIN"

I was first introduced to SURJ's rings of engagement model during a virtual meeting of the Buffalo group in September of 2021. The model was depicted with concentric circles in which the bull's-eye was a movement's "core," the next circle "passive supporter," followed by "disengaged," "passive opponent," and finally arrows pointing out to "hostile," not technically on the map. I would go on to see a similar principle introduced across SURJ spaces, though sometimes using slightly different language and visuals. These are an adaptation of Martin Oppenheimer and George Lakey's spectrum of allies, first presented in a strategy manual for civil rights organizers.[28]

The purpose of introducing this idea in the Buffalo meeting was to practice having conversations about racism and other potentially divisive matters with people in our lives. We were prompted to select someone we might wish to engage and identify their position along the rings. We were then offered a list of considerations for successfully embarking on such a conversation. These included listening with empathy, curiosity, and humility; remembering to consider the place and time of the conversation; as well as accepting pointers on tonality and word choice, such as avoiding sarcasm and jargon. We were also encouraged to remember that our primary aim was to maintain the relationship, to position this conversation as being the first of many. In much the same way as a canvassing script ends with a specific ask—to vote, to donate, to join an organization—these conversations also ended with a request: to "keep talking" and to schedule a time to do so.

Talking to one's personal contacts about racism may seem quaint as a means of confronting racism and certainly would be insufficient as a stand-alone technique for seeking to dismantle white supremacy. This training nevertheless captures important elements of SURJ's organizing approach. This includes the conviction that across any given public, including people who are white, there is diversity of experience and circumstance as well as potential fluidity. People's allegiances are complicated, and their commitments may not be as fixed as they first appear. Most organizing traditions require that people learn how to talk to others, to pull out important stories, values, and motivations, and this certainly informs SURJ's approach. Helping participants name and frame white supremacy as they seek to have these conversations with other white people, and to confront the collective impacts of white ignorance and dominant white socialization, requires participants learn fairly sophisticated dialogue techniques, ones that require nuance and care. In teaching members about the rings of engagement and helping them practice conversing across difference, this session also exemplifies SURJ's investment in political education across its sites and activities.

Pam McMichael, executive director of the Highlander Center when she helped to launch SURJ, explained "the combination of education and action" by drawing an infinity sign in the air with her finger: "That's a figure eight. Those have to go together." Many liberation traditions, and basic sociological insight, suggest that people living under systems of dominance require tools for understanding their situation otherwise. Moreover, behind the strategy of organizing in predominantly white communities is an acknowledgment that white people have been recruited to align with white supremacy at great cost to society and themselves, and they need opportunities to both see and dismantle these investments.

Dahlia explained how rarely such opportunities are made available: "If we are white, we don't really have spaces to be able to learn what is happening around us. Political education, particularly for white people, is severely lacking."[29] This insight builds on the many thinkers who identify whiteness as a form of socially structured, and often willful ignorance.[30] Dahlia continued, "because we have the benefit of whiteness, we get to choose when and when not to engage with this." This is clearly an important niche that white affinity groups can fill and is one of the undergirding logics for their existence.[31] Nevertheless, when the learning becomes an ends unto itself, white people can, as Dahlia put it:

> get in this trap, that I was in, which a lot of white people default to, which is you get awoken, and then you turn to the books. You get your closest friends into a book club. You do a lot of talking, and then it kind of stays in that bubble.[32]

The book club model does little to bring people who believe themselves interested in racial justice into collective action, and it can be off-putting to white communities that do not yet understand their role in movement work. As a distinct approach, Dahlia clarified the need for "rooting the political education with the action."

Participants in this study often used the term "political education" to refer to sustained opportunities to learn about different bodies of thought that can help members make sense of systems of dominance. Examples might include workshops and study groups on racial capitalism, prison abolition, or disability justice. This definition of political education comes out of specific organizing traditions, often credited to the civil rights movement, but with important predecessors among the formerly enslaved and worker organizations, practiced then and still at places like the Highlander Center.[33] I think of political education a bit more expansively, as encompassing the range of opportunities, from formal study to experiential learning, by which participants acquire the many forms of knowledge needed to act towards collectively desired social change. While such a definition might seem unduly broad, I adopt it to underscore that the learning obtained through grassroots organizing is foundationally about resocializing people so that they might imagine and act together to shift relations of power.

By this definition, much of this book is about political education. A full accounting of the formal learning opportunities I encountered in three years of fieldwork could constitute a second book altogether. Nearly every activity I attended, from orientations and general meetings to actual campaign activities, included structured lessons with opportunities to apply and practice new ideas and skills. I offer instead a few patterned examples of formal learning I encountered to demonstrate what kinds of training might be useful for preparing predominantly white communities to move into antiracist collective action.

As the opening of this section suggests, one of the most common skills discussed and practiced across settings was political communication, such as speaking with personal contacts and strangers at their doors. This makes sense in an organizing strategy that understands that identifying and explaining how white racism sows division and collective harm is not just an ethical obligation but central to good political strategy. Understanding how to communicate also extends to bringing demands to important decision-makers. For example, SURJ Buffalo's efforts to monitor the sheriff's office included regularly preparing for legislative hearings. In one such meeting, volunteers were first introduced to some of the principles of abolition before being shown how the county budgeting process connects to an expanding carceral system. They then learned how to structure effective and coherent testimony, developing and practicing what they planned to deliver. Importantly, such trainings are rooted in a grassroots, participatory learning orientation, in which members learn and teach each other, in this case about theories of liberation (abolition), how governing processes work (county budgeting), and applied political skills (how to speak to legislators).

Collaborative research and learning processes were common across the groups in this study and are key to how political education in grassroots organizing has worked for SURJ's movement antecedents.[34] As one telling example, when Kelly Sue described the early months of the Bedford County Listening Project, she referred to participants as grassroots researchers of a kind:

> [These were] poor and working-class white moms, living in shitty housing, who [had] been knocking doors in Shelbyville for probably eight months now, collecting data and surveys that they designed to take a study to tell the media and to prove to city council that the housing is substandard.

While learning how to engage in formal processes of governance, such as how to testify in legislative hearings, is important, trainings in political action were not constrained to traditional channels. Rather, I witnessed a broad range of tactics explored and employed, such as training and planning for direct and arrestable action, explored further in the next chapter.

Not all movement participants require the same forms of political education. For instance, Erin Heaney explained how the organization diagnosed a need among its national staff for particular forms of learning around political theory, as this group "may have the organizing skills but not the deep analysis around the political orientation we're taking." SURJ staff have thus "done sessions on racial capitalism, more deeply understanding the economic system and how race is used to maintain it" as well as "a lot over the years on disability justice." Such an approach is generally not sufficient for local groups, where many are newer to movement work and do need to learn basic organizing skills. As Carla Wallace put it, "chapters are not necessarily made up of organizers. People don't necessarily have the skills around 'How do you develop new leaders?' 'How do you bring people in?'" This is where the role of formal training, coupled with campaign activities, can be helpful.

Partners regularly named their appreciation for SURJ's learning spaces and approaches. Longtime organizer Shameka Parrish-Wright of Louisville, for instance, described sending white people to LSURJ who had come to her with an orientation of, "'I want to be an ally. What can I do? Who can I talk to? How can I get better at this?'" Shameka did not necessarily mind being approached in this way and noted, "I can give what I see as a Black woman." Nevertheless, she believed that

LSURJ could provide a community of similarly situated people seeking dialogue and learning as well as an organizational structure equipped to move white people into practical action:

> When people reach out to me, and they say they need help understanding racism and their role, LSURJ can give them the training and development and somebody to talk to. Somebody to have those hard conversations with and say, "You know what, I could have said something when my uncle was being racist to that guy, but I didn't even know where to start."

Attica Scott likewise described directing people to LSURJ's "monthly educational sessions," remarking that, "training is so important. They [LSURJ] really invest a lot into training and education." Attica continued by reflecting on the skills-based training that LSURJ does before canvassing. During her campaign for US Congress, which LSURJ endorsed, Attica emphasized with some humor that, as far as LSURJ was concerned, "you were not going to go canvassing if you did not participate in the training beforehand!" At one level, Attica thought this was "great," and explained how role playing "a good door" and "a difficult door" are both important, as volunteers "need to know what it's like to come upon someone who says something extremely horribly racist. How do you talk through that?"

Nevertheless, Attica admitted her own initial misgivings that the level of training might be redundant for seasoned canvassers: "Like I'm one of those people, 'I've run for office so many times. I know what I'm doing! I'm just gonna go out to these doors. I don't need a training!'" Attica swiftly learned, however, that the LSURJ training was about more than just how to knock a door. "It wasn't only the technicalities." She continued:

> When I was a part of it, it was also about how do we build our relationships with one another? I was able to be a part of building that relationship with these amazing volunteers, who were gonna go knocking on doors for me.

In this instance, Attica suggested that LSURJ's organizing orientation, which prioritizes relationships in its approach to growing and sustaining movement work, was an important lesson for her as well.

Participants across groups were clear that organizing work was an unending process of learning, both at the individual and collective level. As Amelia exclaimed, "I am always learning with KPU!" enumerating a list of skills she had developed:

> I've learned how to facilitate meetings, how to do one-on-ones, how to be more mindful when I'm discussing things.... I've been given opportunities to grow my skills as a leader, to learn how to delegate tasks, ask for help, maintain posting schedules (for social media).

These are all things that, as Amelia put it, "I never thought I'd ever do in my whole life." Here Amelia demonstrates how the learning that happens in organizing is not merely about skills acquisition. Rather Amelia finds herself capable of forms of action and agency that were previously unimaginable.

Elliot also suggested that through KPU they had learned everything from basic civics knowledge to specific organizing skills. Through KPU's housing justice campaign, Elliot reflected, "I've learned how bills and ordinances are passed. I've learned how things get on the agenda to be voted on." Elliot continued, "I also didn't know anything about running campaigns until I joined KPU. I've learned the steps of a campaign, how to start and progress—identifying the problem and then identifying the issue, how to do a power analysis and build strategy and tactics." Pausing to consider these lessons, Elliot concluded, "I've learned how to bring people into the movement." While acquiring new forms of analysis and skills, Elliot comes to conceptualize themselves as politically effective in the sense of bringing others into collective action for social change.

Indeed, when we spoke, Elliot was helping to distribute forms of collective learning across organizations in Ashland, having recently led a training on the organizing tool of one-on-one meetings with Ashland Pride, a local LGBTQ organization. This migration across organizations of knowledge, skills, tactics, and strategies is an important hidden product of organizing, and it is precisely the kind of cross-fertilization that SURJ hopes to create, particularly among predominantly white communities in the rural South. As Kelly Sue understood it, equipping movement participants with important skills and knowledge in one place and time can pay dividends in the future, often in unexpected ways: "it's never wasted time to train people. That's part of organizing: train people, always train." Kelly Sue continued that such training is essential to the organization's long-term vision for collective liberation:

> [building] a bench of organizers that live in towns across the South, who are trained in this work, can build others' leadership, can build campaigns, can use all of those different tools to build and fight for like basic needs for one, but also a fighting chance to stand in their dignity, and in their ability to fight back.

Such an approach is in line with the organizing tradition of Ella Baker, who emphasized cultivating local leadership, building "leaderful" groups, and entrusting ordinary people with the abilities to make the best sense and strategy out of their lived conditions.[35] Achieving such ambitious aims certainly requires intentional, structured forms of training, which are built into nearly every feature of group work. Yet many participants traced their most important lessons to campaign activities themselves.

LEARNING IN ACTION, ENDING CASH BAIL

For the past several years, Louisville SURJ had focused its energies on ending cash bail, a practice that requires people who have not yet stood trial to pay to be released from jail. Because cash bail has been shown to disproportionately harm BIPOC and low-income communities as well as swell the ranks of those incarcerated, its elimination has become a policy target for some abolitionists.[36] Louisville's cash bail campaign, like similar efforts in Los Angeles and Buffalo, provided an opportunity for the group to organize out of mutual interest and in partnership with Black-led organizing efforts. Moreover, the two most enduring features of LSURJ's campaign—the Court Watch program, where volunteers observed weekly arraignment court, and ongoing neighborhood canvasses—provided participants a range of skill-building and awareness-raising opportunities.

Court Watch tended to attract LSURJ participants with more flexible schedules, often those with some class privilege, but was an applied and helpful way for white people to wield forms of racial and class privilege towards collectively beneficial ends. By observing the procedures by which elected judges hold near complete discretion to determine conditions for pretrial release, including setting bail, Court Watch accomplished a number of aims simultaneously. First, it provided an immediate ameliorative measure, bringing witnesses into a process that often goes unobserved by those outside the system. Many involved in the work of the courts, including public defenders, reported that LSURJ's presence beneficially impacted the pace, thoughtfulness, and fairness of judges' decision-making. Second, Court Watch was a form of grassroots monitoring and collective research that provided the broader group with necessary forms of data to bolster their campaign efforts. During courtroom observations, volunteers documented factors that may inform a judge's decision-making, such as the defendant's perceived race and the presence of a public defender versus private attorney. This information was then used when meeting with willing judges to review observed patterns and also helped with candidate endorsements come election time.

Though neither its primary nor secondary goal, Court Watch also served as an important site of political learning for its volunteers. During a focus group I conducted with eight Court Watch participants in January 2022, volunteers reflected on the "shocking" rapidity of courtroom processes and found "the level of jargon and lack of care" from judges to be astonishing. One participant reflected that, coming from her own place of racial and class privilege, which included "no interaction with the criminal justice system at all, not even a parking ticket," the experience "kind of radicalized me." Another elaborated that "observing court is condensed evidence of intersecting oppressions building on top of each other," explaining her understanding that "most people who've ended up there got there based on racial bias, and zip code, and income.

You're seeing a pinpoint of all of these oppressions at once." All agreed that seeing the criminal punishment system's more mundane forms of violence was a moral shock that reignited their political commitments.

LSURJ's cash bail campaign also prioritized ongoing door-knocking efforts in predominantly white working-class neighborhoods over several years. Carla described this as "listening to people's struggles with housing, or the criminal justice system, to identify their shared interest in joining together across racial lines for the change that will benefit them too." LSURJ would then invite people to take action with the group, such as by signing petitions, sending postcards to county judges, or expressing support to end cash bail at local media events to end cash bail. The group has found cash bail to be a particularly salient way to do door-to-door political education and move white people into collective action at the intersections of economic justice and prison abolition. As LSURJ member Sonja reflected on door knocking around cash bail:

> You're really having conversations with people about race *and* class and the whole system because cash bail affects so many people. It's a great lens with which to see the class *and* race inequality in our system.

During their first major electoral push in 2022, when all thirteen county positions for judgeship came open, the group found that 75 percent of those in Louisville's majority-white, poor, and working-class neighborhoods agreed that cash bail should be eradicated. This viewpoint often transcended partisan lines, as "even among registered Republicans, about half" opposed cash bail.[37] While seven of LSURJ's endorsed candidates won, LSURJ understood this electoral success as but a step, if an important one, in creating more favorable governing conditions under which to end cash bail. Days after the election, the group invited all new judges to meet so as to continue "building relationships and accountability."[38]

The cash bail campaign has secured concrete political achievements, while giving SURJ participants and their audiences a range of opportunities for political learning, sometimes in unexpected ways. Sonja, for example, told a story from her canvassing efforts during the multiple years the group has been working to end cash bail. In this instance, she was door knocking with her teenage son. The two were standing on the sidewalk getting ready to approach a house, "and this guy came out. He had an NRA [National Rifle Association] t-shirt on," which today many might interpret as signaling alliance with the political Right. Sonja turned dubiously to her son, who challenged her to approach the man anyway. As soon as they started conversing, the resident was immediately receptive. He shared the story of being arrested while in high school with three friends, all of whom were Black. All were accused of the same infraction, but as the man recalled, "'the difference is, I got to leave that night. And they didn't. Because they had a bail, and they couldn't pay it. It was so clear to me that the only reason I was leaving was because I was white.'" The man signed the petition, wanting the literature and "campaign swag."

This anecdote exemplified for Sonja the learning that comes with campaign work: "I love it when I get challenged with stereotypes. That happens a lot when you door-knock because, you know, people are complex." I now turn more squarely to the role of door knocking for the groups in this study, examining it as a site of participant learning as well as an important tool in the arsenal of white antiracist organizing.

DOOR KNOCKING

White People for Black Lives (WP4BL) member Allen admitted that until he began canvassing, he spent most of his time with like-minded people. This experience is not atypical, particularly for those who are most engaged in the political process. Nevertheless, Allen observed such ideological silos are a "dangerous" place for the Left to be in general, and for white people on the Left in particular. Allen therefore credited door knocking with some of his own most important political learning, particularly in terms of "clarity around moving people." Allen suggested that when those who seek social and political change fail to speak to a broad swath of the public, they begin to misunderstand key aspects of the terrain of struggle: namely, how to move people from differing backgrounds to become movement sympathizers or even constituents.[39]

Allen recalled a particular conversation with a homeowner who "really [believed] in jail because 'people need to be punished for crime!' [He believed] in more police 'because homelessness is a problem.'" When Allen probed the man's own relationship to jails and prisons, however, this homeowner was clear that his own brother, arrested at twenty-one for a cocaine violation, needed help for an addiction. By asking that resident to reflect on personal experience, Allen was able to evoke the commentary that "'jail didn't help us. It was terrible! I wish that there was a treatment program that actually would have addressed [my brother's] humanity, rather than just punishing the worst parts about him.'" Allen was not naive about this exchange, laughing, "maybe I'm not like bringing that guy to the next White People for Black Lives meeting, or, you know, organizing him." At the same time, Allen believed that "those conversations move people" and asked the rhetorical question of, "What does it mean to talk to someone who has a BLM sign in their yard, but also just called the cops on homeless people?" In alignment with the concept of rings of engagement, SURJ believes that not everyone needs to become a committed organizer for a movement to track progress.

Most organizing approaches prioritize going out and finding people where they live, work, and socialize in an effort to move them into some form of collective action. While the techniques for doing this are multiple, there is a long tradition of starting at people's homes. Indeed, writing about organizing in the U.S. civil rights movement, Charles Payne suggests:

> Maybe canvassing is the prototypical organizing act. It is the initial reaching out to the community, the first step toward building relationships outside the circle of those favorably predisposed to the movement.[40]

Some participants described canvassing as uncomfortable work that is nevertheless worthwhile for reaching a broader and more diverse contingent of white people. I again turn to my conversation with Sonja of LSURJ as instructive. Sonja began, "I've always loved door knocking," and then quickly caught herself, began to laugh, and continued, "you know, it's funny. I say, 'I've always loved door knocking.' I hate door knocking! But I love it too because it's so effective." Sonja explained being "an introvert" and finding it quite nerve-wracking to go speak to strangers.

At the same time, Sonja saw door knocking as an important antidote to the ways in which movement groups can become insular and routinized, tendencies Sonja deemed "depressing." She described a typical scenario "when you're with an organization, you have an event, and it's all the same people, and you're pretty much having the same conversations." Sonja acknowledged that groups can use tools beyond canvassing, such as digital outreach, but believed knocking on people's doors held a particular value because of "how alienated people are and isolated people are, knocking on people's doors, it's really powerful." In a society highly segregated by race and class as well as increasingly mediated by digital tools, showing up at someone's door to engage in meaningful, civically oriented conversation might even be understood as a radical act.

Kelly Sue took this insight a bit further, explaining that important and counterhegemonic conversations can happen at people's doors. She explained, "something that I think is very important when you knock on a door is having these conversations with each other, which we don't have normally . . . talking about the things they don't want us to talk about." In this way, Kelly Sue conceptualized the role of door knocking within an organizing drive as an opportunity to build relationships premised on opposing the dominant power structure while developing and sharing forms of insurgent knowledge.

Among the city-based groups in this study, participants regularly identified door knocking in predominantly white communities as one of the more important tasks for white people in multiracial movement. Much like Sonja of LSURJ, Josie of SURJ Buffalo explained her personal discomfort with knocking on strangers' doors: "it hits my anxiety button, and I have to do a lot of fake it till I make it sometimes, leaning into what can be really awkward conversations and just not knowing what's going to happen if a person opens their door." At the same time, Josie believed that reaching out to people through door knocking "is what's so necessary. . . . I'm so committed to canvassing," because of its ability to grow the movement's base of support. Josie noted that for her personally, door knocking, even more so than risking arrest, is a way of "putting something on the line," defined as "getting down and dirty," "using time and resources . . . access and opportunity and identity as [white people] to do the work with other folks in this movement, both locally and nationally."

In this way, and particularly in urban groups, door knocking is understood as one mechanism by which white people might productively deploy the fact of their whiteness as part of multiracial movement work. This is an interesting twist on the notion of white privilege discussed in the last chapter. Seeking to organize in a range of white communities with an opening salvo that points to whites' racial privilege may not be effective. At the same time, and without necessarily naming it as such, the fact of having white racial privilege foundationally structures how a number of city-based participants in this study made sense of their tactical choices.

Indeed, Carla Wallace, SURJ co-founder, cited the need to door-knock in majority white communities as an important rationale for the white affinity model itself. Carla recalled some of the pushback the network received early on from activists concerned by the prospect of organizing in predominantly white formations. She reflected, "I come out of organizing, right? You can't organize without knocking doors. Growing means we got to talk to people we don't know." Given this premise, one of the questions SURJ would pose to these early skeptics was, "are you saying that Black people should go knock the doors in these white neighborhoods?" Rarely did someone suggest this was a good idea.

A number of Black partners concurred that having white people be the ones to knock on white doors was important. For example, Phylicia Brown, who at the time of our interview was executive director of Black Love Resists in the Rust, SURJ Buffalo's strategic partner, explained:

> I think of all the things that happen during door knocking. And I'm like, Black people don't need to be subjected to whatever white people want to say, or their feelings about something, in a way that is not aligned to our survival.

On one level, then, having white people canvass predominantly white neighborhoods is understood as a way of mitigating the potential for white racist harm.

Black partners also named their sense that such an approach is simply more politically effective because of how white racism makes it difficult to earn legitimacy. Jerome Scott, a lifelong organizer and founder of Project South, who serves as an advisor to SURJ, asked rhetorically, "You know what happens when a Black person goes into a white neighborhood?" He continued, "white folks are automatically—their defenses go up, particularly if they don't know you. And I'm not talking about *bad* white people [laughter]." Jerome continued that when Black people try to door-knock in white communities, "it takes so long for you to win over an ability for them to just listen to you . . . nothing else, not even agree with you, just listen, hear what I'm saying."

Phylicia of Buffalo assessed this dynamic as, "People listen to people who look like them, right?" Ashanti Scott [no relation to Jerome], a youth organizer in Louisville, likewise surmised that "white people receive conversations about racism better when it's white people having those conversations with them . . . they're more comfortable having those conversations when it's someone who looks like them."

Attica Scott—an elected representative, organizer, and Ashanti's mother—situated such an observation within her own campaign efforts in predominantly white parts of Louisville. She explained, "I've knocked on white people's doors when they didn't answer. But looked out the window, saw me. Then the next week opened that same door for white people who came to the door." Such a dynamic certainly raises concerns about the ultimate efficacy of knocking on this person's door as part of any racial justice effort. If someone will not even open the door for a Black candidate, how likely are they to ultimately vote for one, even if the person that comes to talk to them is white? Still, in line with numerous organizing traditions, SURJ assesses that most people's commitments are complex, often contradictory, and potentially malleable. One way that white people can contribute to multiracial justice work is by approaching other white people in order to hold conversations, build awareness and relationships, and ultimately move sufficient numbers to begin to question, and ultimately more actively, resist racist logics, policies, and politics.

For this reason, partners often named door knocking as one way in which SURJ groups contribute to multiracial movement strategy. Attica Scott recalled her first memories of LSURJ in 2012: "they were knocking on doors and canvassing communities and neighborhoods and talking to white people about racial justice." Once Attica started seeing yard signs in support of the Movement for Black Lives, emblazoned with a SURJ logo in predominantly white neighborhoods, she recalled thinking, "oh, this is huge!" A decade later, some critics would evaluate such yard signs as merely "symbolic or expressive forms of antiracism" that do little to shift the balance of power.[41] While this is a critique many in LSURJ might also share, such iconography was nevertheless meaningful in that place and time.

Ashanti agreed that LSURJ's commitment to canvassing demonstrates courage and is an important contribution to multiracial movement work: "one reason why I love [LSURJ]," is because "they're not afraid to go straight to [a white person's] door and talk to their neighbors. They've been canvassing for a long time, canvassing white areas of the city."

With this said, SURJ's racial division of door knocking is more commonly observed in the urban formations in this study, which generally operate in more clearly delineated cross-racial and cross-organizational partnerships than do SURJ's rural projects. By way of contrast, Amelia—a leader of Kentucky People's Union, "a mixed woman, African American and white"—described door knocking as likely the most meaningful part of her work with the group. In the poor and working-class areas of Ashland where KPU did most of its canvassing, and where Amelia herself resided, Amelia explained, "nobody's talking to these people. They feel like nobody cares. But we do care." Amelia's race was not necessarily top of mind when she canvassed. Amelia continued that in her work with KPU, "we knock on any door," though the canvassers "usually choose low-income neighborhoods over ones that seem more affluent." When asked about the presence of flags or other iconography that could suggest the resident is hostile to her or the group, Amelia explained that while KPU canvassers "always go out in pairs" and "never have to knock on a door if we don't feel safe," she rarely chose not to approach a house.

To be certain, this is not because Amelia believes her race immaterial in Ashland. She explained that spending most of her life as a mixed-race person in a predominantly white community has been "hard, really hard." One of Amelia's first memories when her family moved to Kentucky from Florida was a classmate warning her, "'Be careful. My uncle is part of the KKK.'" Amelia was nine years old at the time. "I didn't even know what the KKK was!" Such explicit racism has also punctuated her adult life when, for instance, she was called racial slurs at the town park. Yet Amelia has found door knocking, and her organizing with KPU more generally, to be something of an ameliorative to such experiences. Amelia has discovered that many people, whites included, "actually align with KPU's values" when invited to do so.

Amelia noted that her neighbors nearly always express surprise and appreciation when she comes to their door: "'Wow, you've actually taken time out of your day to talk to me!'" For Amelia, "that feels like I've made a difference in this person's day. And hopefully I can make a difference in this person's life." If this sounds idealistic, Amelia was speaking as an organizer, seeking to reach out to new people, to help them identify their shared interest in dismantling white supremacy and other intersecting systems of oppression, and then, as Amelia put it, to "give them the space to take on a role with me to actually make a difference." Amelia's experience lifts up the complexity and contextual responsiveness that SURJ prioritizes. Organizing in predominantly white communities towards multiracial liberation does not look the same in all sites, nor carry identical meanings for all participants.

ORGANIZING IN MOVEMENT TIMES

Organizing is both the thing that we have to do because we don't have enough power or money to win what we need otherwise *and* organizing is the thing that will actually get us free . . . [because] we basically have to rebuild our society.

—TARYN HALLWEAVER, SURJ National Organizing Department

This revolution is necessary, therefore, not only because the ruling class cannot be overthrown in any other way, but also because the class overthrowing it can only in a revolution succeed in ridding itself of all the muck of ages and become fitted to found society anew.

—KARL MARX[42]

SURJ's organizing approach seeks to grow a base of enduring white support to join with BIPOC in advancing a multipronged liberation agenda. This strategy centrally includes going out and finding new people while building the collective capacities of those already involved. Campaigns for economic justice and abolition bring participants into "communities of action" where they can refine their understandings of systems of dominance while becoming the kinds of people capable of collective political action.[43]

To tell SURJ's story, however, one cannot lose sight of the social and political context in which the organization has grown. This centrally includes the rise of the Movement for Black Lives along with new indicators of consolidating fascism, underwritten by a majority-white base.[44] The organization saw major moments of growth following the Ferguson uprisings of 2014 and again in 2016, with high-profile police killings as well as Trump's 2016 election.[45] Many term 2020 "the summer of the whirlwind" when, following the police murders of Breonna Taylor and George Floyd, unprecedented numbers of people flocked to SURJ. In June, the Buffalo group had 600 people attend their virtual meeting. The Los Angeles chapter counted between 3,000 and 4,000 participants. The national network convened a number of video calls with 10,000 to 12,000 in attendance. As Erin Heaney described it, SURJ has been "growing and organizing in movement times, which means everything is extra dynamic."

Receiving those who come to a group willingly may seem easier than going out to find those who do not. Incorporating newly activated people into more durable formations nevertheless comes with challenges. Indeed, it is not uncommon for leaders in mass movements to recall worrying that the revolution would not come quickly enough only to feel that it has come to soon, and they are underprepared when it arrives.[46] As Pam McMichael reflected on the past decade's mobilizing moments, people come with "a wide range of experiences . . . wanting to talk about how to get involved, wanting to be connected to other people, wanting to do something." Pam believed that one strength that has allowed SURJ to grow and endure is a consistent and strategic responsiveness in such times, which she described as "holding space for people to move . . . [creating] different on-ramps that are needed for people in motion." SURJ has created the infrastructure to bring new people into supportive communities where they are invited into learning and action quite swiftly.

Many in this study termed this the work of "absorption," a framework that can be traced to the Momentum training institute, founded in 2014 by organizers from movements that range from Occupy Wall Street to Black Lives Matter. Backed by empirical study, Momentum explains absorption as "the systematic process of bringing newly activated people into the movement so that the movement grows in capacity and can escalate with greater impact over time." In essence, absorption seeks to turn mobilizing moments into deeper organizing opportunities, funneling new participants into contexts where they can take meaningful action, deepen commitment, and hone skills and analysis.[47]

Liz introduced the concept of absorption to me with some of the questions WP4BL had to address in the summer of 2020. First, she set the stage: "we have this like sea of people, and how do we absorb them all? How do we keep them?" She then described some of the specific psychosocial and logistical considerations that absorption entails: "How do we get every single person to be able to have some connection to this work and care about it, regardless of accessibility needs, childcare, or time and capacity? How do we find a way to plug every single person in?"

Taryn understood absorption within SURJ's "concerted effort to shift the organization from a reactive ally place to a more proactive power-building base-building campaign-running organization, where we're actually taking responsibility for going out and organizing our own." There is something necessarily reactive in the work of absorption insofar as it requires receiving people after moments of mobilization that no organization can fully orchestrate. Planning for absorption, however, means understanding which events are likely to inspire mass grievance and clarifying procedures for when they occur. Taryn posed the questions that have shaped the organization's more intentional posture in this regard: "How are we anticipating those moments and building the structures in advance to catch people and move them into action?" Some of the more predictable of these might include dates on the electoral calendar.

In many ways, the work of absorption is quite similar to that of proactive base building, though distinct in terms of pacing and scale. For the organizers I spoke to, it generally includes three interconnected tasks: transitioning painful emotions into more sustainable dispositions; asking people to take on practical tasks; and fostering relationships between newer individuals and more deeply involved participants. Liz described the work of moving people from their outrage and panic at the height of mobilization into a more durable orientation. She used the example of 2020 when white people flooded WP4BL with the realization, "'Fuck—I just figured out I'm white! What do I do? How do I deal with this now that I know?'" In response, Liz explained, "our role, as we've seen it, is to not just tell them something in the moment to kind of calm them down." Instead, the approach is, "How do we make people realize that this is lifelong work?" coupled with the acknowledgment that what that means "looks different for everyone." This means identifying practical steps that align with each participant's skills, interests, and capacities while bringing them into relationships with members of a group.

One way such an effort can be scaled is through group-level orientations for new members, in which participants are introduced to the organization, its approach, and a campaign they can join. The three urban groups in this study regularly hosted such orientations. They also prioritized more individualized relationship building, often accomplished through the common organizing technique of a one-on-one meeting. In the work of absorption, one-on-ones usually mean that a more experienced group member asks to meet with a newcomer in order to identify their motivations while beginning to invite them into community. For example, when we spoke in 2022, Connor of SURJ Buffalo was doing a number of one-on-ones with new participants after sixty-seven people had attended the group's general meeting following "the May 14 massacre," in which a white supremacist shooter targeted a grocery store in a predominantly Black neighborhood.[48] Connor reflected, "we haven't had those numbers since probably 2020." Connor described these one-on-ones as "just building a relationship a little bit," while also seeking to identify new participants' interests and skills. After the meeting, Connor would send his notes to "someone on the leadership team [who] will follow up with them to get more involved."

Following the mass mobilizations of 2020, Josie of Buffalo credited her group's process of absorption with bringing in "a lot of new people, completely new" and ultimately generating "a shift in leadership" in the group. As she explained, "we were able to absorb folks into our chapter, [people] that got activated in June of 2020, who have been part of this work since then." At the same time, she acknowledged moments of mass mobilization as the "ebbs and flows" of movement life. Not dissimilar from the rings of engagement idea, many participants understood that even once mobilized, people may be highly variable in their ultimate levels of commitment to movement work. As Halle of WP4BL put it, not everyone the group invites to participate "has to really grow as an organizer within our organization as opposed to taking *some* action with us." Getting people to tackle even a small step is a success and can sometimes become the seed of something more.

The organizing tradition seeks to be wide and deep, to pull a growing number of white people away from their investments in white supremacy, while honing the analysis, skills, and commitment of more active participants. Through sustained training, deliberation, relationship building, and tactical trial and error, ordinary people can collectively become those with whom power has to reckon. The next chapter turns its focus to how this organizing orientation operates in cross-organizational and cross-racial partnerships, particularly for the urban groups in this study.

5 ACCOUNTABILITY IS AN ACTIVE THING

PAIGE INGRAM OF THE NATIONAL Movement for Black Lives (M4BL) organization recalled her first encounter with a SURJ group, laughing at her own misunderstanding. In 2016, Paige had signed up to participate in a two-day antiracism workshop in her hometown of Minneapolis, not realizing that it was SURJ conducting the training until after it was over. While Paige and her friend had been the only Black participants, it was not an all-white group. Moreover, as Paige explained, predominantly white movement spaces were not particularly unusual in Minnesota. "I learned a lot," she reflected of the training, "So much grace. Such wonderful people." Paige stayed connected with the group in the years to come. "Their mailing list was poppin.' SURJ Minneapolis—they were on top of things."

As Paige's involvement with M4BL deepened over the next few years, she heard more about SURJ both locally and as a national organization and assessed that they were doing "education and unlearning (racism)" with white people while working to "flank Black organizations," essentially offering support to the organizing of Black-led partners. Paige reflected that, "in that context, they were responding to the demands of the moment. But I wouldn't say that they were trying to build power." In the years since, Paige has watched the organization "doing hella work to transform into something different, something that *is* about building power, a commitment to reaching folks that would not normally be reached in movement." In other words, Paige has watched the organization transition into a base-building entity, bringing in new constituents while deepening the skills, analysis, and commitment of those involved.

Paige acknowledged that there are a lot of SURJ chapters and affiliates around the country, and that "just like every other chapter-based organization, your experience of them can vary completely from place to place." She was also clear about why after so many years, at least at the national level, "I roll with SURJ. I do. I'm not gonna lie":

> I just see them continuing to bring a level of commitment and rigor and collaboration that I think is really critical. You kind of have to know people to be all in on something like this. I have seen [SURJ] be consistent, stepping up, leaning in. Those are the folks that you want in your corner, trying to build something against some very difficult odds that we're in right now.

Paige's words anticipate some of the central themes I trace in this chapter, in which I explore how the urban groups in this study have built and maintained long-term partnerships across race and organization.

Paige highlights the importance of demonstrated consistency and commitment. She also suggests that organizational relationships need to be anchored interpersonally, that trust is built through knowing people. Perhaps most importantly, she acknowledges the importance of context. The educational and flanking aspects of SURJ's efforts in 2016 responded to a particular moment—the early years of the Movement for Black Lives when some Black organizers were quite clear that white people needed to "stay in their lane." By 2024, movement conditions were different, and Paige assessed that SURJ's work had evolved. The organization she had come to trust was particularly valuable in its orientation, at least at the national level, to building political power, in part by organizing communities that other movement groups have not.

Research points to the negative impacts experienced by activists of color when working with white people in mixed-race organizations.[1] These include a sense of burnout as well as frustration with white proclivities to water down radical analyses and approaches. We know less about the experiences and assessments of organizers of color that work in separate but partnered formation with predominantly white antiracist groups. Moreover, explorations of alliance building in social movements have given more attention to external dynamics like political opportunities and threats than to the interactional practices that participants use to build and sustain relationships across difference.[2] For example, while trust is widely accepted as a key element for building and sustaining productive alliances, less is understood about how such trust is forged and maintained, particularly when activists collaborate across boundaries of race, ethnicity, and class.[3] The long-term cross-racial and cross-organizational partnerships held by the urban groups in this study therefore offer helpful lessons to scholars and movement participants alike while raising open questions faced by a race-based model of organizing.

This chapter begins with the origin stories of the cross-racial and cross-organizational partnerships held by the urban groups in this study and then discusses two central practices that Black and Latinx organizers emphasized as helping to build and sustain these partnerships. These include local white participants' engagement in high-risk protest and the tactic of solidarity fundraising. In these instances, the role of racial privilege in white people's antiracist efforts continues to emerge, and to do so in complex ways. That is, Black and Latinx partners suggest that when white participants, particularly in urban groups, wield forms of white racial privilege into politically useful action, they help to forge and grow cross-racial and cross-organizational trust.

The second half of the chapter turns to some of the more complex relational dynamics that arise with a race-based organizing model. One is the need for white groups to balance their own initiatives with responsiveness to their partners. Another emerges from the fact that partnerships are maintained interpersonally. If there are great strengths that accompany this reality, such as a firm basis with which to navigate conflict, there may also be challenges when partnerships continue to be held by a small few.

LOUISVILLE

The Louisville SURJ chapter was formed in 2012, a good three years after the launch of the national network. Even so, many partners in Louisville struggled to distinguish between the two entities, likely in large part because Carla Wallace and Pam McMichael, SURJ's co-founders, have deep roots in Louisville and have spent decades in multiracial movement efforts, as outlined in Chapter 2. One of the more powerful examples of this is Carla's long-term relationship with Black organizer Shameka Parrish-Wright, as the two were introduced to each other by mentor Anne Braden. Shameka recalled how Braden "was really intentional about the people she connected.... Anne said, 'I want you two to meet and see how you work together. You both bring so many different skills, and I want you to work together.'" While Shameka and Carla were only able to get together twice before Braden's passing in 2006, Shameka described how she and Carla

> kept those meetings going. And those meetings grew into a friendship, grew into partnership, grew into using each other to break down doors and barriers and understandings and then built a beautiful relationship that I've come to adore in all these years.

Thus, Shameka explained her initial trust in SURJ as quite personal, even as she also saw the project as useful on its own merits:

> I know who Carla is, her actions. So when the whole thing of Showing Up for Racial Justice came about, I felt like it was timely, it was needed, and I wanted to support it in any way possible.

Longtime organizer Attica Scott, a member of the Kentucky House of Representatives at the time of our interview, also highlighted the importance of personal trust with those involved in the Louisville group. Attica met Carla in 2004 while working as an organizer for Jobs with Justice in Louisville and recalls first hearing about the idea of SURJ about five years later, in 2009. Attica explained the conversation she had with Carla "about this thing that she was going to be a part of helping to create [that] grew out of a lot of the racial justice movements. Trying to figure out what do white people need to step up and do." Attica continued, "a little while later, it launched. And a lot of good people that I know, and I'm close to, were a part of it. And I was like, oh, this thing, it's got to be real. It's got to be a good thing."

Alicia Hurle, the executive director of the Commonwealth Alliance for Voter Engagement in Kentucky at the time of our interview, described her early trust in the Louisville group because of how the effort was both explained and initially implemented. Alicia recalled having a conversation in which "Carla [was] . . . checking in, explaining an ask from folks like Alicia Garza [for] somebody to organize white people, so they can stop coming to [Black organizers] and asking us what they should do." The group had emphasized that their efforts would proceed, as Alicia put it, "in conversation and collaboration with Black and Brown organizers" at multiple organizations, rather than just seeking the input of one person or one organization. While such an approach is strategically important for operating in a diverse social movement ecosystem, Alicia highlighted its personal importance to her as a Black queer organizer who had "been tokenized a lot in this work, especially working for predominantly white organizations."

Alicia emphasized that LSURJ was action-oriented from the start, recalling that one of the group's first projects was joining with Black women organizers who were trying to halt the construction of a methane plant in their neighborhood in Louisville. Alicia recalled how the group was poised to respond to feedback about how they could best support the effort. Alicia, along with the women leading the campaign, had suggested that the white activists "be more out and open and like trying to be more in the public eye" as a tactic for moving white audiences in the city who, despite the obviously racist implications, were liable to be more receptive to other white people opposing the methane plant. The group did heed this advice, reaching out more proactively to mainstream media outlets.[4] Alicia recalls, "they definitely took a lot of [our] ideas and thoughts to heart. And I actually saw that show up in [LSURJ] strategy." The methane plant's construction was ultimately halted, with the community going on to pass local ordinances to prevent toxic facilities from being located close to residential areas.[5] Alicia reflected, "That was a great victory for those Black women organizers. And I think LSURJ and we [Kentuckians for the Commonwealth, Alicia's then organization] were a small part of that." This campaign effort thus stood as one of LSURJ's first opportunities for cross-racial and cross-organizational collaboration. The group demonstrated its commitment to action and openness to feedback.

Attica also highlighted practical actions as cementing her confidence in the group, recalling two of LSURJ's early efforts, in both 2016 and 2017, to join with Black and Latinx organizers in Louisville to oppose two pieces of legislation. The first effort was to contest the so-called Blue Lives Matter bill, which named police officers as a protected class eligible for hate crime protections.[6] The second effort in 2017 opposed the "gang bill," which enhanced penalties for those believed to be involved in gang activity. Along with a number of organizations, including the Louisville Urban League and ACLU-KY, LSURJ understood both pieces of legislation as a frontal assault on the Black Lives Matter movement and communities of color.[7] While both bills were ultimately signed into Kentucky state law, Attica believed the group's effort was important for demonstrating that "a lot of white people didn't support either of those bills and didn't think they were necessary." This included a small number of police officers who Attica suggested also opposed the legislation. Given the time and context, Attica described these efforts as "huge," despite the campaign losses. She added, "they were not only doing the work and canvassing and talking to folks but also making it visible."

Karina Barillas, who had been a leader in immigrant justice work in Louisville for decades and was the director of La Casita Center when we spoke, also recalled trusting the group because of who was involved as well as their approach. Karina admitted to not knowing "LSURJ as a name until at least 2016 but recalled a group of individuals whom she had worked with for years, coming to her with generosity and humility. She explained:

> It's so very interesting, because if I will look into my memory, it isn't really until recent years that I learned about the name [LSURJ]. But

in my memory is these white allies, always willing to give us a hand, to use their white privilege to support us.

It is interesting here that a partner names white participants as using their white privilege in tactics of support. While SURJ activists might not understand themselves as inviting white people into racial justice work through the semantics of white privilege, partners still named the fact of the tactical use of white privilege as important.

In 2017, as Donald's Trump's promises to terrorize immigrant communities began to take shape, Karina recalled different members of LSURJ "coming to visit me and just say, 'What do you need from us? Do you need money? Do you need accompaniment? We're here, think about it.'" Karina juxtaposed this approach to experiences with "regular white people," who have come to the immigrant and Latinx communities in Louisville with unsolicited and often demeaning advice. She explained, "for someone that is not white, it takes double or triple or five times the work to be believed [or heard]." She imitated her sense of being approached by white people who purport to want to help but seem to say, "'You have an accent. Do you have an accent in your brain? Are you smart? I don't understand . . . you don't make sense.'"

Those who formed SURJ and ultimately LSURJ were broadly respected by many Black and Latinx organizers in Louisville with whom they already held long-term relationships. Thus building cross-organizational and cross-racial trust was not a big lift. Alicia laughed as she explained the humility of these white organizers:

> They're so humble. They don't brag on themselves a lot. I don't think I realized the scale of SURJ until the last few years. I kind of just knew what was going on locally. . . . So it's just like, "Oh shit. Y'all started a massive national organization and have like all these organizers and chapters."

Even with such esteem among a number of Black and Latinx organizers, white participants consistently back up their explanations with practical action. They have shown a willingness to work in white communities on both winning and losing campaigns as well as to be responsive to partner feedback. I now turn to the Los Angeles context, where the effort to forge cross-racial and cross-organizational partnerships took a bit more tending, requiring as one organizer put it, that white activists move "at the speed of trust."

LOS ANGELES

The group that would become White People for Black Lives (WP4BL) held its first meeting in Dahlia Ferlito's living room in late 2014 following a national SURJ phone call convened in the aftermath of the Ferguson uprisings. Similar to Louisville, the early organizers of WP4BL held preexisting relationships with Black and Latinx organizers in Los Angeles that had been forged through movement work. Dahlia, who is nonbinary, explains themselves as being "dialed in" to those foundational to BLM LA's early organizing efforts. Jason, who helped to start the AWARE-LA network and later WP4BL, was also close friends with at least one founder of BLM LA, having shared in multiracial organizing work with her for over a decade.

Distinct from the Louisville story, WP4BL took a lot of direct instruction from BLM LA during its early formation, in part because of the particularly acute political moment. Dahlia recalled:

> That first year was like a lot of rapid response because things were on fire and felt that way. So everything that we did, was like "okay, there's blockades. There's jail support. Take these supplies to this. Make these phone calls for that." It was lots of asks and everything.

WP4BL's first year was centrally oriented towards building trust through meaningful action. Dahlia explained that these early months "focused on fostering the relationships [with BLM LA] to figure out what are the ways that we can show up that would be in support." Many of these efforts were about creating organizational structure and managing logistics, "filtering those calls to action within the networks that we started, [creating] the mechanisms for all of us to be in communication, and to be able to show up and build trust and do actions and everything."

Dahlia named and then quoted adrienne maree brown, a Black feminist organizer, theorist, and SURJ supporter, to describe how WP4BL approached building its partnership with BLM LA: "we moved at the speed of trust."[8] Elaborating on how this worked in practice, Dahlia explained:

> Early on, it was like, "here's the little lane for white people that we've carved out for you. Do that." They would tell us very precisely what they wanted us to do at an action. And then slowly, it got bigger and bigger and bigger. [Then] "you could just be in the room, while we're planning this." [Then] "plan alongside us. Do you agree with this tactic? Let's think collectively about the strategy" and things like that. We moved along, but those [steps] are based on trust.

The importance of practical action to building cross-racial and cross-organizational trust was reiterated by Michael, who organizes with BLM LA and has been in movement spaces with WP4BL since 2015. In our interview in 2022, Michael admitted having initial suspicion about the race-based organizing model SURJ espouses. He explained, "I'm gonna be very honest. I was like really weirded out about White People for Black Lives when I first encountered it." Even as the model was explained to him, Michael recalled:

> It took me a while to really understand [that] Black folks need their own space, and white folks need their own space. And not because white people and Black people shouldn't interact or be together, but that there's some issues that Black people need to handle within their own communities that are not something that white people need to necessarily be a part of, or understand or have a voice or a say in, right?

Akin to the reflections of those in Louisville, Michael was ultimately convinced by seeing how WP4BL operated in practice, doing what Michael termed the "unglamorous work . . . that is about helping facilitate Black spaces, helping to create Black spaces, helping to keep Black spaces Black."

During our interview, Michael was participating in a BLM LA occupation of City Council Member Kevin de León's house, in which protesters were calling for de León's resignation after his support of a fellow council member's anti-Black remarks were leaked to the public.[9] Michael used that protest as an example of what unglamorous work looks like:

> White People for Black Lives right now they're [helping] buy supplies and food and other things [for] this encampment. So yes, we're the ones who are organizing. We're the face. We're the people on the microphone, on the bullhorn, but White People for Black Lives are the ones that are doing the work [to] make sure that things are organized for us, stepping up to supply those needs and help us so that we can stay focused on the fight that we have.

Another common form of unglamorous work is the tactic of traffic blockades. In these instances, white activists use their bodies to help create the physical space for Black-led protest, often in ways that interrupt city traffic or prevent undue police repression. Reflecting on WP4BL's early years, Liz explained how BLM would regularly ask the white activists "'to be a physical barrier between us [Black protesters] and the police . . . and so White People for Black Lives folks showed up and they stood between BLM LA and the police." Liz added, "that's still something that we do pretty regularly: [stand] in front of traffic and [block] cars to make sure that we [can] shut down an intersection." Liz continued to list a range of ways that WP4BL supports BLM LA: "we provide financially. We provide labor. We sort of provide whatever support is asked for that we're able to do, and we're able to do a lot because we're a big chapter with a lot of capacity." Of course, as the partnership has evolved, WP4BL now does much more than these supporting tasks, executing its own initiatives and campaign efforts.

WP4BL has also developed so as to hold accountability relationships with other organizations, even as BLM LA continued to be the group's primary partner throughout data collection. For example, WP4BL had joined the JusticeLA Coalition for prison and police abolition. This had become one venue by which WP4BL's communications with its accountability partners were formalized and routinized through "weekly meetings" and regular "text threads." Liz explained in 2021 that over its first seven years, WP4BL had "taken the time to develop those relationships, showing up consistently." Liz suggested that building cross-racial and cross-organizational trust was a fairly straightforward undertaking, if not necessarily an easy one: "You have to go to things and become familiar over time and be dependable and reliable. And we've done that. And now that we have those relationships developed, it's much easier to maintain."

BUFFALO

Like the groups in Louisville and LA, SURJ Buffalo was begun by white activists with a depth of multiracial movement involvement. What makes the Buffalo case distinct is that white organizers founded their chapter in tandem with the Black and Latinx organizers who formed SURJ Buffalo's sole accountability partner at the time of data collection: Black Love Resists in the Rust (BLRR), originally Just Resisting, a Black and Brown member-led, abolitionist organization.[10]

Phylicia Brown, BLRR's executive director at the time of our interview, explained this genesis:

> It was [the two founders of Just Resisting] and Erin Heaney, who is now the director of SURJ national. [They] got together and wanted to develop . . . a cadre of folks who were thinking and talking about organizing. And so the decision was made for [them] to found Just Resisting, which would be a space for Black and Brown folks. And then Erin and some other folks worked on establishing SURJ Buffalo.

Akin to Los Angeles, those in Buffalo recalled that this partnership was forged amidst great urgency during the early months of 2015. Phylicia explained, "we were doing a lot of protests in the beginning . . . there were a lot of direct actions." Linnea recalled how she got involved about a year into SURJ Buffalo's work. It was the winter of 2016, and Linnea received a phone call from Erin Heaney, a friend from previous movement efforts. Erin asked Linnea if she could make it to a gathering, "and that Saturday, I walked into the church basement at 8 am. It was full of people and an intro question was, "who's ready to get arrested?'" SURJ

Buffalo had organized a day-long intensive training on direct action in preparation for then–first-time presidential candidate Donald Trump's plans to convene a rally in Buffalo.

Trump's campaign visit was finally solidified for that April. Linnea explained that the plan "was white people go inside; that was the ask from our partners, "You all go inside.'" Meanwhile, Just Resisting

> had planned a totally different kind of action outside of the arena, where they were going to be having like a celebration . . . the vision was like Black joy prevailing in the face of white supremacy. They had music. And "white people, go inside. Go get your cousins, maybe get [in their] face."

When SURJ Buffalo members "formed a line and got on the floor and were yelling [with] locked arms," they were removed by security, and two participants were arrested.

Many of the tactics that SURJ Buffalo has deployed in support of their partner organization are similar to those described in Los Angeles. Akin to traffic blockades, Phylicia noted the importance of "SURJ using their bodies as a barrier" in order to support Black and people of color–led protest in Buffalo. Phylicia also described SURJ Buffalo's support during the summer of 2020 when BLRR occupied downtown Buffalo's Niagara Square. Similar to the unglamorous work described by Michael of BLM LA, Phylicia explained the white activists providing a "twenty-four-hour security detail that they planned and organized." They served as liaisons with the police and ran interference with "a lot of white agitators who would be in the square at night."

In reflecting on important features of the relationship between the two groups, Josie, of SURJ Buffalo, and Phylicia, of BLRR, both highlighted the importance of reliable, responsive, and consistent action, akin to their counterparts in Louisville and Los Angeles. Josie framed this by explaining that "accountability is an active thing, like an active relationship that is very dynamic and also ever growing." In practice, Josie highlighted that this means "responding to [BLRR's] calls when they really need white comrades to show up." Phylicia agreed that SURJ

Buffalo has built and maintained BLRR's trust through this responsiveness, explaining that "nine times out of ten, if we [at BLRR] call on [SURJ Buffalo] to do something, they will say, 'yes,' they will come."

Both Phylicia and Josie also highlighted the dynamism of accountable relationships. Phylicia explained how the partnership between the two groups has evolved to respond to shifting leadership and campaign priorities, requiring communication between the two groups to take different forms in different moments. For instance, at certain times the collaboration between the groups has included "monthly meetings between SURJ leadership and BLRR leadership." At the time of data collection, however, most communication was being done less formally, via "a phone call or a text message," even as a member of SURJ Buffalo sat on the board of BLRR and served as the central liaison between Phylicia, as executive director, and the SURJ Buffalo membership.

Especially as the political and organizing context shifts, Josie emphasized the importance of open communication and continuous relational work between the two groups: "checking in regularly, being in consistent communication with one another, and also working towards building relationship between leadership from our chapter and leadership from their organization." Years into this partnership, BLRR relied on their white partners in SURJ Buffalo to develop their own strategy and campaigns and to take leadership in the work of organizing predominantly white communities towards abolition and economic justice. Josie laughed that "[accountability] doesn't mean we like metaphorically sit by the phone and wait for our accountability partner to tell us what to do." While SURJ Buffalo continues to consult with BLRR about where they can "be filling in or supporting in the most robust, rigorous, and principled way," SURJ also developed its own plans to take to BLRR, with the ethos of, "'Hey, this is what we've got cookin.' What do you think? Does this make sense to you?'"

When exploring how productive and sustainable political partnerships were forged in the three urban groups in this study, it is clear that these groups were built on a bedrock of movement experience. Those who first formed these particular organizations held relationships with Black and Latinx organizers because of years and sometimes decades of shared social change work. According to the literature, this is a somewhat predictable finding; successful coalitions often emerge where there are preexisting interpersonal relationships and deep trust.[11] This also makes it a bit difficult to offer suggestions to white antiracist organizations that might wish to form outside of these already existing relationships. Even so, these cases also demonstrate the ongoing, interactional work necessary to forge and strengthen cross-organizational and cross-racial alliance. White activists need to demonstrate their ability to put words into action through tactics that are reliable, consistent, and responsive to their partners. There is also an important undercurrent involving tenor and approach that can be applied more broadly. The white activists in these groups were willing to take initiative but to do so in a way that demonstrates humility and a capacity to respond to feedback, a point I develop later in this chapter. I now consider the forms of white antiracist action that help to forge and strengthen cross-organizational and cross-racial ties.

HIGH-RISK ACTIVISM

If building productive relationships across race and organization depends upon white people prioritizing action, this section focuses on forms of high-risk direct action, in which protesters seek to confront those in power through extra-institutional channels.[12] This often includes activists putting themselves into contact with state force and the potential of arrest. Such activities hardly capture the entirety of SURJ's activities, and generally they seek to respond to urgent conditions of state violence and injustice. Nevertheless, they were undertaken at different points across the study's cases and were identified by many Black and Latinx partners as a key means by which SURJ participants instantiate solidarity and earn trust.

The history of all political struggle is punctuated by examples of people willing to put themselves on the line, often at great personal risk. In the U.S. context, this tradition has included some white individuals and their groups incurring hardship for the cause of racial justice, such as in the examples of abolitionist John Brown, the Weather Underground, and white participants in the Student Nonviolent Coordinating Committee.[13] Few participants in this study were engaged in practices likely to lead to a lifetime of imprisonment or execution by the state and vigilantes. Nevertheless, high-risk activism has long been one important way that activists deploy unearned privileges in ways that challenge systems of dominance.[14]

The fact that high-risk activism has been an important part of the work of some SURJ chapters also introduces an important layer to the discussion of white privilege from Chapter 3. SURJ organizers suggest that the framework of white privilege is ill-suited to recruiting a broader base of white participants into sustained and politically impactful action. Nevertheless, many SURJ participants described engaging in tactics that wield white racial privilege against structures of injustice. Moreover, Black and Latinx partners often described valuing the efforts of SURJ participants precisely *when* they directed their white racial privilege towards impactful action.

A first example of this is when white participants helped facilitate humanitarian response in the face of state violence. Karina explained the Alerta Roja network organized by grassroots groups in Louisville to confront the first Trump administration's escalation of immigration enforcement operations. Karina explained how the multiracial and cross-organizational network operated in practice:

> People would call us to say, "la migra is at this and this place." And then the Alerta Roja, "the red alert," comprised by our white siblings will get a group of people and go to the place where la migra was present . . . just go there, put their bodies [there], observing, videotaping, and watching.

Karina believed that having white people present to document the actions of immigration agents was a crucial part of the response: "[ICE] realizes, 'oh, I'm being observed by all these white people, oh, wow, this is not in the dark anymore.'" Karina assessed that having white collaborators in LSURJ, people willing to exercise their racial privileges and protections, was integral to the network's success. She continued:

"it was through Carla (Wallace) and other white siblings that we could put together a network." As a Latina woman, Karina explained that she could not interact with immigration enforcement in the same way as the white participants: "you know, even if I am a U.S. citizen, I cannot put myself [in front of ICE] because it doesn't work that way, right? Like [I] put my life in danger." The presence of those with white racial privilege serves to potentially mitigate against the worst of immigration enforcement's outsized and unscrupulous measures.

Alerta Roja required the participation of various groups in the city, exemplifying the benefits of cross-racial and cross-organizational alliances. After immigration enforcement had completed their operation, Karina emphasized the need to handle "the aftermath." This included a range of tasks: "[making] sure that the family [has] information so we can [help with] the bond, or they needed food, or they needed mental health [services], or they just needed to cry with someone, then we come into the picture." Those at the forefront of these efforts were, appropriately, organizers from the Latinx community.

In addition to serving the urgent, practical needs of humanitarian response, the Louisville group had also deployed white racial privilege in protest actions. Attica Scott discussed what she saw as an important contingent of white activists in Louisville's 2020 protests following the murders of Breonna Taylor and George Floyd. As one example, she named the fact of "older white people, you know, grannies who literally took lawn chairs and sat on the front lawn of the Attorney General Daniel Cameron [and] were stitching blankets."

Cameron became a target of Black-led protest when he refused to bring charges against the two officers who shot and killed Taylor.[15] Attica explained the power of these older white women protesters:

> They were willing to put their bodies out there. And while they were sitting there, like they knew that their older white bodies had privileges that ours didn't. And so they were granted grace to be out there for a much longer time than the Black people on his front yard.

When these white grannies were "gently taken into custody and treated very differently," Attica believed that many audiences were forced to witness the racial differential in policing practices. This had particular importance, she added, for those "white people who didn't want to acknowledge that there was a difference in how we [Black people] were treated." White grannies knitting in civil disobedience thus served as an important form of public education, particularly for white audiences. It proffered immediate evidence of the racial disparities in how protesters are handled by police, challenging the racist biases by which white observers perceive such policing.[16]

Attica also highlighted how this action served as a powerful model to others aspiring towards antiracist practices:

> It showed what it looks like when you do actually show up for racial justice and don't just talk about it. You're about it and you're willing to put [yourself] on the line, just like the Black folks have been doing.

Taking a step back to assess the ramifications of such tactics on building cross-racial and cross-organizational trust, Attica continued:

> white members of LSURJ are willing to put their bodies on the line for racial justice. . . . [W]hen white people get arrested, they're gonna be treated differently, like they just are. And even the arrest process is going to be different. And so I feel like here, white people understand that, and are willing to put their bodies on the line where they're needed to be put on the line. And so that's been important to me.

When white people use the fact of their embodied privileges and protections to stand up to state violence, they can play an educative role, revealing to themselves and their audiences the racial disproportionality of state violence. They also demonstrate a level of commitment that is important to their Black partners.

A number of organizers in Louisville also cited LSURJ's participation in the 2018 nationwide Occupy ICE campaign as formative for strengthening cross-racial and cross-organizational partnership. In response to the first Trump administration's family separation policy, Occupy ICE staged protests at ICE administrative offices, transport centers, and immigrant detention facilities around the country. Louisville's involvement began in early July, when activists set up tents in front of the Heyburn Building where the city's ICE offices and immigration court are housed. Led by what Karina termed "Latinx millennials," predominantly those involved with Mijente Louisville, in collaboration with Louisville's BLM and LSURJ activists, the encampment was swiftly dismantled by federal agents. Yet the protesters remained for over two weeks until the Louisville mayor and local police department forced their removal.[17]

On July 26, protesters continued their efforts by staging a direct action in the Heyburn Building's lobby for which they knew they would likely face arrest. Linking arms through plastic piping, they encircled the elevators, making it difficult for ICE and immigration court employees to reach their offices on the eleventh floor. One participant in the action, LSURJ member Sonja, explained, "so we managed to shut down the Heyburn Building for pretty much the whole day." All of the protesters were arrested and spent the night in jail. Sonja continued:

> Louisville had never experienced this kind of thing before . . . that police presence was enormous. [But] it brought attention to the situation. It was on every news channel, all the stations. It really was effective in bringing up the issue of the families being torn apart by ICE, all of what was happening at that time.

Reflecting on the Heyburn protest, and the decision by some activists to take the charges to trial, Alicia recalled:

> That was another huge moment [of] LSURJ really being at the forefront of white people risking arrest very strategically. . . . Folks did get arrested, did have to go to court, all those things.

Attica concurred, noting that throughout the Occupy ICE protests:

> LSURJ members were present regularly, so that if law enforcement were showing up and started harassing people, [law enforcement] would have to know that there are white people right there, ready to be arrested, which would probably get even more attention. Because some of these white folks are wealthy and well-connected, right?

Despite the fact that some LSURJ members, though certainly not all, might also have financial and social capital connected to their racial privilege, this does not mean that they are immune from state repression. In fact, Black and Latinx leaders emphasized their understanding that white protesters are not guaranteed safety during high-risk tactics. In the case of Alerta Roja, and given the emboldened immigration enforcement under Trump, Karina assessed that LSURJ members "were willing to put their lives, their presence on the line for this." Attica also highlighted the legal, financial, and personal risks faced by all participants in the Occupy ICE actions, including those raced as white. She remarked, "This is ICE, this is a federal entity . . . these are federal grounds that people were occupying. And that had a huge risk that went with it." While the risk of state force is racially stratified, Karina and Attica suggest that white people are still putting a good deal on the line. This demonstration of commitment helps solidify respect and trust.

It is important to note that Black partners do not always want white participants risking arrest. As Dahlia described of the "early days" in Los Angeles, white people "were not meant to get arrested because it would detract from the attention that Black folks were really trying to draw in and lead." This did not mean that WP4BL avoided ambitious tactics to raise public consciousness. Rather, in 2014 they began "banner drop Wednesdays," which BLM agreed was an appropriate form of white-led direct action for the moment. WP4BL met every Wednesday, and at the height of morning rush hour, dropped large signs from the overpass bridges that straddle downtown LA's major freeways. The banners named Black people killed by the police and posed provocative questions, such as "White people, what will we do to end our legacy of violence?" Dahlia recalled that the aim was

> to raise as much awareness as possible about the BLM movement and the atrocities of police murder. . . . [I]t was like the first time [many white] people were actually being able to see . . . the consistency of the brutality . . . that this is part and parcel of the American system: police are not what keep us safe, despite how we have been socialized to believe.

Through their regular banner drops, the group sought to educate large audiences and enact practices of solidarity while adhering to their partners' wishes. Dahlia added that as the partnership evolved and the political context shifted, BLM LA did ask WP4BL to "move to arrestable actions."

Not every movement moment and context calls for white people to undertake high-risk action. Nevertheless, when SURJ participants put their bodies on the line, they facilitate a number of aims that their Black and Latinx partners find important. In the case of traffic blockades and protest security, white people can be a frontline defense with law enforcement and vigilantes. White bodies can also facilitate humanitarian response networks, such as Alerta Roja's response to immigration raids. Moreover, when white people use the fact of their embodied privileges and protections to stand up to state violence, they deepen both their own and their audience's comprehension of the racially disproportionate use of state force. Black and Latinx partners also understand that no protester is guaranteed protection in the face of the state, regardless of white racial privilege. In their willingness to take on these risks as part of their antiracist practice, white activists earn deeper levels of trust and respect from partners. Thus, even if, as articulated in Chapter 3, "white privilege is not an organizing strategy," it does play a role in the broader tactical repertoire of white antiracist organizing. I now turn to a different form of practical action that SURJ pursues as part of its commitment to cross-racial and cross-organizational partnership: collaborative fundraising.

FUNDRAISING

Another way that white participants take practical action in support of Black and Latinx-led organizations is through fundraising for partners. In urban groups, where participants' whiteness is often more likely to be tied to access to wealth than in SURJ's rural groups, this is also a way that white participants can wield privilege in an economically redistributive fashion. For the Los Angeles group, fundraising for accountability partners was central to the group's origins. Dahlia told about the first big event that white activists in Los Angeles planned of their own volition: a fundraiser for BLM LA hosted in February of 2015. This was early in the partnership, before the group that would become White People for Black Lives (WP4BL) even had a proper name. Dahlia recalled the group seeking approval from Black Lives Matter (BLM) LA, who responded with, "'look, if you want to raise money for us, go for it.'" The event, a dance party, ultimately raised $3,000 for BLM LA, which was the greatest sum that had yet been donated to the group. Dahlia continued, "and then we continued fundraising events to be one of the central features of our work."

Over years, WP4BL massively scaled up its capacity to raise monies, with one of the more creative efforts launched in 2021. Termed "Study and Action," WP4BL hosted two seven-week programs in which predominantly white participants pursued a curriculum that covered topics ranging from racial capitalism to queer liberation. They engaged in dialogue, introspection, and even arts practices, such as making collages to depict abolitionist visions. Most centrally, they learned about the importance of relational fundraising as a way to resource grassroots organizations and practiced these skills. As Bethany of WP4BL, who helped to develop the program, explained:

> We wanted to experiment in ways that we could ask our friends, ask our loved ones, just different ways that we can fundraise. So many participants have come up with so many different, creative ways, like having garage sales, where they also talk to the community about WP4BL and about the content that we're learning about.

Over two efforts, the eighty WP4BL members who participated in the program raised $31,000 for their partners.

While many SURJ groups conduct stand-alone efforts to fundraise for partners, efforts to funnel monies into BIPOC-led organizing were also built into more routine practices. This fundraising model (which participants call solidarity, collaborative, or companion fundraising) can be situated within the longer discussion about raising resources and hiring staff that SURJ began in earnest about five years into its formation, as laid out in Chapter 2. As a basic principle, when groups fundraise for their own initiatives, they ensure they are raising monies for partners. SURJ Buffalo, for example, often explained during fundraising asks that they would be doing a 20/80 percent split, with the larger share going to Black Love Resists in the Rust. Across the groups in this study, participants ended meetings and campaign events with an ask for member donations. This generally included situating the importance of grassroots financial support in terms of allowing organizations to be flexible, responsive, and member driven. Some groups would also name how the silence around socioeconomic class in dominant U.S. society can make fundraising an uncomfortable discussion topic. Participants were then offered concrete tools in order to gauge how to make a contribution that is "generous" but does not "create hardship." Such fundraising discussions often included directions on how participants might split their intended donation to include a SURJ group's partner organization. At other times, SURJ members were told that their donations would be routed to partners as well. The solidarity fundraising model is one that was mentioned and appreciated by many of SURJ's partners. Shameka of Louisville, for instance, explained, "I love that LSURJ, if they do raise money, they try to give that money to Black and Brown-led organizations, which is so important."

Solidarity fundraising has been used not only to support existing groups but also to help launch new organizing projects. One example of this is the effort to launch two Kentucky-wide projects in partnership: Black Leadership Action Coalition of Kentucky (BLACK) and Kentucky People's Union (KPU). Alicia of Louisville, an early facilitator of BLACK, explained how she and Beth Howard, SURJ's Appalachian organizer, "went to major donors in Kentucky and did like [the] 'ask' together. Beth told her story, I told mine." This began a process that would ultimately raise over a half-million dollars for BLACK. Alicia believed a central piece of what made raising such monies possible was "leveraging the relationships with people of wealth" that some white SURJ members maintained.

This fundraising effort was tied to a larger vision for multiracial organizing throughout the state. Alicia described her conversations with Beth in which they discussed how SURJ is "training up poor and working-class white folks and organizing with them. [BLACK is] doing that with Black folks and really preparing them for leadership in these spaces." In practical terms, solidarity fundraising allowed both BLACK and KPU to each hire a full-time organizer in spring 2022. These two staff organizers held monthly calls, sharing experiences and offering each other advice and support, "really kind of starting their time at the organizations already in relationship and alignment." The ultimate goal was to seed a multiracial, poor, and working-class organizing presence across the state, allowing for what Alicia termed, "work that can happen together across race and class, that we haven't seen in a really authentic, sustained, and scaled [way] in Kentucky . . . in my lifetime anyway."

NO ONE ROLE

Practical action is critical to helping the urban groups in this study forge cross-racial and cross-organizational trust. At the same time, and as is the case in all political alliances, the partnerships in this study must navigate some complex relational dynamics. For instance, participants widely accepted that those most impacted by the injustices a movement seeks to confront should be in leadership. This idea is often articulated along the lines of "those closest to the problem are closest to the solution."[18] How precisely this principle should work in practice, however, raises important questions for all organizations, and particularly for white activists seeking to align with Black-led struggle. On the one hand, white people in racial justice movements have a history of taking too much power, replicating the features of white supremacist socialization, such as entitlement and authority. As a corrective to this well-recognized pattern, many white-identified movement participants understand themselves as supporters and followers in racial justice work. Too much white deference, however, can reproduce the very dilemmas that white affinity organizing is designed in part to solve. One of the key reasons for organizing in predominantly white formations is to be able to bring a critical mass of white people into antiracist struggle in a manner that does not ask organizers of color to do this political, emotional, and intellectual labor. Predicating white people's antiracist action on clear and specific mandates from BIPOC does little to lessen this burden.[19] For this reason, both SURJ organizers and partners were clear that white activists should ultimately be taking initiative in organizing their own communities while becoming fuller collaborators in multiracial struggle. As Phylicia of BLRR in Buffalo put it, "I think it's up to white folks to do their work, and to be studying and building and doing the transformative organizing work within their spaces."

Black organizers discussed this need in terms ranging from prefigurative and visionary to specific and tactical. For example, Nana Gyamfi in Los Angeles was clear that white people need to move into a place of full collaboration with their Black partners so as to pose questions and sharpen strategy. She began, "just because people are Black people doing good work, doesn't mean that they're on point all the time, or that they're doing the right thing all the time." One way Nana believed that white antiracist organizing can and has gone wrong is when "white people that are trying to support Black people . . . get a little automatron-y. Like, the Black Nana said we should do X, Y, and Z, so we should do it. And it's like, 'no, because Nana could be wrong.'" Nana assessed that this kind of unquestioning stance among any contingent of activists "could be leading you down the road to perdition." Nana continued:

> We need to be in relationships in which you can say, "Huh, that doesn't quite make sense to me. Can you explain that? Can you explain that again?' It may never make sense to you. It may be something about being Black that makes something make sense. But just to follow what Black people are saying, I think is also foolishness.

Nana's analysis is nuanced, suggesting that participants in multiracial movements must contend with a great deal of ambiguity and complexity. On the one hand, she is clear that the strongest political strategies require collaborative questioning and correction. The basis of this, in turn, must be relationships with a high level of trust and honest communication. At the same time, cross-racial relationships and political strategy cannot always be predicated on white comprehension, as being racialized as Black may avail organizers of perspectives and insights that white collaborators cannot quite see.

The onus on white participants here is not straightforward, requiring they be able to assess when it is useful to challenge Black partners and when it is necessary to trust and follow. There is no recipe for navigating such a balance beyond the specifics of particular political relationships and conditions. As a broader principle, however, Nana concluded that a racial justice movement requires full participation from all of its members, white people included, for both strategic and prefigurative reasons, "because the world I'm looking for is not the world in which Black people are the masters now. That's not the goal."

Attica of Louisville adopted a similar perspective, explaining her distaste for the term "role" when discussing white people in multiracial movement. She explained that "it feels like you're putting people in their place." While differentiating activists' roles in a given action might make sense for reasons of clarity and efficiency, Attica believed that the language of "role" failed to adequately capture how people needed to show up in movements over the long term. She continued that the concept of a role is limited because "it's not relational; it's fixed." Instead, Attica suggested that all movement participants need to be ready to take on different positions in response to context and relationship.

In terms of a specific quandary that can arise when white activists become too rigid in their deference to Black organizers, Shameka reported having observed white activists "waiting for a Black-led organization to tell them their next move [and that] Black-led organization [doesn't] have a next move ready or [is] working out some internal issues." This is a dynamic that tends to be more common during the early stages of building cross-racial and cross-organizational trust.

Shameka was sympathetic to the impetus to first seek approval from partners, noting how "so much has been taken from Black organizations and Black-led work. I get it that people want to be cautious." Shameka nevertheless emphasized that the instinct to await instructions and even feedback needs to balanced with the pacing of political opportunities. Her advice to white activists has been to generate a plan and then commit to direct communication alongside action:

> Make sure that you check in, let [organizational partners] know what you're going to do, and then you go do it. Because timing is of essence . . . the things that we're doing are far too important. Always be intentional, but make sure that you are keeping it moving.

Carla likewise assessed that cross-racial and cross-organizational partnerships are most effectively forged as white participants hone and pursue a strategic vision for working in predominantly white communities. She explained that in terms of

> the accountability relationships across lines of race, the more clarity we have had around our strategy and what we're doing, and the more that we have actually moved from saying to actually building something, the clearer the relationships get, because then it's like, "aha, there's a strategic value that SURJ builds. We want that in here."

While such an orientation seems relatively straightforward in theory, balancing white initiative with Black leadership is not always so clear-cut in practice.

Dahlia explained a real dilemma that emerged when WP4BL in Los Angeles decided to develop and pursue their own deep canvassing effort around the abolitionist policy Measure R. WP4BL had taken their proposal to partners for feedback and received broad support. As the group invested the vast majority of its volunteers' time and energy towards the campaign, however, Dahlia explained "some differences emerged because our movement partners were like, 'Yeah, go ahead and do it. But we still have real requests that don't have anything to do with this.'" WP4BL was at capacity organizing weekly canvassing efforts out of multiple locations, while also providing childcare, transportation, and food to make the effort as accessible to its members as possible. Meanwhile, BLM LA was still holding a weekly action calling for the ouster of District Attorney Jackie Lacey after her failure to charge law enforcement officers in a number of cases, amounting to hundreds of police murders in LA County. WP4BL, once able to send thirty supporters a week to the BLM action, was now lucky to summon five.

Certainly, this generated complex negotiations with accountability partners. It also surfaced difficult conversations among WP4BL's own membership, some of whom felt "really uncomfortable ever saying no to anything our movement partners say because that's legitimacy. It's our relationship to our movement partners that gives us legitimacy as a white organization." At the same time, many agreed that holding too much of the organization's capacity for responding to partners' requests was also an untenable option. Dahlia explained this dilemma as "waiting for our solidarity partners to tell us what to do [and] then we're just sitting around a lot of the time. We could be doing something else." While this is less of a binary choice than a balancing act, many do assess difficulty in maximizing responsiveness to partners with developing independent initiatives, even if both elements are desired by all parties. With this complexity in mind, I now turn to questions of intergroup communication, considering what it looks like to solicit and integrate feedback.

INCORPORATING FEEDBACK

If successful cross-organizational and cross-racial partnerships require white activists to balance taking their own initiative with being responsive to Black and Latinx leadership, albeit imperfectly, open and honest communication between partners is key. Indeed, much research examines how racial justice efforts are thwarted when white participants are unable to hear and incorporate feedback from activists of color, often due to white defensiveness and other displays of "white fragility."[20] In order to navigate the imperative to take action of their own with the need to remain open to their partners' feedback, it is instructive to consider Carole Barlas and colleague's concept of "critical humility." This stance seeks to give white people an entry point to racial justice work in which they must navigate a paradox—white people need to take action, and at the same time that action is likely to be flawed due to dominant forms of white racial socialization. Critical humility is proposed, then, as a means by which white people might prioritize action and risk taking while "remaining open to the fact that our knowledge [as white people] is partial and evolving."[21]

Without using the language of "critical humility" per se, SURJ organizers indicated their commitment to imperfect action alongside receiving and integrating feedback from partners as central to building and sustaining partnerships. In fact, when asked how a group like SURJ has responded to the range of criticism white antiracists have historically received, organizers indicated that being receptive to feedback, particularly from organizers of color, was the only reasonable antidote.[22] Many with whom I spoke over the course of this study also suggested that the network was actually receiving less generalized criticism than it had five or ten years prior. Liz of WP4BL attributed this in part to the 2020 uprisings, which she believed marked "a real culture shift and a consciousness shift around white people's role in this work and what we should be doing." Grace added that the decline in generalized criticism should be attributed to the relationships and track record that SURJ has established:

> I think [the decline in criticism] has to do with really deep relationships that a lot of people on staff have with other POC organizers. There's trust there. I think SURJ has delivered on a lot of things that we've said we're gonna deliver on, as far as moving resources and showing up in campaigns and bringing white people along.

Grace and Liz also emphasized SURJ's commitment to integrating feedback from people with whom groups are in direct relationship. Liz offered a juxtaposition between integrating the commentary of movement partners and trying to respond to general observers:

> We are in deep relationship with our solidarity partners. We take feedback from them, and we work to support them. And if they give us feedback, we certainly respond to that, [but] not like someone who doesn't know us saying that they sort of in general don't like what white people are doing.

As Grace quipped, "there's always gonna be like internet criticism, you know?" SURJ assesses that it is a strategic mistake, as well as a waste of finite resources, to seek to respond to every public criticism their organization might face.

SURJ organizers' examples of receiving feedback from partners ranged from individualized guidance to questions of campaign strategy. As an instance of the former, Sonja reflected on an early moment during the Alerta Roja effort when the urgency of the situation prompted her to act swiftly without considering the project's commitment to empowering the state's most direct targets. Sonja recounted, "on one of my first runs, I ended up making the call to the lawyer." Sonja was gently corrected by a Latinx leader:

> I can't remember if she said, "hermana," but some kind of a loving thing, "you know, we want to empower people. So you're not the one supposed to make the call. You help *them* make the call. You make sure *they* make the call." And she just made it very clear.

Sonja assessed, "it was wonderful. It helped me do my work better, you know?"

If Sonja appreciated the tenor of this corrective, she clarified that she held no expectation that Black and Latinx partners frame their feedback so gently. White people have often demanded BIPOC express their grievances in a polite and palatable manner, as if this will earn them access to more equitable treatment, which it does not.[23] Sonja reflected on other urgent moments when communication between partners sounded quite different:

> I've definitely been in situations organizing on the streets, in an arrestable action ... someone in Black leadership gets pissed off at the way someone white is doing something ... that is where my job is to try to hear what that person is saying, however they're saying it.

She added with some laughter, "And then if I have some shit I need to deal with, go deal with it with someone else. You know?"

SURJ organizers also reflected on soliciting and integrating feedback on questions of campaign strategy and tactics. One example of this includes the Measure R campaign in Los Angeles. In addition to some of the challenges of balancing the actual campaign with other requests from partners, WP4BL had to navigate with partners a question of whether to conduct research. Kristen, a seasoned organizer who had played a leadership role in the Measure R effort, was a doctoral student studying the efficacy of deep canvassing at the time of the campaign. The promise of conducting research was that it might help assess the relative efficacy of deep canvassing for moving white people to support abolitionist policies. The drawback was that the research would require fielding a placebo condition, a more generic script less likely to win white votes. Kristen explained how the leaders of color on Measure R "were feeling this pressure to just maximize the number of voters" and so did not want WP4BL to divert resources to an experiment. While "it was a very hard conversation," Kristen recalled, "we all decided together . . . that now was not the time to do the research." WP4BL went on to launch the research as a stand-alone project a few years later, assessing the most effective canvassing techniques for shifting white attitudes towards police and prison abolition, but without the pressure of needing to win actual votes.[24]

Another form of campaign feedback that SURJ groups have received in more than one instance, and to which their responses have varied, is the call to do electoral organizing in *favor* of a particular candidate. As discussed in the last chapter, such an orientation cuts against SURJ's early stance of only entering into electoral races in order to end the campaigns of candidates the network opposed. Erin Heaney used the case of Buffalo's 2021 sheriff campaign as an example of how the response to such feedback might work. Because the seemingly less harmful candidate, Kim Beaty, was nevertheless a lifelong law enforcement officer, the initial instinct among SURJ Buffalo participants was not to support Beaty. Erin explained, "we're an abolitionist organization. And so our initial orientation was to be against the other guys as opposed to for the person." Yet Kim Beaty was also a Black woman candidate, and Black Love Resists in the Rust asked SURJ Buffalo to consider running a proactive campaign to support her. Erin reflected that, across the country:

> particularly when it's candidates of color, we've gotten feedback from partners that like, "you need to actually be *for* the person, es-

pecially if you're talking to white people about a Black candidate because of the additional layer of attack that this candidate is going to get around race, and in [the Buffalo] case, gender."

Reflecting on the decision made in Buffalo, in which the group did ultimately elect to run a proactive effort for Beaty, Erin added, "I think the way that [Beaty was] attacked, it was really helpful feedback. I think we as white people are not quite as grounded in the many kinds of attacks you're going to get as a Black woman running."

At the same time, local groups and the national organization have not always adhered to their partners' preferences. Rather, participants undergo an intentional deliberative process, "taking it to whatever the leadership team is, to work through it and make a decision about how we're gonna pivot or not." This process does not always generate the same result, as Erin explained: "with different groups and at national, when we've gotten the feedback in different ways, sometimes we've taken the advice and sometimes we've said no, and gone back to our partners and explained the why."

In this way, predominantly white groups seek to balance deference to BIPOC partners with autonomous initiative, to be responsive but not obsequious. I now turn to the mechanisms by which such cross-organizational communication takes place, as well as a broader discussion of how partner relationships are held.

HOLDING PARTNERSHIPS

If SURJ's national partnerships are fairly formalized, the urban coalitions in this study are both less structured and less uniform, no doubt largely because they are volunteer driven. Research suggests that clear hierarchies and paid employees facilitate cross-organizational collaboration.[25] These features are not present for the groups I am considering, making them an interesting case study. In practice, many local partnerships rely upon specific interpersonal relationships. While having a small subset of individuals anchor cross-organizational coalitions is not unusual,[26] it does inform a range of dynamics from how feedback takes place to the ways in which members interact across organizations. It also generates diverse, and sometimes conflicting, interpretations of what is effective practice and where potential troubles might lie.

Take for example the actual mechanisms by which partners offer each other feedback. When asked how Attica in Louisville would go about giving feedback to members of the local LSURJ group, she was clear that "it happens organically because of our relationships." Attica gave the example of an incident years earlier, when her friend David, who later would go on to join LSURJ, was helping to organize a local faith gathering. Attica had been invited to speak at the conference, but upon looking at the program, she noted that she was to be the only person of color, as well as one of very few women. Due to having a preexisting relationship with David, she was "able to call [him] and say, 'you know, I love you, but what's happening right here?'" David swiftly went to work addressing the issue, and Attica ultimately decided to participate.

Karina also explained offering feedback to the particular people in LSURJ with whom she had longstanding relationships. She recalled two specific instances in which white men affiliated with LSURJ came up with ideas about how they wanted to work with the Latinx immigrant community in ways that La Casita Center believed would create problems and put vulnerable people at risk. Karina turned to those in LSURJ with whom she had built long-term, trusting relationships and asked them for help. She explained:

> In those two incidents, the only thing that I did was say, "my siblings, this is what happened. I don't want to be in the middle of this. You gave me permission to share what happened, here you go."

On both occasions, Karina found the issue was addressed quickly and without drama, though my data do not reveal what happened on LSURJ's end.

Despite these somewhat similar experiences of offering feedback to trusted individuals and feeling that the issue was resolved, Attica and Karina had different interpretations—both regarding how LSURJ structures opportunities for communication and about what best practices should be. Attica, on the one hand, reported that she was "not aware of mechanisms for [partner] feedback" that LSURJ has implemented as part of its organizational structure. She suggested:

> That could be an opportunity for growth for LSURJ is to create . . . some kind of formal structure for that kind of feedback rather than just assuming that it will happen because we do have relationships.

While certainly a reasonable suggestion, Karina's experience contrasted with Attica's, suggesting that such a structure is, at least at times, in place. When asked how communication between LSURJ and La Casita Center works, Karina explained her organization being invited to engage in formalized feedback sessions, "Sometimes they call it, bless them, 'accountability meetings.'" Karina laughed some at the idea that her group would enter a meeting with LSURJ under the auspices of "we want to hold you accountable." Instead, she suggested, La Casita Center's feedback for LSURJ is "we love you. Thank you. You don't have to do this [accountability meeting], but thank you, right?" Reflecting more broadly on the best way for feedback to be issued and integrated, Karina suggested that formalized measures felt somewhat forced and unnecessary. Instead, she believed that the partnership between the two groups is rooted in "organic, non-traditional friendship, sisterhood, siblinghood, if that's a word. That's how it happens, you know? It's just very organic. It flows. No need for something formal, just flows." In this case, it is quite clear that partners, even those who are in relationship with the same group, have differing perspectives on whether and how to formalize intra-organizational communication.

A thornier question was raised by a few of the white participants in this study regarding the fact that intra-organizational relationships tend to be held interpersonally, and often by those who have the longest history of movement involvement. These participants worried that group members in white affinity spaces were not engaged in much cross-racial interaction, politically or elsewhere. For example, Sonja of Louisville noted, "I just feel like there's a couple people who have the accountability relationships. And the rest of the people don't really even interact with those groups or those individuals." Sonja suggested that when LSURJ does its regular social events, such as picnics, those in attendance are predominantly white. She compared this to her time with the John Brown Anti-Klan Committee (JBAKC), a group that worked in solidarity with Puerto Rican independence and Black liberation groups in the 1980s: "we would do stuff together, their organizations and us, whether it was eating together, whether it's studying together, whether it was being in some meetings where we talked about our work together." The JBAKC was a relatively small and militant organization, with a vision and strategy quite distinct from SURJ's effort to pull as many white people into antiracist organizing as possible.[27] Nevertheless, Sonja worried:

> Because we live in such a segregated society, it's like there are people in LSURJ who don't even have any relationships with people of color. That feels weird to me. I don't know what to do about it. It just feels like a very strange thing.

Joe, who had organized with WP4BL in Los Angeles for around four years, shared a similar assessment. Though they had not been involved with the group since 2020, they perceived that aside from the key leaders who hold decades-long relationships with Black partners, "very few people in White People 4 Black Lives are in [those] relationships where on a daily basis, they're feeling the impact [of racism]." Joe, who personally had a very multiracial social network, was concerned with the political ramifications of this. Joe suggested that when white people do not have close relationships across race, they lose key insights and skills as well as a sense of urgency around their movement work.

Some of my data do complicate these accounts. For instance, just as Joe was not living a racially segregated life, a good number of those whom I interviewed in the urban groups were in long-term, cross-racial romantic partnerships, often raising biracial families. Indeed, a patterned reason that participants found their way to a SURJ group was because of wanting to more lovingly and responsibly show up in their cross-racial close relationships. These participants' clearly do not maintain racially segregated personal lives.

Allen's experience in the Los Angeles group is an interesting reflection on these concerns, demonstrating how different movement moments, and the tactics they require, may facilitate more or less cross-racial interaction. While Allen did not have a racially segregated personal life when he joined WP4BL, he understood his work with the group as offering him a first opportunity in his life to forge "relationships with Black folks and other racialized folks in any type of *political* sense." Allen believed, however, that this was because of his somewhat atypical early engagement with the group. As a stay-at-home dad with a more flexible schedule, he was able to regularly attend Tuesday morning police commission meetings with participants from a number of Black and people of color organizations. Allen reflected that this "was important for my trajectory because I built relationships with folks in that space, finding community with some of the folks from the orgs that we [at WP4BL] organize alongside and in solidarity with." Allen continued: "I wouldn't have necessarily built those relationships in that time frame that I did [by only] going to White People for Black meetings and events."

Allen's involvement in a predominantly white antiracist organization was certainly the conduit to cross-racial interaction. Because of his SURJ group, Allen received notice of and motivation to attend a multiracial tactic, even as it was not itself necessarily a priority WP4BL event. Moreover, Allen assessed that as his group transitioned to "actual organizing versus just showing up places," white participants often had less opportunity to build these political relationships across race. In essence, as white affinity groups become more strategic, and arguably effective, at amassing political power, participants may (perhaps temporarily) spend less time in multiracial spaces. If the end result is always to engage in multiracial movement building, attending fewer coalitional tactics designed by partners can mean white activists are less likely to build personal, cross-racial relationships through their political work.

Scholars identify this as a potential dilemma of the white affinity organizing model, though perhaps in exaggerated terms. Amie Thurber and colleagues, for instance, suggest that, "choosing an independent, White-led movement-building strategy may also reinforce White supremacist comfort and preference for living racially segregated (or shallowly integrated) lives."[28] The groups in this study would contest the idea that they are leading movement-building strategy independently from

BIPOC, and with good reason. Within the life of local groups, however, the question of white comfort in living segregated lives is a potential risk. Perhaps more importantly, and as a strategic matter, the groups in this study seek to equip their participants with the skills and competencies they need to engage in collective action for racial justice. A central competency that white people require in a society segregated by both race and class is how to build meaningful relationships across racialized difference. These are skills that become more difficult to practice within the confines of predominantly white formations.

Carla saw such concerns a bit differently, framing it as a matter of prioritizing interpersonal gratification over building political power to change systems. She began by reflecting on her work several decades ago on school desegregation when "so many progressive Black people said to me, you know, 'we've seen the benefit [be] very one-sided. The white people feel good because their children have gotten to be around our children. But we haven't seen the progress.'" Carla also recalled that after Obama's election, "the Black people in my life, were all like, 'Oh, my God, Carla, all these white people want to be friends with me. I do not have time!'"

Referencing the same social events that Sonja suggested are predominantly white, Carla reported a common occurrence in which a newer white participant would report, "'Carla! It was so wonderful! I had an hour-long talk with'—and then it would be a Black person or Latinx person." Carla did not denigrate this, adding, "and I appreciated that. I was like, 'that's so wonderful. I'm so glad.' I see the longing there. Absolutely, that is real." At the same time, Carla believed it to be both superficial as well as a manifestation of white entitlement for white people to pursue interpersonal relationships across race because they feel good without also struggling against the broader systems dividing people by race in the first place. She continued:

> White people long for something different. And we just have to say, "yeah, and it's because of white supremacy that we don't have it. And so let's work for that." And then, "hey, let's talk about some spaces for people to come together." But there has to be a basis of doing the

work together. Otherwise, I don't feel genuine. I don't feel genuine just making Black friends if I'm not doing the work.

The requirement that one be actively struggling against systems of oppression as a white person in order to earn the right to cross-racial relationships might strike some as a high bar. At the same time, Carla's analysis is bolstered by a range of studies in which white people pursue cross-racial interactions as a kind of commodity item. Particularly among the middle and owning classes, where race-based segregation is generally most pronounced, such interactions are often pursued because they enrich white people and white institutions, while proffering evidence of purported moral goodness.[29] In this way, Carla is not alone in suggesting that seeking out cross-racial relationships for private enjoyment, without also challenging the systems that continue to sort and segregate people by race, does little to combat white supremacy.

Thus, where Carla sees the dilemma centrally as white people longing for the psychic rewards of cross-racial relationship, others worry that racially separate organizing might authorize white activists to choose racially segregated lives. This is an enduring dilemma to which the model of white affiliate organizing does not offer easy answers. Black organizer Alicia Hurle introduced a different perspective, and one that focused more on pragmatic considerations. Alicia agreed that in her work with the Louisville group, she had mostly communicated with the same person. She contextualized this, however, as common to all organizing for reasons of efficiency and effectiveness:

> I do think that [participant in LSURJ] has just been my touch point because we have that relationship . . . it's just like, "okay, who's gonna contact this person, who's gonna contact that person?" It's "well, I'm gonna contact [participant] because I know their gonna pick up the phone."

At the same time, Alicia believed that the Louisville group was quite intentional about "their infrastructure and how they scale engagement and their leadership team and having those types of meetings [with accountability partners]." Liz affirmed that in the case of the Los Angeles group, time, organizational experience, and more opportunities to collaborate meant that it was no longer a tiny cohort anchoring cross-organizational partnerships. She reflected that seven years into the organization's evolution, "there are just more people [in WP4BL] who have more relationships and deeper relationships than there were."

Alicia added to this consideration the fact that those who hold the accountability relationships within groups are often socially positioned to have more free time due to limited work or care-taking obligations. Movement scholars term this "biographical availability . . . defined as the absence of personal constraints that may increase the costs and risks of movement participation, such as full-time employment, marriage, and family responsibilities."[30] In reference to her point person with LSURJ, Alicia continued, "there's a privilege that she has that allows her to be in a lot more spaces, [to] have time and intentional relationships. There's some SURJ folks that work full time and have kids and family, you know?" This observation was reiterated by Liz in Los Angeles, who explained how those who anchor the accountability relationships might have "a day job that allows them to do a lot more organizing" than other people in the group.

In practice, it makes some sense that those who serve as liaisons across organizations would have the greatest biographic availability. Being accessible and responsive to their partners is a central way in which white affinity groups build and maintain cross-racial and cross-organizational trust. Moreover, it is not uncommon for those with a depth of movement experience and reputational esteem to serve as "bridge-builders" between organizations, helping to facilitate the interactive processes that sustain cross-organizational partnerships.[31] In the case of SURJ, which seeks to bring ever more white people into multiracial movement, such bridge-builders might also be a kind of buttress, allowing those newer to the work to learn important skills for confronting their white socialization before they are brought into political relationships with Black and Latinx partners. Indeed Karina's explanation from earlier—in which she needed to give feedback to those whom she trusted in LSURJ when other participants were overstepping—suggests this is precisely how the partnership can operate in practice.

The contrasting argument would be that white activists earn invaluable political skills and knowledge through cross-racial relationships.[32] There is also some tension between bridge-builders being those most biographically available, often due in part to class privilege, with the organization's strategic emphasis on organizing poor and working-class whites. Finally, and hardly unique to this case, there is always a risk to movements that conflate organizational positions with particular persons. Yet I also do not wish to belabor these concerns. It is worth noting that only white participants raised these matters, not Black and Latinx organizers, and a rare few at that.

As a final perspective, then, I turn to Buffalo, where there was great fluidity to race-based organizing in practice. For example, Shontay, a Black woman, understood herself as a member of both SURJ Buffalo and its partner organization, Black Love Resists in the Rust. Shontay chose to do most of her political work with SURJ Buffalo because of its focus on the sheriff's department but explained how she turned to BLRR, "when I have those feelings where I really need to be amongst my people." Importantly, Shontay herself was not the liaison between the two organizations. That position rotated and was held by others in the groups.

Phylicia of BLRR also suggested that the two organizations interface with some frequency for both social and political reasons. Scholarship points to the importance for social change coalitions of having both informal and formal spaces in which differently positioned members can comfortably interact and learn from each other.[33] Phylicia explained how among the BLRR membership "we'll be having a birthday party in April. And so I'm sure a lot of SURJ folks will come to that . . . [and] there's a conversation about the Erie county jails coming up. And so BLRR and SURJ folks will be at that conversation together." Espousing the sensibility that organizational co-mingling tends to be most fruitful when it is responsive to political or social context, Phylicia explained, "when the moment makes sense, I think we come together, but we don't try to force it."

All social relationships are dynamic, evolving, and often messy. This is no different in the case of the cross-racial and cross-organizational partnerships examined in this study. While many of these partnerships are grounded in longstanding interpersonal relationships, ongoing interactional processes also support productive alliance building. Black and Latinx partners clearly value when white activists take action in ways that are responsive, reliable, and consistent. They also identify the fact of white participants' racial privilege, valuing when white activists wield such privilege proactively towards movement aims, such as in the case of high-risk activism. There also remain open questions for the race-based organizing model explored in this chapter: balancing independent initiative with availability to partners; determining if formalized feedback mechanisms are a help or a hindrance; and deciphering if some instantiations of white affinity organizing authorize participants to live racially segregated lives. These are important matters around which the groups in this study continue to grapple, experiment, and evolve.

The next chapter turns more squarely to intragroup dynamics, examining the cultural practices by which the urban groups in this study create an ethos of welcoming, experimentation, and risk taking. In their efforts to bring more white people into multiracial struggle, while deepening participant commitment and growing their political skills, the groups in this study assess a need to move away from some of the tendencies that have historically characterized white people's antiracist efforts.

6 WHAT IF WE GET CALLED OUT?

IN ORDER TO EXPLAIN THE need for a culture shift in white people's antiracist movement work, Sonja DeVries and Carla Wallace each told a story. The stories, which take place thirty years apart, both feature a white person sitting in a chair. The setting for Sonja's story is that of a predominantly white organization with which she organized in the early 1980s, a group that worked in solidarity with Black and Puerto Rican liberation struggles. Sonja reflected on the cultural norms in the organization at that time: "we're talking serious calling out. If folks made a mistake, or said something that was perceived as racist, their white comrades [would] just bash them." Sonja was clear that this punitive culture was "a white people thing . . . I didn't see my Puerto Rican comrades doing that when they were organizing." Asked for an example of what this looked like in practice, Sonja recalled:

> I remember one woman who was—God, she was such a committed, really principled, young activist and had been involved for a long time. I can't remember the mistake she was perceived to have made. But I remember people kind of surrounding her and just berating her as "being bourgeois, having all this racism" . . . it was like a verbal beating up. And I just remember her shrinking. . . . That person turned away from activism.

Carla's story takes place at an early SURJ retreat at the Highlander Center around 2010. Then SURJ leader Scott Winn, who was very tall, "maybe six foot six," according to Carla, "curls his body into the littlest knot he could." This tiny, coiled up position was meant to demonstrate how Scott felt when he started in racial justice work. Carla reported how Scott explained it to the group: "'I was taught that [being antiracist] was to disappear—to be as small and unnoticed as I could be.'" Scott then stretched his body out and explained his realization over time, that "'the work calls us to actually be our full selves.'" Carla laughed at this memory: "it's hilarious because there's no way he cannot be this huge, white—he's queer—but white, cisgender man." To Carla, this act beautifully illustrated "what all of us at some point, or continue to, feel about the anxiety in this work. About 'who are we? Are we going to do it right? Or what if we get called out?'"

These two accounts stand in obvious contrast. In the first, a committed activist made a mistake and was berated to the point where she physically shrank. She ultimately left the movement altogether. In the second, a committed activist used his body to demonstrate what it might look like to be one's whole self in a movement space, imperfections and all. These stories also emerge from two seemingly very different strains of white antiracist practice. Sonja's discussion is of the militant white Left in the 1970s, which engaged in direct action and occasionally staged tactics as extreme as bombing the sites and symbols of U.S. racism and imperialism.[1] Scott's explanation reflects on a kind of antiracist training that focuses on white privilege and awareness-raising and is often criticized for lacking an action focus altogether.[2]

These two stories nevertheless demonstrate an important commonality. White militant activists held sessions in which participants took turns being aggressively and often abusively berated for acting too "bourgeois" or white.[3] The "privilege confessional," a frequent component of antiracist learning spaces since the late 1980s, has likewise demanded that white people confess to the many ways they are complicit in perpetuating white racism.[4] Across very different examples, then, we see the far reach of what participants would today term "call out culture," though in a very particular sense. White activists flagellate themselves and other white people, confusing the performance of moral right with the aims of amassing political power.

It is certainly the case that emotional distress often accompanies whites' recognition of their complicity in a white supremacist system.[5] Indeed, experiences that rupture one's sense of comfort with the status quo can become important catalysts for whites to move into action for racial justice.[6] At the same time, there is a risk, particularly in white people's antiracist efforts, of approaching discomfort, guilt, and shame not merely as understandable features of the work for racial justice but instead as emotions to be cultivated in their own right and as an ultimate ends. SURJ adopts a range of alternative approaches, both for processing such emotions as they may arise, but also for facilitating learning, community building, and intragroup accountability. Building on the language and framework often originally attributed to reproductive justice activist and scholar Loretta J. Ross, SURJ organizers discuss the culture shift they are seeking to create as a move towards "calling people in" as opposed to "calling people out."[7]

SURJ understands this imperative for cultural shift on a few interrelated fronts. First, a culture that shames and blames individual white people is based on a faulty analysis. Bringing white people into the project of dismantling white supremacy is not primarily about fixing problematic individuals but about building collective power to confront structures of domination. This requires the acknowledgment that everyone has been socialized into a system of white supremacy. The corollary to this is a belief that, while everyone has the potential to confront the ways in which this socialization shows up in their own lives, doing so is an unending process. As Sonja suggested, "we've all been marinated in white supremacy, and we continue to imbibe it because it's everywhere. The work of antiracism is a lifelong commitment, externally and internally. It's something we have to constantly work on." Carla concurred, "I believe we will be on a personal journey until we die. And we cannot wait until we die to start the work."

Shifting movement culture also has strategic import for building a critical mass of white people to engage in antiracist political struggle. Carla reflected:

We cannot do this work and grow this work in the way it needs to be grown unless we have culture shift within white antiracist work. Because the culture that we inherited within white antiracist space was so fear based, so perfectionist based, so shame based, elitist, attacking of each other.

It is also the case that a central logic behind the white affinity model of antiracist organizing, such as that adopted in the urban groups in this study, is that it can offer white activists opportunities to make mistakes and to learn without risking harm to BIPOC.[8] Ideally, such spaces for learning and introspection are simultaneously rigorous, equipping participants with the skills and competencies they need to be effective and principled organizers, while also creating contexts in which people want to stay involved. As Sonja asked rhetorically: "Why would you want to be a part of something where if you make a wrong step people shred you? It's just not a way to build anything sustainable."

Research demonstrates that the movement features that draw activists most enduringly into struggle are often social relationships and cultural practices as much, if not more, than an individual's personal ideology.[9] In other words, building ties with others, and finding a collective context that *feels* right, may actually be more important to an activists' trajectory than their personal ideas about what is good or just. For those raced as white, having supportive interpersonal relationships with others who share an antiracist stance, regardless of race, serves as a critical, and likely necessary, source of personal fortitude.[10] In this sense, the way a movement group operates internally—the relationships it supports, the practices it routinizes—is not merely incidental to the political project at hand. It is essential.

This chapter examines the practices by which the urban groups in this study seek to build welcoming and inclusive organizations, in which a broad range of participants might cultivate relationships, be supported through learning and conflict, and deepen their movement involvement. I focus here on the three urban groups in this study as the sites where my fieldwork and interviews are able to show introspective and community-building practices as they unfold. I also turn to some of the dilemmas of growing and sustaining movement organizations, a difficult task no matter the conditions. I pay special attention to how groups balance the impetus to embrace participants from a variety of social and political backgrounds while simultaneously responding to political conditions and coalition partners. While some of the challenges faced are generalizable to other kinds of grassroots organizing, specific predicaments can arise when organizing in predominantly white groups.

BEING CALLED IN

Dahlia tells the story of first being "called in" while they were part of a multiracial activist group. Raised in Massachusetts, Dahlia ultimately moved to California where they would become the only white member of a queer organizing collective. Due to an errant text intended for someone else, Dahlia learned that the group had been struggling with the way Dahlia's "white privilege" was manifesting in problematic ways, from dominating group conversations to being presumed the leader of the group by those outside of it. Upon learning that those in the collective had not come to them directly, Dahlia was hurt and defensive, and not initially receptive to evidence of how they might be doing harm. As Dahlia put it, "cue Robin DiAngelo's white fragility responses."[11] They were also confused by the term "privileged," having grown up working class:

> I was like "privileged?" because white people equate privilege with class privilege or wealth privilege, and not the benefits that one acquires by having white skin, which is different. But I didn't know that at the time.[12]

In the ensuing weeks and through other social connections, Dahlia was handed a flyer for AWARE-LA's Unmasking Whiteness Institute, which they decided to attend. Dahlia described the four-and-a-half-day "intensive" institute as designed to explain the social construction of whiteness, to give language to what white privilege really means, the history of white supremacy as like a system that affords benefits to white people at the expense of others, what the process was of assimilation and why my roots of Italian ancestry have been whittled down to like eating lasagna on Christmas.

The institute was transformative—"I felt like I was a changed person"—but it also brought up a range of emotions that Dahlia struggled to navigate. They felt overwhelmed by their new awareness, embarrassed and ashamed as they tallied their seemingly endless list of blunders. They were also "afraid of reproducing the same harm" they now understood themselves to have perpetuated to the point that they went "silent . . . turned into a person that didn't speak at all."

This was where the weekly Saturday Dialogue spaces, also hosted by AWARE-LA, provided Dahlia with a continuing place for "self-study." Dahlia explained:

> I found community there, found witnessing there, found love, found connection, and [that] was exactly what I needed after this four-and-a-half-day experience. And still organizing with this collective and still being the only white person and still trying to figure it out.

It was also through regular participation at Saturday Dialogues that Dahlia was able to begin to integrate a key lesson that was first presented to them during the four-day training, one that they now consider formative to the ethos of calling white people into the work of racial justice: "guilt is a place you visit, but it is not the place you live." As Dahlia reflected today of their organizing with whites, "guilt is not a tactic that we rely on. It is not something that keeps people in movement spaces."

Dahlia's story demonstrates many key features of what it means to be called in to the work of racial justice as a white person. In this account, a well-intentioned white person is nevertheless unaware of how their behaviors and public reception are shaped by white privilege. They find a space of intensive introspection and learning, identifying what it means to be white in U.S. society and how this has socialized them to be complicit in harming others. For Dahlia, as is the case for many, such a realization generates a great deal of discomfort and even some temporary paralysis in terms of knowing how best to move forward. Through a loving community of people that share the experience of trying to be committed to antiracist struggle as white people, however, Dahlia ultimately begins to find new anchors for antiracist engagement beyond guilt and shame. They participate in various forms of multiracial action and organizing and ultimately go on to host the first meeting of AWARE-LA's action arm, White People for Black Lives, in their living room five years after first being called into the work.

Among the groups in this study, AWARE-LA was by far the oldest and largest, as well as the only group that had an entire infrastructure designed solely for introspective work, including its weekly dialogue spaces and biannual intensive institute. Nevertheless, elements of Dahlia's account resonate across the groups in this study. Each integrated some level of introspection and reflection as a means for deepening participant commitment, forging a sense of community, and preparing members to show up in as principled a manner as possible in multiracial struggle. Josie explained of the Buffalo group:

> Something that we strive to consistently do is to provide space both for personal reflection and for learning, for interrogating and thinking about the way in which white supremacy permeates our cultural norms, has shaped our viewpoints, who we are, how we experience the world, and also the institutions, what we have access to, the systems that we've been entirely ingrained in throughout life.

One of the most common entry points by which each of the groups in this study invited participants into such reflection was through the introduction and discussion of SURJ's core values. "Calling people in" was often listed as the first of these values. The other values included "take risks, make mistakes, learn and make amends, and keep going"; "growing is good"; "accountability through collective action"; "organize out of mutual interest"; "center class"; and "there is enough for all." This list of values was generally introduced to participants early on in their engagement with a SURJ meeting or training.

During a general membership meeting of SURJ Buffalo, for example, Richard, a white man in his seventies, introduced these values and then homed in on "calling people in" to introduce the day's "skill-builder." Richard recalled how he first joined the group, which had been canvassing in his neighborhood. Someone showed up at Richard's door with a Black Lives Matter lawn sign, explaining to him that SURJ Buffalo was "an outlet for those who cared about this stuff and wanted to stay involved." Richard highlighted what calling in meant for him: "I'm here because people accepted me with my mistakes, or my misconceptions." He continued by explaining how he always felt comfortable asking for clarification when there was something he did not understand. Participants in the meeting were then asked to reflect on how they had been called into the work of racial justice before moving into a training and practice session for calling in others.

The first half hour of Louisville SURJ's monthly meetings likewise focused on reflecting and building community around this list of values. Before doing campaign-specific planning and skill building, participants had the option of beginning the meeting early, with a more introspective session. During the first LSURJ meeting I attended, Kate, a white woman in her thirties, introduced the value of "organize out of mutual interest," with the provocation to a seemingly all-white group, "How does white supremacy, or living in a racist society, hurt you?" Participants brainstormed a list of possibilities together, offering affirmation and learning from one another's experiences.

In another similarly structured meeting in Louisville, Paula, a white woman likely in her sixties or seventies, asked us to consider the rather lengthy value of "take risks, make mistakes, learn and make amends, and keep going." Paula then gave further context for the value: all white people are going to make mistakes in this work. It is impossible not to do so. The notion of "taking risks" was contextualized with the acknowledgment that "people of color take risks everyday just in living their lives, in moving through the world." Before inviting others to share their own reflections on how they might engage with this value, Paula gave an example of making mistakes in her own antiracist practice. She reflected on co-facilitating a series of conversations about racial justice with a Black woman at her church. Over these sessions, Paula recalled how her co-facilitator had to correct statements that, as Paula reflected, had been made from a place of her own ignorance: "I would apologize and wonder, 'why do I see things so differently?'" Paula named these moments in which she had made a mistake, apologized, and learned as profoundly important, if also uncomfortable, learning opportunities. Participants were then invited to share about their own often painful moments of making mistakes and learning lessons.

One of the more important roles of white affinity spaces in multiracial movements is providing white people a space for making the mistakes that all learning requires, and for doing so in a way that does not expose BIPOC to extra labor or potential harm. Certainly this requires that such affinity spaces provide white people opportunities for information gathering, self- and collective correction, and growth. Ensuring that participants have opportunities for sharing in vulnerability and imperfection, however, is also important. Structured opportunities for introspection allow participants to find role models and validation for movement work that can be quite emotionally difficult. This can offer an antidote to the forms of isolation that those raced as white often face when they decide to act for racial justice.[13] I now turn more explicitly to how the groups in this study seek to signal and practice their commitment to collective learning and growth, where people are welcome no matter their background.

"A SPACE TO TRY"

The Los Angeles group's "down speech" in many ways exemplifies the ethos of calling people in. What would become a central opening statement in all White People for Black Lives (WP4BL) meetings traces its origins to right after Donald Trump's first election, when the group happened to have their monthly membership meeting. While a typical showing at these meetings was twenty or thirty participants, over a hundred people were in attendance. The room was uncomfortably crowded.

Those already in the group understood the moment as a potentially pivotal one. No matter how people had found their way there, they were mobilized and ready to take action. Dahlia reflected, "I wanted people to feel welcome, and I wanted them to come back." Dahlia recalls beginning to speak, articulating a set of principles fairly spontaneously. They began, "White People for Black Lives isn't one of those spaces where you have to prove how *down* you are in order to be here. This is a space where we welcome you, where you're at, and we want you to keep coming back because this fight is for the lifetime." This is how the down speech was born.

I did not myself witness the down speech until five years later, when seventy people came together for a special seven-year anniversary gathering of WP4BL. We gathered on Zoom due to pandemic conditions. The first fifteen minutes of the two-hour gathering had been dedicated to a number of practices with which WP4BL regularly opens all of its meetings. At least ten people took turns introducing everything from the video conferencing technology and how to best communicate with each other to the meeting agenda and the groups' "commitment to taking outward, bold, and visible antiracist action." Other practices included a guided meditation of sorts, termed a "grounding exercise." This was followed by a fairly extensive land acknowledgment, which we learned had been compiled through research and conversation with Indigenous partners. The presenters explained why it was being presented, making plain the contradiction inherent to white people seeking to engage in antiracist struggle even as "we are currently on occupied and unceded land of Indigenous peoples that was stolen through violence and colonization." Other discussions included an explanation of why participants introduce themselves with personal pronouns, "to acknowledge and respect the spectrum of gender identities," and a discussion of the group's commitment to accessibility, including protocol for how to secure American Sign Language interpreters for meetings. Participants were also offered a glossary of common terms that might emerge during the meeting, with vocabulary that included terms such as "abolition" and "NIMBY."

This amalgamation of practices could be viewed as signaling the very activist culture that the down speech itself seeks to trouble: participants engaging in a litany of rarefied, socially conscious rituals. At the same time, every step of the process was introduced carefully and intelligibly, offering a precise logic for its inclusion. By the time Dahlia introduced themselves to the group, they were clear about the intentionality behind such an extensive set-up: "we do what we always do because it works, opening up our meetings in a way that's grounding and in a way that welcomes everybody to be here." There was certainly evidence that this approach was working in some important ways. AWARE-LA had existed for over two decades. WP4BL had been around since 2014 and was continuing to grow in size and capacity while earning concrete victories with and for its Black and people of color–led partner organizations.

Dahlia then transitioned to the specific nugget that has been termed the "down speech," here presented in abbreviated form:

> We recognize in White People for Black Lives that there are going to be white people of all stripes that come to our doors, wanting to get organized, wanting to figure things out, wanting to throw down and take bold and visible antiracist action. And we also recognize that often times in organizing spaces, there can be the sentiment that makes you feel like you gotta be a certain way. You have to have the right language. You have to know how to write a thesis on cis-het-heteropat [stumbles over the word "cisheteropatriarchy" and laughs at how hard it is to say]—see I can't even say it!
>
> Or [prove] how long you have been in social justice movements. Has it been ten years? Twenty years? Fifty years? How many arrests have you had? How down are you for the cause? Because you gotta prove it to be in that space. But for us, we feel like that sense of downness really creates a sense of exclusion when we're really trying to organize as many white people as possible to take antiracist action.

While the down speech and portions of how WP4BL opens its meetings are unique to them, each of the groups in this study took steps to make plain that their space is *not* only for deeply experienced activists or those who have perfected their antiracist analysis. Groups would regularly name that all participants show up imperfectly and that everyone can grow through their engagement in SURJ's range of trainings, campaign activities, and spaces for more focused introspection. They took pains to use accessible language, explaining each key concept or step of a group process as if to newcomers, even when many in the room were seasoned organizers. As Josie explained at the beginning of her facilitation in a meeting of SURJ Buffalo, "we don't want to be a small, perfect group of people; we want to be a big, messy group of people wielding power."

Facilitators regularly modeled what imperfection and growth can look like, often reflecting on their own trajectories. During a Buffalo orientation for new members, for example, the facilitator explained the concept of calling in through personal anecdote:

> I have to admit: I have spent many years calling people out. And I always felt very brave doing it. SURJ has taught me to temper that, and really work on calling people in. It's how we want to be with one another as white people. It is recognizing that we all mess up, and we are speaking from this shared experience.

In this moment, exemplary of many others, facilitators introduce a value or concept through their own experiences. This facilitator shared the mistakes she has made and how her views have shifted, the learning she has undergone.

Josie elaborated on the theory behind this approach in her interview with me:

> If we're only going to look for people who are perfect [or who are] already coming in aligned with us, we're gonna have a really small movement. And that's not what we're about. We're about building a collective, building a bigger and more powerful "we." That means really moving through action through the messiness with people.

If dismantling white supremacy requires bringing a critical mass of white people into impactful and sustained antiracist action, this requires fostering an environment in which those raced as white can learn and grow.

In formal materials, the national organization elaborated on the practice of calling in with suggestions that included "recognizing we all mess up and speaking from this shared experience. Being specific and direct. Talking to people in times and places that support conversation and learning." What is clear from this list is that the aim is not to ignore mistakes or troubling behavior. Instead it offers a set of principles by which participants can hold each other accountable to learning and growth.

Halle of Los Angeles was clear that even as "the culture feels so supportive and so empowering" in her group, these features were not about ignoring the way white participants have likely done harm, even if unintentionally, simply by virtue of being socialized as white people. She described the group sensibility:

> It's not, "we're going to support you because we are pretending not to see harm you've contributed to" but instead, "we're gonna support you because we see you clearly. And you're a human who's showing up, who cares about this work." And support looks like accountability, and chances for growth, and love and care.

Halle continued with an example of how this might look. During the "whirlwind" summer of 2020, when the group was convening huge groups online due to the pandemic, Halle was facilitating a webinar with an unprecedented 500 attendees. The person in charge of running the video conferencing was new to the technology, which hit a glitch. The person admitted that they were uncertain about what they were doing. Halle recalls how the other facilitators immediately jumped in, some supporting the person to figure out how to do the task in question. Another announced to the audience, "'You all, look at this person trying something new. They're learning. They're like bravely learning right here in front of us, with all of us.'" While this example may seem fairly banal, and even Halle laughed at the fact that this instance stuck in her mind, this anecdote was clearly about much more than celebrating someone as they learned how to fix a technical error. Halle continued, "that moment was so distinct for me. Like we can only grow power and build this new world if we support people in trying. And trying means all kinds of making mistakes . . . we [have] really created a space to try."

This example also demonstrates these groups' emphasis on learning through doing, a practice that often begins at the relatively low stakes but critical work of facilitating meetings. When many people can help facilitate, the specific labor and responsibilities of each meeting are spread across the collective, making the workload more sustainable. Moreover, as individuals practice the skills and confidence to take leadership in one domain—that of running a meeting, for example—they often find themselves empowered and ready to experiment in other areas as well, such as with specific campaign tasks.

Of course, not every instance of seeking to bring someone new into a leadership role is seamless. In addition to what SURJ groups tend to view as the generative opportunities to let people make public mistakes and support them lovingly in their learning process, there are instances in which someone brought into a facilitation role engages in behavior that is actually at odds with the group's aims. Halle gave an example of this kind of instance and how WP4BL went about addressing it.

Halle had invited someone newer to the group to help facilitate a phone bank. This person explained the attack on the U.S. Capitol on January 6, 2021, as a positive event: "essentially he just said, 'the fascist act that happened at the Capitol was a good thing because it really raised awareness.'" Other members of the group staunchly disagreed with this assessment. They saw the events of January 6 as evidence of the dangers of a descent into authoritarianism, supported by a majority white base. They believed the event needed to be named as a deeply troubling instance, if also one that could be used to frame the importance of organizing white people to resist an extremist right agenda. Halle continued that while the phone-bank participants were neither a large enough nor a new enough group that this facilitator's commentary "needed to be interrupted in the moment," leadership knew it had to address the situation. The group developed a multipronged approach that would productively encourage the participant to remain engaged but to get "more coaching before they were asked into a role like this again."

The strategy included identifying a member of the group "to build more trust in a relationship with this person" and then to encourage the participant into "the political education spaces of White People for Black Lives, and then some of the Saturday Dialogue spaces," both of which are designed for white people to engage in further political learning and personal introspection as they cultivate their commitment to antiracist practice. Halle concluded, "I think the model is really about [how] as we grow trust, and support, that's the place from which change and shift can happen. And it's really fundamental to build relationships." I now turn to a deeper exploration of the role of relationships and community-building for these groups.

FINDING POLITICAL HOME

Hannah attended her first meeting of the Los Angeles group in December 2016. She had heard of SURJ in a few different places and was ultimately looking for a way to channel her grief, shock, and "guilt" after Trump's first election. Upon arriving at her first meeting, Hannah recalled feeling "out of my depth" when hearing people she would later befriend speak about the group's work. This sense of "intimidation," however, was coupled with a conviction of, "'Oh, these are my people, and this is where I need to be.'" Hannah explained that, before this moment, her sense of connection to Los Angeles, where she had lived off and on for a few years, had felt rather thin. She was there because of people she loved, but "finding White People for Black Lives was like, 'I could do this, and I could stay here . . . This is a community that I feel is a home.'" Hannah began attending the monthly general meetings. Even five years after she first found the group, Hannah explained, "I still try to go to every general meeting. I think, for me, it's a really kind of grounding piece, having that consistency of being in space with people."

During the first meetings she attended, Hannah mostly listened and learned. A turning point came a few months in, after a political education session on class identity, where participants had filled out surveys about their own socioeconomic class. When someone remarked that there was not yet a plan for how to record the survey data, Hannah saw an opening to contribute to what she perceived to be a low-stakes, concrete task. At the end of the meeting, she approached a facilitator and volunteered to do the data entry. Hannah was told that someone else had also volunteered and that the two of them should work together. Hannah laughed that the "type-A perfectionist in me, who did so much of the work in so many group projects, was like, 'I don't want to! Okay. Fine.'" Hannah approached the other person and proposed that the two split the work. The other volunteer, a more seasoned leader, responded, "'No, let's not split it up. Let's meet and talk about it and figure it out.'" Hannah begrudgingly accepted. The next week when the two met over coffee, they discussed the surveys for about five minutes and then proceeded to "chat" for three hours. The dreaded group project became the seeds of a profound relationship. Hannah reflected, "we have been like dear, dear, dear friends ever since."

Hannah explained this part of her trajectory as "dipping my toe in." Soon she was regularly volunteering to manage other lists for the group. She also joined a book group on class identity, which launched her into a months-long process of personal revelation around her own class status. Hannah went on to help form the group's class committee, discussed later in this chapter. Less than a year after she attended her first meeting, Hannah was asked to join the group's steering committee. Her response was to think this invitation was both "such an honor and also like a major imposter syndrome moment where I was like, 'you can't possibly need me.'" She ultimately accepted. From there, Hannah began to get "deep into the leadership of the org," and has taken on "varying capacities of leadership since then."

Hannah's story demonstrates a number of themes that emerged for participants in this study regarding the way that their group fosters a sense of belonging and community, while encouraging people to learn by doing. If coupled with some overwhelm, Hannah finds in her group deep interpersonal connection, a space that privileges relationships over accomplishments, and a recurring invitation to hone her leadership skills as she takes on new and greater organizational responsibilities in a supportive community. One of the ways Hannah narrates this experience is that of finding her "political home."

The term "political home" was one that I first heard when interviewing participants for this study, many of whom describe their relationship to their group in this way. Steph of the Buffalo group described a political home as, at one level, being an organization where you "trust the direction it's going in, and I think it's worth my time to invest in the goals and the actions they're doing." Steph added that, as a political home, "SURJ goes a little bit deeper" than the other organizations she had worked with, which included a "rural antifracking group, an urban housing group," and her labor union. Steph explained that "organizing work in other places, it can get really exhausting and emotionally draining." Where she believed "SURJ work—at least in the SURJ Buffalo stuff I've done"—differed was in offering "space to process emotions around the work, which makes it feel more sustainable and personal." Steph added, "it feels like I can be my full self there," experiencing feelings and reflecting on personal experiences in ways that are "not necessarily honored in other organizing spaces." For Steph, these other spaces are often quite focused on accomplishing their practical obligations but do little to acknowledge, much less nurture, the personal and emotional lives of their participants.

Others explained the concept of a political home as something akin to a chosen family, though in a political sense. For example, when the Los Angeles group was vetting my research project, they asked me if I had a political home. When I asked for a definition, they explained it as a community of people who will embrace you, flaws and all, while still helping you identify how you can learn and grow and supporting you in doing so. This sense of "family" also highlights something potentially longer term and less transactional than many political relationships, though not without its own set of potential dysfunctions. The idea is that one's political home holds them accountable to their own as well as the group's broader political vision.[14]

While I failed to ask participants about the genealogy of the term, its traction in contemporary movement spaces is likely connected to the writings of organizer and movement intellectual adrienne maree brown, whose work SURJ leaders often cite. brown describes political home as "a place where we ideate, practice and build futures we believe in, finding alignment with those we are in accountable relationships with, and growing that alignment through organizing and education."[15] Described as such, it is clear that the concept of political home includes a prefigurative dimension. It is a site in which participants both dream about and enact the ways of being they wish to see enacted in society writ large.

Josie of Buffalo highlighted her groups' prefigurative sensibility, and connected it to the principle of loving people through the mistakes they will inevitably make in the process of movement learning:

> We want to create a culture that really mirrors our best vision and dream for the world that we're building . . . where people can also just like fuck up in the ways that they're going to . . . there is a lot of caring and loving community to move together through that learning and just meeting folks where they're at.

Some participants noted that building prefigurative culture requires a good deal of intentionality. In a Los Angeles meeting, Dahlia explained the group's many opening practices as being done in order "to make sure that we're grounded and we're doing this based on principle, based on love, based on connection and community. It's with intention that we open up our meetings." They continued by connecting this to what the group itself seeks "to prefigure," using this as an opportunity to teach participants what the term "prefiguration" means:

> We need to live out the world we want to live in. We got to do it now. Because we know it's not everywhere, but we have to start practicing it in the spaces that we have control over, and we have control over this space. So you're gonna see us practicing out the liberated world we are working to create.

A few participants emphasized the importance of seemingly small features of group practice, which might otherwise be dismissed as trivial or even contrived, as having a prefigurative dimension. Some saw these as akin to spiritual practice; others believed they helped build emotional capacity for challenging social and political work. Steph described SURJ Buffalo as a bit "church-y" in "the attention" paid to small details, "like a little song or a poem or some piece of beauty" that the group often shares at the beginning or closing of a meeting or campaign activity, "tapping into like my deep feelings about what I want my life to be about." Indeed, nearly every meeting or campaign event I attended online included carefully selected music played at the beginning, during breaks, and at the end. In-person campaign work often began and ended with chants and songs from U.S. labor organizing and the civil rights movement. It was quite common for facilitators to share a short poem or quote from important leaders in movements for racial, economic, and gender justice as well as various anticolonial struggles.

Sonja reflected on the fact that when the Louisville group gets together with one of its partners, "every meeting is opened with a kind of a ritual of connection and love, and it's just beautiful." Ella, who had helped bring "breath work" and physical movement practices to the Los Angeles group, explained such efforts as helping participants develop the embodied skills that might allow them to stay engaged in collective struggle for longer. She explained the importance of this, particularly in predominantly white spaces, as needing to "build the capacity to hold the fact that you're going to [make mistakes] . . . to build a capacity literally in your body." Numerous healing traditions understand that psychological challenges also manifest bodily. Working against structures of oppression and violence requires endurance on numerous levels, including the psychic and visceral.

Importantly, many who would come to describe one of the groups in this study as their political home did not necessarily feel this way at first contact. They instead explained a process that required building relationships and experiencing transformative forms of learning, often through collective action. Even Hannah, who described an intense sense of attraction to the Los Angeles group, recalled having to overcome her sense of intimidation. Over a period of several months, she engaged in a set of group practices that allowed her to build relationships and take on greater responsibilities. This afforded her the confidence to see that she too could participate on equal footing with other leaders whom she admired.

Josie of Buffalo admitted having few clear memories from her first

SURJ meeting, but recalled engaging in something of an exploratory period, testing her own willingness to take on risks as much as her desire to remain in the group itself. Josie recalled, "I didn't immediately think, 'Oh, this is my political home,' you know, which is definitely how I feel now." Nevertheless, Josie remembered resonating with how SURJ was explained to her early on, both in terms of the values, which "really made sense," and in the idea that the group was "doing the work of putting something on the line, white people fighting racism in a way that's accountable and grounded and part of a larger movement." Josie was curious and wanted to meet the challenge, "to lean into this, take advantage and see what this is about." More than anything, though, Josie suggested it was the community in SURJ Buffalo that was and continues to be what cemented her sense of the group as a political home: "just talking to people, connecting with people. It's really the people that stick out."

Steph also reported going through a process of engaging in action, tackling risks, and building relationships before she would come to see SURJ Buffalo as a primary political home. In fact, Steph acknowledged that she first got involved in the group because of a friend's invitation to engage in direct action, not because she herself understood SURJ's work as urgent. As a labor organizer, Steph was not new to political activity. She nevertheless believed that it was only *after* she had been arrested in an action with SURJ that she began centering racial justice in her own political commitments. This trajectory, in which personal contingencies rather than deeply held convictions lead one into movement practice, is not unusual. In fact, studies suggest a somewhat counterintuitive causality: it is often the experience of movement life itself, frequently in the form of direct action, that ignites participant motivation, as opposed to the inverse.[16]

Steph's arrest happened at a protest organized in conjunction with Buffalo's partner organization, Just Resisting. Participants had prepared for the event, training with a veteran organizer from ACT UP, an AIDS activist organization that prioritized disruptive protest activities, particularly in the 1980s and 90s.[17] Due to circumstances outside of the protesters' control, Steph ended up being one of only two people who were arrested. The event was covered in local media, and Steph was something of a recognizable figure as a well-known labor organizer. Steph reflected on the arrest, that it "changed my identity." A few people called the union office to demand she be fired, but Steph also received some outspoken support. Regardless, Steph explained that because of her position and the visibility of the action, "I had to start talking about race, and talking about that part of my political identity, which I certainly was not comfortable doing."

Even after playing a key role in a number of SURJ campaigns over more than six years, Steph revealed that she "still [did not] feel terribly articulate about race issues." She understood this as emerging from being socialized in a family that "made it very clear that I wasn't supposed to be racist, but it seemed like the only thing I was supposed to do is just to not talk about race as a thing." Given the level of commitment and engagement I had seen Steph demonstrate with the group, which included leading trainings for people new to door knocking, her self-assessment seemed surprising. It also potentially suggests something important about her group itself. Despite continuing to feel quite humble about her ability to speak in alignment with what Amanda Ball has termed "the 'high culture' of the racial justice field,"[18] Steph is situated within a community that supports continued engagement in political struggle as a space for learning and growth. Steph remains committed and engaged despite her sense of not being "terribly articulate."

The idiom of political home suggests a space in which participants find belonging and support. The ultimate aim of such a community is that it fosters the means for learning and growth while sustaining long-term engagement. If political homes are akin to a chosen family, however, it seems inevitable that conflict will also be part of the package. What do SURJ groups do when a participant is regularly engaging in practices that are troubling or problematic? And what happens when it is more than just one individual, but rather many individuals, who hold differences of vision or tactical disagreements within the group? The next sections explore one group's approach.

ENGAGING IN CONFLICT

When asked about the first lesson he had learned in his two decades of antiracist work, Jason did not hesitate: "Be prepared for conflict." This, he suggested, had not always been intuitive to him. Instead, Jason explained how the kind of welcoming culture that AWARE-LA was early to embrace and that other SURJ groups now seek to cultivate can actually lead to what he termed "a little bit of naivete" around the need to have a set of mechanisms in place when conflict emerges. Reflecting on his own presumptions, he recalled thinking, "We'll be fine. Like, we love each other. What could we ever possibly fight about that would be so bad?'" When AWARE encountered its first in a number of "breakdowns and breakthroughs," however, things did not feel fine. Jason was clear that loving each other is hugely important and also not a sufficient strategy for conflict. "Conflict is part of the process," Jason explained. It is both "normal" and even "potentially generative." Weathering it nevertheless requires a set of agreements and protocols as well as "[having] people who are ready all the time to help facilitate that." This lesson was offered graciously, as Jason thought his own naivete "might be shared among other white activists, particularly people that don't have a lot of experience in organizing and are just getting involved."

The most robust model I found for conflict engagement during this study was within the Los Angeles group. The reasons for this are likely due to size and historical precedent. Of the groups I examined, White People for Black Lives has by far the most people and therefore capacity. Moreover, with roots in the larger AWARE-LA network, white affinity organizing has been present in Los Angeles for longer than in the other places in this study. This means there has been more opportunity for conflicts to arise over time. Perhaps most importantly, the AWARE-LA network originated with the kind of dialogue and introspective practices that are generally central to conflict resolution, meaning that many who formed WP4BL brought to it both skills and experience in conflict engagement.

Naomi, who joined WP4BL in 2015, concurred with many of Jason's points. She explained that the restorative culture approach in the group, which she played a part in helping to shape, is characterized by "assuming . . . conflict is an inevitable part of life," which requires "practices and agreements in place so that we can engage in healthy, generative conflict and repair and healing and growing." Naomi also connected the group's internal practices for conflict navigation with the group's political commitment to abolition:

> The alternative to locking people up is actual accountability, actual healing, actual relational practices. So, if we actually want to live in a world where we've abolished prisons and police and jails, etc., we're going to need very strong skills to engage in restorative practices with each other.

For Naomi, having this strong set of practices for engaging in conflict was also central to the prefigurative dimensions of her group, what she termed "prefigurative liberation," defined as "being in a community . . . where we're trying to build the work as we do it and really live the way we want the world to be."

WP4BL had an established series of restorative justice principles around conflict resolution. They also maintained a "restorative culture team" that both conducted regular skills trainings for members and helped facilitate conflict navigation processes as necessary. In terms of skill building, the restorative culture team offered both stand-alone trainings as well as a "the restorative culture skill builder." In this yearlong program, participants met monthly to, as one participant explained it, "practice skills related to restorative culture and generative conflict." The skills included active listening, "the anatomy of an apology," and how to communicate using "I" statements (as well as address "pushback" to these statements). A week before the actual meeting, the facilitators for that month would send a message to the group introducing the skill, prompting participants to come to the session with a particular, thorny scenario to engage. Group time included an overview of the skill, time to practice through role play, and then a collective debrief. One participant assessed that through the skill-builder, "we're building muscle of how to communicate better and how to be in conflict in a generative way together." This person also suggested that, even in one year, the program had had a huge impact on their own life and relationships.

In addition to such skills training, WP4BL responds to emergent interpersonal and organizational conflicts through the process of "restorative circles." These facilitated dialogues require a great deal of work and intentionality, as members of the restorative culture team scaffold a multistage process. In addition to the facilitators, those involved in a restorative circle generally include at least one person who has been "impacted," at least one person that has "done the harm," and then "witnesses," who are invited to serve as "emotional support" to those who have been harmed. In preparation for the actual circle process, the facilitators meet individually with all of the participants, supporting each person in preparing a statement that can be shared during the circle. The circle itself then proceeds through multiple stages in which statements are presented and participants are given opportunities to respond. One participant explained to me that after these steps, those involved are asked to share what they want moving forward, in which "you can say anything you want" with the knowledge that "you might not get it." During the final stage, the facilitators review all of the requests made and help the group arrive at "a plan about what it looks like to move forward from this situation in a way that works . . . we'll get to a place where we say, 'Yes, we all feel good about this plan.'" All aspects of the process are carefully planned, down to the seating and speaking order. After the circle process is completed, the facilitators continue to be in communication with all participants to ensure that the agreed follow-up steps are going as planned.

Having participated in three restorative circles with the organization over the past seven years—which, she laughed, "might be a record!"—Hannah was clear in her assessment that such processes are integral to sustaining the organization. Speaking emphatically of her own experience, she suggested that such facilitated processes were "the only reason I'm still part of the group." The processes that Hannah had participated in ranged from one in which a man in the group was trying to have inappropriate relationships with women to one in which there was widespread hurt and disagreement about approaches to accessibility in the organization. She continued: "I did not have the skills to work through the conflict and the feelings that I was having. Without [the circles], I would have been out . . . I would have been out probably after a year." Hannah concluded that even as the restorative circle process could not resolve all forms of hurt that an organization might endure, "it is an incredible tool [and] imperative to a healthy, functioning organization."

GROWING PAINS

One form of organizational growth that was explained to me as being ultimately generative but beginning with some hurt was the process by which WP4BL sought to become more accessible to poor and working-class participants. Eric recalled that his "most vivid memory" of this process began at an early meeting he attended, when he was confronted by the fact that the group's membership was predominantly "owning class and upper-middle class folks at that time." While he did not recall what had prompted a participant to do so, he remembered a member of the group standing up to announce, "'I have never had to worry about money in my entire life.'" Eric recalled being disgusted and enraged by the comment as "that day, I literally had to decide whether I wanted to eat lunch or go to this meeting because I had to either get gas or get food." Eric was apparently not alone in finding the public declaration galling as well as symptomatic of WP4BL's class culture. Hannah concurred that during her early years with WP4BL, she had experienced a sense that she needed to engage in "masking" as well as her sense of "just feeling a little out of place if you're not middle class."

Eric and his life partner, along with Hannah and a few other working-class participants, turned to what Eric termed the "great restorative team in the organization" to help facilitate a circle process and important healing. Nevertheless, this occasion also made clear that organizational change was required. Around that time, Eric's partner flew to North Carolina for a poor and working-class gathering hosted by the SURJ national network. She returned with a deep conviction that WP4BL needed to, as Eric put it, "center poor and working-class people in this work," and had come back to Los Angeles with a number of practical ideas for how to do so. A small group thus formed the "class committee" in order to, as Eric put it, "make [WP4BL] more of an inviting place for working class and poor folks to attend."

The class committee started with small steps. This included drafting what Hannah explained as "an accessibility statement that includes class that we read at every meeting." The group turned meetings into potluck affairs because, as Eric explained:

> Our friends who organized in the South were shocked when we told them that we didn't have a potluck at our general meetings. They were like, "What are you doing? . . . you have to offer people food if you're telling people to come and sit and listen to stuff for two hours!"

WP4BL started to offer childcare and to reimburse transportation and parking costs. The results were widely popular. Eric recalled, "the potluck was a hit! Childcare was a hit!"

While the class committee began its focus on what Hannah called "tangible stuff, org related," group interest in developing a class analysis continued to grow. Hannah explained how the glossary that WP4BL offers at its meetings came out of this work "because a lot of the terms that you hear in activist spaces are super academic and really not accessible." The class committee started running workshops for all WP4BL participants that included identifying "the ways that middle-class people show up in spaces that can be harmful and antidotes to that." Hannah recalled how the class committee was sustained as a group of between twelve and fifteen participants for its first few years but tripled in size after the summer of 2020 and began "talking about mutual aid . . . about socially conscious financial literacy." The growing attention to accessibility in terms of class also increased group members' awareness of questions of ability status.[19] While no one claimed that the socioeconomic composition of WP4BL's leadership had undergone a radical transformation in the years since the class committee began its work, most participants agreed that the group had become a more welcoming space for those across class backgrounds and ability statuses.

WP4BL's trajectory around class accessibility and inclusion was not unique in this study. Sonja also explained that those who were involved in the Louisville group's early work "were more people with class privilege . . . and so there were some people who were working class who really felt [class] wasn't being addressed." Newer and often younger participants pointed out that meeting times were not being held at hours that were feasible for those seeking to balance full-time work and care obligations. They expressed a need for childcare during campaign activities. Sonja reflected that even as some of the conversations were "hard," they "raised some really good discussions [that] ultimately benefited the work," pushing the group to adjust its procedures so as to become more inclusive. Sonja suggested that the results were quite impactful for Louisville SURJ, which now has "a lot more working-class folks involved and in different leadership positions."

At the same time, participants raised interesting questions about the processes and practices that seek to make a SURJ group as inclusive as possible. For instance, some participants in Los Angeles identified an uneasy balance between a prefigurative ethos and the exigencies that accompany political organizing, particularly as a group of white people accountable to BIPOC partners. Such a tension was made resonant when the group dedicated the majority of its members' time and resources over many months to the project of deep canvassing for their major ballot measure campaign, Measure R. A number of committed participants—particularly those who had to work on weekends due to financial constraints or who could not physically tolerate the hours of standing and walking required for door knocking due to illness or impairment—began to find little role in the organization. This was exacerbated by the fact of having their regular contact with others in the group rather suddenly eliminated, since those group members were committing huge amounts of time and energy to the campaign. Some participants felt abruptly disconnected from close personal friends as well as an organization that had been deeply important to them, often for many years. Feelings were hurt, and some suggested the campaign was not as inclusive as it might be, particularly to those of different class and ability statuses.

In this instance, neither the group's more recently adopted approaches to inclusion nor its restorative circles process provided easy remedy. Jason reflected on this, noting that, "the challenge is that a lot of those tools [used in restorative processes] come from community building and interpersonal conflict. And it's really hard to find the nuanced way of doing that when things get politicized." The line between personal grievance and structural exclusion can become blurry. Not being able to participate in a central tactic because it takes place during working hours is experienced as a form of organizational exclusion.

WP4BL had a number of political commitments it was trying to accomplish simultaneously. Jason identified how this created an uneasy balancing act. On the one hand, WP4BL wished to pursue "a robust way of organizing in an inclusive way to people who want to do the work." This impulse, however, can create tension with maximizing the group's broader political impacts:

> I understand issues of inclusion and bringing everyone in when you're building a community of people. [But] when you're trying to hit political goals, trying to end jails, and the tactic is deep canvassing, direct action, and involves people's bodies, there are certain people who might not be able to participate.

In this way, prefigurative practices can sometimes be in tension with a larger political vision.

Another participant, while empathetic to those who felt that "your beloved community should never hurt you," was also uncertain that a sense of love and support within their community should be "*the* organizing principle; there's just maybe some tension about how much that should be centered." Jason agreed, adding that at core, there is a potential contradiction in seeking to practice prefiguration in an all-white or predominantly white group: "there's something that I appreciate about prefigurative politics but, if you're building a prefigurative politics in a whites-only group, it's not liberatory . . . we're not a multiracial group."

Here it might be worth delineating between prefigurative practices and prefigurative formations, which are linked but separable concepts. There is certainly value in building community and working through conflict in ways that balance accountability with kindness and support. These are the prefigurative practices that have value for all movement participants, regardless of race or relative privilege. What it means to prioritize an inclusive approach, particularly in terms of marginalized, intersectional identities, in an all-white group, however, is less straightforward.

Certainly, those privileged by whiteness are no monolith and bring their multitude of social positions to the movement struggles they join. This is a fact that the groups in this study seek to acknowledge and organize around in creative and often generative ways. Yet in seeking to be as inclusive as possible, some SURJ groups, particularly in city spaces, also exist in order to organize people who share the fact of being white, and to do so as part of a larger multiracial justice movement. These groups' founding logic is to organize in predominantly white communities *in order* to support the vision and organizing begun first and foremost by BIPOC leaders.

For Jason, this acknowledgment was fundamental when understanding WP4BL's political commitments:

> Our solidarity partner needs us to do this thing that is very important to these long-term goals of transforming our society. The tactics we have to employ themselves are not always going to be inclusive to everyone.

WP4BL participants did acknowledge that there are a number of potential roles for people to play in a campaign tactic, even if they cannot put their bodies on the line or take time off from work. Most also agreed that the more people that *can* participate in a campaign, the more politically powerful it is likely to be. There is, nevertheless, an uneasy balance of prioritizing the needs of a group's own participants while pursuing a collective, political vision that is accountable to organizational partners. Jason explained his concern that there are ways of approaching group-level inclusion that begin "to give up fidelity to the tactic [if] we are centering like the individual, or the hypothetical individuals, who won't be able to do that thing": in essence, prioritizing a small group's needs over and above what movement strategy may require.

Another participant—who identified as white, "queer nonbinary," and raised with class privilege—agreed, adding their assessment that "for me, the goal is not to avoid people ever having a bad experience. ... I don't believe in unnecessary suffering, but I think it's okay to struggle, especially in this work, especially as like an enormously privileged person." The line between discomfort and real suffering is a highly subjective one, of course. In terms of principles, SURJ itself is clear that the value of calling people in is not about ensuring participant comfort. Indeed, a strong commitment to learning and growth generally requires participants experience discomfort, even as they are supported by a foundation of caring relationships. In practice, however, seeking to construct cultures of care can risk recentering white feelings and white comfort, which have been demonstrated to derail racial justice efforts.[20]

Yet, the opposite extreme—in which feelings are dismissed because they are expressed by white people—may also be harrowing for movement groups. In the case of Louisville, Sonja identified how important questions around making the organization more inclusive to those across class status were sometimes funneled into interpersonal blame. Sonja observed that some of the critique around class inclusion became "very personality oriented . . . certain people were being attacked as perpetuating class privilege, class dynamics instead of 'how are we dealing with this as an organization?'" The group ultimately benefited from integrating a deeper class analysis into its culture and structure, but the process to secure such gains likely included more interpersonal hurt than was necessary.

Building organizations that are welcoming and inclusive to those from various backgrounds, bases of knowledge, and even political orientations holds clear strategic and psychic benefits. Nevertheless, this approach is not without challenges and tensions. Some of these are clearly generalizable across movement groups. For example, it is not uncommon for important organizational questions to manifest as interpersonal conflict. Moreover, it is difficult to combine a big tent approach with organizing around a specific political vision, and to do so in a coalition with other groups. Other dilemmas are more particular to the project of organizing predominantly white participants in racial justice efforts. There are likely no catchall answers to these dilemmas, but they can certainly be wrestled with in particular sites of struggle.

And in spite of such dilemmas, the groups in this study find good reason to keep building an inclusive culture across their efforts. I now turn to how the disposition of calling people in works beyond the internal life of the organization.

"THERE'S LOVE IN ALL OF IT"

Sonja had many stories about being part of the white Left in the 1980s. In this one, she recalled when her organization was distributing their newsletter in a small town in western Massachusetts. Her fellow activist approached another white man and asked if he wanted to read about the threat of KKK organizing, an offer that was refused with the excuse of, "No, sorry, I don't have the time." Sonja laughed as she remembered the scene that unfolded, "this [activist] started running after him [yelling], 'Are you a racist or something?'" The disposition of calling people out not only impacted dynamics within groups but extended to white activists' efforts to reach outside their organizations.

This chapter has thus far examined how the ethos of calling people in functions within the groups in this study. Call in culture seeks to welcome all-comers and to forge supportive communities without ignoring the harms of being socialized as white. The emphasis is on learning and growth, anchored in the inevitability of individual and collective imperfection and conflict. As a matter of movement strategy, the groups in this study understand this culture shift in white antiracist efforts as the best way to grow and sustain more white people in practical struggles for racial justice. This approach is also undergirded by a sociological truth: white supremacy is socially structured and cannot be reduced to individuals' moral failings. Approaching mistakes with scolding and righteousness misunderstands both the systemic nature of racial injustice as well as the ingredients necessary to build and sustain movement groups.

It is also worth emphasizing that SURJ's adoption of the principle of calling in aligns with a Black liberation vision. Certainly the language itself can be attributed to the work of Black reproductive justice activist and scholar Loretta J. Ross.[21] Far beyond this, however, study participants explained the ethos of calling in as being aligned with the needs, desires, and strategies articulated by BIPOC organizers.

Some recalled conversations in the early 2000s, before SURJ was formed, in which BIPOC organizers clarified that white people's fear at making mistakes was preventing them from being full movement participants. This was viewed as a strategic impediment. Clare Bayard, co-founder of Catalyst, reflected on the common understanding, often promoted by white antiracist activists, that "white people need to shut up and be in the back of the room." This approach has important value during different movement moments, always determined by actual context, relationships, and the tactics selected. Catalyst's BIPOC partners nevertheless raised concerns about this as a default approach:

> We definitely got pushed early on by comrades of color who were like, "Yo, if your version of check your privilege is that you step back so far that you remove resources, which also includes skills and experience, that is not constructive. So find a different way to do it."

Clare recalled in particular the words of Paulina Helm Hernández, then the co-director of Southerners On New Ground (SONG), a queer BIPOC organization that, incidentally, SURJ's own co-founders had helped launch in the 1990s. Clare explained of Hernández, "declawed was the metaphor she used. She was like, 'you white people need your claws for these enemies who are trying to kill our people.'" Call in culture seeks to be something of an antidote to this "declawing."

Shelly of AWARE-LA similarly reflected on her group being one of the first white antiracist spaces that was actively pushing for a "non-shaming, accepting approach." Certainly, this orientation emerged because of the limitations white organizers themselves had confronted in antiracist movement and education spaces. Importantly, Shelly noted that a space for supporting white people through imperfection and growth was also a response to "the people of color in our lives who were clear that they didn't expect us to be any less human than them." Shelly extended this analysis to suggest that calling each other in, at least to her mind, "meshes with abolitionist culture . . . we are not abandoning other white people, even if they're not totally on board yet. And we're not gonna abandon white people who are still too new to do things right." Shelly was clear that this was not a hard and fast rule, so much as an undergirding principle, acknowledging, "we have strategic choices to make about who we work with, and when. That's the nuance and complexity, of course. This isn't a free pass for anybody."

LA-based Black organizer and attorney Nana Gyamfi agreed with this assessment, noting that, from her vantage point, AWARE's approach aligns with abolitionist principles. Nana explained:

> For me, [AWARE is] a great example of the values of abolition in practice in terms of setting up community and building trust, talking about and addressing issues that come up in this effort to engage in this dismantling [white supremacy] but in ways that are not like "shame-y blame-y" but still are squaring up with stuff. They're not hiding from things.

It is worth noting that the strategy of calling people in can be interpreted and implemented in ways that do not in fact align with the visions of SURJ's BIPOC partners. Kate of the Louisville group explained how there can be a fine line between making racial justice campaign messages, or aspects of a Black liberation vision, palatable to white communities versus distorting such messages altogether. She explained that "one piece of feedback that we heard from [our] accountability partner conversations ... is that sometimes white folks water down the messaging." Kate used the example of "defund the police," in particular, and how it is "so easy for slogans to get co-opted." Kate was clear that when Louisville SURJ uses the words "defund the police," it actually means that this is the end goal, even if it may not happen "tomorrow." Stepping back, Kate reflected that this was "a really important piece of feedback because sometimes you want to water stuff down from a good place, like we want to make it accessible for people who are new." This is part of creating a sense of openness and welcoming to participants from a range of backgrounds. Kate continued, "But there's a real danger there of letting movements be co-opted." Kate assessed such a danger in very measurable political terms, concluding, "then we get legislation that's not very powerful, and doesn't get passed anyway."

Connected to this critique, some BIPOC partners admitted some initial consternation about the prospect of calling white people in to the work of racial justice. Attica Scott of Louisville was frank:

> Honestly, when I first heard the calling in language, I was like, "oh, my gosh, are you gonna like tiptoe through this, and make white people feel comfortable for their mess!?!" I was like, "oh, my gosh, no, please! We're going to water it down!?!"

Over time, however, Attica shifted her assessment:

> It's taken me a long time to get to the point where I was comfortable with that language [of calling in] because I've seen what it means. For some people, that's what has to happen for them to not run away, right? You have to call people in.

While Attica seemed to understand calling white people in as something of a necessary tactical compromise, Nana understood it a bit differently: as the most reasonable approach to organizing a broader base. She surmised that in its efforts to reach beyond the core of the organization, the Los Angeles group was "very intentional" but also maintained "flexibility." She continued:

> Some people may get it, some people may not get it. . . . [The group]'s actually engaging folks, seeing where people are, talking with them, and planting seeds and opening paths, without shoving. . . . The person may keep going down that path, and they may stop right there. But you're not dragging people down the road, not the way that White People for Black Lives does it.

Attica likewise saw the tactical value to calling white participants in, particularly for broadening the base of white support for racial justice, but she also believed the practice of calling people out required contextualization. She explained:

> What sometimes gets missed in racial justice work that's led by Black people and other people of color is that calling out is so much of what we have had to do because people in positions of decision-making

weren't listening. We *have* to call [them] out. What choice did we have? And so that became the way that we operated.

This analysis is one that the SURJ groups in this study widely share. Organizational materials and participant explanations clarify that white people should not ask BIPOC to call them in. They also explicate that calling in is not the approach groups espouse when communicating with those in power. The purpose of organizing, after all, is to put pressure on key decision-makers. The strategic use of public shaming is sometimes valuable in this regard.

Attica continued that even as BIPOC communities have been required to call people out in order to get necessary attention, an approach that is often portrayed in dominant society as a "more negative, almost violent thing that we've been doing, we've always done things out of love for our communities." Regardless of whether the approach was calling in or calling out, Attica believed this deeper ethic of love undergirded both efforts:

> The calling in of LSURJ, I think, has shown people that there's love in all of it, if we just do the work in different ways. And because of our different privileges, we're able to approach it in different ways.

Here, Attica lifts up the importance of using multiple approaches on multiple fronts—from "conversational" to "confrontational"—"you got to have all of it. Because if we all operated in one way, we're still not going to get what we're fighting for." Through her organizing experience, Attica advocates for a level of political dexterity that is attentive to each tactic's targets in the power structure as well as the range of potential audiences.

A number of SURJ leaders also deployed the language of love to describe the practice of organizing. SURJ staff member Grace Aheron, who described herself as a multiracial Asian American southerner, reflected on how she uses the term rather provocatively when she speaks to white people involved with SURJ. Grace began: "I like to get in front of white people and say, 'I love white people.' And people are like, 'Oh,

God, why!?!'" At one level, Grace's assessment was a practical one: "white people hating themselves about being racist is not going to get us anywhere." At the same time, Grace was clear that the project of organizing white people was one of combining good strategy with a larger vision anchored in love: "strategically, white people are the ones that are making racism happen. But also organizing comes out of a deep love of people and wanting them to be free and to be a part of this free world."

Kelly Sue, the Bedford County Listening Project's staff organizer, agreed with this, explaining that love anchors the work of organizing:

> In order to be an organizer, you have to love the people you organize. And love doesn't have to mean being okay with everything they do. But love them, believe in transformation, and believe we can build a different world despite the fact that it so clearly looks like we can't! Like just no matter what the odds are.

Kelly Sue's discussion of love evokes some of the same principles participants associated with the concept of political home. Just as one's political home functions as something akin to movement family, ready to support people while holding them accountable to learning and growth, the kind of love Kelly Sue describes offers a firm basis with which to not "be okay" with harmful thought patterns and behaviors. The love found in organizing is also both clear-sighted and outrageously hopeful, quite akin to Antonio Gramsci's "pessimism of the intellect, optimism of the will."[22]

There is a long and rich discussion of the role of love in movements for collective liberation. Martin Luther King Jr., for instance, wrote of different forms of love—that of romance, that of friendship, and that of a more expansive, "agape" love. Tracing the etymology for "agape" love from the Greek New Testament, King defines it as an "understanding and creative, redemptive goodwill for all men."[23] Agape love is not premised on liking people, but on an unconditional, and in King's case, faithful orientation. This is not dissimilar to the kind of love Attica, Grace, and Kelly Sue locate in their organizing work. Many other movement intellectuals have also identified love as a revolutionary force. In her *Methodology of the Oppressed*, Chela Sandoval reminds us of the ways in which Frantz Fanon, Che Guevara, bell hooks, Gloria Anzaldúa, Trinh Minh-ha, and Cherríe Moraga "to name only a few, similarly understand love as a 'breaking' through whatever controls in order to find 'understanding and community': It is described as 'hope' and 'faith' in the potential of some promised land."[24] Love, for Sandoval, offers access to the kinds of subversive analyses and forms of imagination necessary to make society anew.

This kind of love may well be a political necessity for sustaining movement struggle. It is one thing to hold one's nose while engaging in a necessary tactical compromise, such as having to vote for the candidate who is likely to be less harmful. It is quite another to try to build long-term movement strategy solely out of a sense of necessity and obligation. SURJ's choice to organize white people as part of a multiracial movement cannot only be done out of practicality but requires a more capacious sensibility. Engaging in such organizing, participants suggest, means finding a place of love: love for a vision and the world being pursued, but also love for the people, however flawed, who must build it.

The approach of calling people in seeks to recruit and retain a wider base of white participants, deepen their commitment and engagement, and foster sustainable organizations that can endure the boom-and-bust cycles of movement life. Call in culture prioritizes learning through doing, creating contexts that are supportive while rigorous, so that participants grow the skills and competencies necessary to be effective leaders and organizers. Insofar as this is some of the more individualized and internal-facing work that groups undertake, it comes with inherent pitfalls. Lessons and approaches can be taken on in ways that prioritize individual belonging over collective goals. Group processes that are inclusive, sustainable, and loving are necessary but sometimes insufficient for working towards a broader political vision. Yet there are important reasons to continue to make racial justice organizing appealing and accessible to as many people as possible, including those raced as white.

The priorities and practices traced in this chapter are situated within a broader movement strategy that aims to grow the base of white people willing and poised to engage in politically impactful, collective action for racial and economic justice. Moreover, while the Black partners in this study may not all initially celebrate the idiom of calling white people in, they have come to see its value for meeting people where they are at, understanding organizing as an act of love.

7 FIGHT FOR OUR PEOPLE

TOWARDS THE END OF OUR many conversations, I asked Pam McMichael how she thought Showing Up for Racial Justice differed from previous efforts to engage in antiracist work with predominantly white communities. Pam responded that she is "not a fan of comparative language," and so "that is not the question for me." She then suggested a different line of inquiry: "The question is, what are we doing right? What are we doing well? What do we need to learn?" Pam's redirection of the question is instructive. To overemphasize the differences between SURJ's approach and other efforts, particularly to do so in a normative sense—judging some as good and others as bad—counters an ethos of respect for movement lineage and disregards the way that effective political struggle requires consistent reflection, assessment, and adjustment. The maneuvers that a group adopts in any given moment are responsive and cumulative. Pam extended this thinking:

> Things come out of a context, and things build on each other. Some organization may not have been as effective or not done something, but that doesn't mean that it was a waste or that people didn't learn something in that moment that informed [strategy].

The groups in this study may be engaging in new approaches, or at least different configurations of ones attempted in the past. Pam, however, emphasized that there are always situational variables that shape what choices might seem sensible and important. This aligns with the learning orientation that the groups in this study seek to integrate at multiple levels of their practice. It is also useful for approaching the lessons we might glean from this study. As a general parameter, then, it is worth bearing in mind that all movement approaches need to be assessed within their context. The groups in this book seek to maximize their efficacy by responding to current conditions with the accrued knowledge of what has come before.

As one clear example, the focus on developing white antiracist consciousness in general, and the tool of the white privilege analytic in specific, met important aims for particular audiences. It made whiteness newly visible to those raced as white through clear, tangible, and often personalized evidence—such as drawing attention to the color of available bandages. It may have also been particularly relevant during the ascendance of colorblind racism, following the gains of the civil rights movement. At the same time, these approaches may not do enough to help participants connect the individual manifestations of whiteness to larger power systems, reducing antiracism instead to something of a personal moral quest. Observers have also pointed to the way that antiracist learning activities designed for white people often presume a middle-class experience of whiteness. There is the additional danger that participants come to understand awareness building as antiracism's ultimate end, forestalling important forms of collective action.

Likewise, the sense of perfectionism and cultural gatekeeping that has made white antiracist spaces feel exclusive and elitist arguably emerges from the important impulse to hold white people accountable in ways that dominant society does not. It is not wrong to assess that most people raced as white will need to dismantle key features of white socialization in order to show up in multiracial movements more respectfully, responsibly, and effectively. At the same time, no one can learn if they are not afforded entrance to the process. Moreover, participants require a basis of support and care if they are to take the risks and learn the lessons their movements require.

The approaches in this book are certainly the result of careful study, reflection, and experimentation around the important logics as well as shortcomings of movement practices that have come before. They also respond to the current political conjuncture, framed by consolidating forms of fascism as well as efforts for collective liberation. In the U.S. context, and following the election of the first Black president, resurgent manifestations of organized white racism and rage have seen broadening and deepening support. Today a major political party, with clear demand from the electorate, routinely promotes candidates and policies that embody antidemocratic practices and authoritarian principles, appealing explicitly and implicitly to white entitlement and white grievance. Meanwhile, both major political parties have ushered in responses to accumulating capitalist crises, particularly in the form of neoliberal restructuring, that divest in majorities and invest in a microcohort of the elite.

Half a century into the era of welfare state retrenchment and mass incarceration, the forms of organized abandonment and state violence that have always disproportionately harmed BIPOC are impacting growing numbers of white people as well. White majorities nevertheless continue to support policies that authorize increasing levels of collective destruction, including their own, jealously guarding their whiteness and believing it to be under threat. Into this confluence, the Movement for Black Lives (M4BL), this generation's feminist and queer iteration of the centuries-long struggle for Black liberation, has been one of the more visible and consolidated efforts agitating for a different set of possibilities, politics, and policies. Insofar as movement efforts "come out of a context," as Pam helpfully articulates, these are some of the more proximate conditions shaping the analyses, principles, tools, and tactics that this book explores.

LEARNING FROM MUTUAL INTEREST ORGANIZING

When I spoke to Alicia Hurle in the summer of 2022, she did not sugarcoat the political context in Kentucky. While Alicia had seen many local victories, she had also witnessed many state-level losses. As she put it:

We're seeing what happens when the Right amasses power and the lengths they'll go to to really destroy people's lives. In that context, it can be really hard to hold a vision as you're organizing because you do feel like, "I just have to stop the bleeding."

Asked how she stayed in the work, Alicia emphasized that she still found reason for hope:

The world's always been on fire for most people in this country. Now, some people are waking up to that because they're seeing how—back to mutual interest—"oh wait, this actually might impact me one day." Nobody can run away from climate change, or inflation. . . . More people are coming into the work.

As a long-time organizer in Louisville, Alicia had watched the Louisville SURJ chapter grow over its first decade. She was also collaborating on rural organizing efforts throughout the state, such as the work that birthed Kentucky People's Union. Alicia named these efforts as helping to move the needle:

To have a primary partner like SURJ that is so well aligned and moving in that direction, [I am] seeing the possibilities of that solidarity work in a way that I haven't before. Things are in a better position for actual sustained change than I've ever seen since I've been doing this work. So that's what keeps me going. I'm like, "there's real possibility there."

Alicia was not the only participant in this study to discuss a sense of hope in the face of fairly bleak political times. Nor was she the only Black organizer to attribute some of this hope directly to the collaborative movement-building work being done in partnership with a local SURJ group or the national organization. So what is it that we can learn from the approaches explored in this book, approaches that give Alicia hope? There are likely myriad lessons to be taken. Here I synthesize some primary take-aways.

LESSON 1: CHALLENGING SYSTEMS AS THE PURPOSE OF, AND A SITE FOR, WHITE ANTIRACIST LEARNING

The first lesson is that antiracist practice must incorporate an attention towards systems change, which requires both an analysis of how power works as well as an understanding of how to wield collective action to challenge power relations. These forms of analysis can and should coincide with other kinds of more explicit consciousness raising around dominant white socialization, but educational activities are positioned in the service of collective action and movement building. This is because the groups in this study assess white supremacy as both an ideology that whites need to unlearn as well as a system of actual policies and material arrangements that can and must be challenged.

The groups in this study therefore understand that antiracist organizing in predominantly white communities requires multiple forms of learning. This includes political education as to how white racism operates within a range of interlocking social structures, as well as how white racism can harm movement processes at every level from the interpersonal to the tactical and strategic. At the same time, the antiracist learning we see in this book also incorporates the lessons and skills of organizing: participants come to understand themselves as politically efficacious, capable of joining with others to help determine collective conditions. The precise activities by which these various forms of learning occur can differ based on the needs of each group in their context. What the efforts in this study hold in common is equipping participants to be more politically skilled in their antiracist commitments with the aim of amassing grassroots power.

In this sense, the models in this book also help to complicate the assumed developmental arc regarding white people's engagements with antiracism. Research and common sense generally suggest that in order for white people to become antiracist, they must acknowledge their complicity in a white supremacist system. This is often coupled with the implication that such acknowledgment is either a prerequisite for action or even white antiracism's ultimate ends. For some white audiences who may not initially identify as "antiracist," however, a desire to take collective action for other reasons, even ones that are initially self-interested, can become an opening towards developing more collectivist as well as antiracist understandings and practices. For those white people who are already interested in participating in antiracist work, this book demonstrates how various forms of learning might be situated within an action-oriented approach.

Bringing participants into forms of practical struggle allows them to see political conditions for themselves and to develop new analyses and commitments. Moreover, participants regularly report that their most impactful learning experiences are found through the actual practices of organizing. This does not dismiss the importance of white people's acknowledgment of their whiteness. Yet it permits that white people's antiracist consciousness may not need to precede taking antiracist action and that consciousness alone is insufficient for effecting systematic and enduring antiracist change.

LESSON 2: ACCOUNTABILITY AS RESPONSIVE AND PROACTIVE

The second lesson is that white accountability to a BIPOC liberation vision in general, and a Black liberation agenda in particular, requires balancing at least two important impulses. The first is a responsiveness to context, which often means adapting to specific movement conditions on the ground, often in immediate and direct consultation with movement partners. The second is pursuing a longer range and more overarching vision: the commitment to bring a greater number of those raced as white into multiracial struggle. In the case of specific, local partnerships, there are various practices by which groups build trust and act collaboratively. To fortify these relationships, it is sometimes the case that white participants need to perform discrete, supportive actions, such as serving as human shields between Black participants and law enforcement or vigilantes. The fact of participants' white privilege in these instances is leveraged to promote movement gains. Partners regularly report that white participants' high-risk actions, such as when they risk arrest, are some of their most appreciated ones.

At the same time, the groups in this study generally understand that being accountable to a Black liberation agenda can only be realized at a much more sustained level of movement building. Bringing a critical mass of white people into multiracial struggle for racial and economic justice is in fact the fulcrum of this conception of accountability. These interpretations of accountability—as both responsiveness to actual people and organizations as well as operating at the level of guiding principle—always operate in tandem but can also contradict each other in practical ways. For example, as occurred in the Los Angeles group, choosing to take initiative in the white community to accomplish an abolitionist goal, even one coordinated with partners, can focus group energies away from other specific, supporting efforts that a partner organization might require. Interestingly, this conflict was most divisive within the group itself, as white participants struggled with which understanding of accountability to prioritize.

This is one of innumerable sites across any movement in which abstract principles can collide with practical considerations. The group in question endured and maintained its cross-organizational partnerships, a testimony to its years of practice navigating conflict and developing both intragroup and cross-organizational relationships.

LESSON 3: ORGANIZING WHITE PEOPLE BECAUSE OF AS WELL AS BEYOND THEIR WHITENESS

The white affinity organizing approach is adopted because of the ways that white racism continues to stymie the internal operations of movement groups while overdetermining the political terrain on which such movements mount their tactics. At the same time, the mutual interest approach suggests that bringing white people into multiracial struggle requires appealing to the various subject positions white people hold beyond just their whiteness, and hold in common with BIPOC. This might include, for instance, as tenants, workers, people in need of healthcare, and those harmed by gender-based violence. The groups in this study find a particular importance in the ways that socioeconomic class as well as region shape white identity and proactively seek to organize with poor and working-class whites, especially in rural areas and the U.S. South. This is because these groups of white people hold a very tangible and urgent shared material stake with working and poor BIPOC. At the same time, the legacies of chattel slavery, Jim Crow, and the Southern Strategy mean that white voters in rural areas and the U.S. South hold outsized power in state governance to the extent that they participate in the political process. Helping these communities to identify and engage in multiracial organizing around the widely felt experiences of economic abandonment and state neglect is a crucial step to help shift the balance of power.

Just like any movement practice, however, organizing around mutual interest is not a silver bullet. Building multiracial solidarity in the face of white supremacy has always been an uphill battle in the face of the psychic, cultural, and material enticements of racial whiteness. This is a consideration that the organizers in this study seek to address head-on. They do so by naming and framing how white racism is stoked to sow division. As importantly, they bring participants into forms of practical struggle where they can experience forms of empowerment, dignity, and social connection that outweigh the wages of whiteness. As one example, KPU is functionally multiracial, affording participants opportunities to build meaningful relationships across many socially structured differences, including race.

The work to create more welcoming and inclusive organizations is another way of operationalizing the idea that white people need to be organized beyond just their whiteness. Particularly for the urban groups in this study, there is great intentionality to recruiting and retaining a diverse contingent of white people by class, ability status, and gender identity, for example. As some participants discuss, however, prioritizing inclusivity in predominantly white groups can risk recentering white feelings and white comfort in ways that contradict larger political aims. Moreover, sometimes good political instincts, such as efforts to make group practices more accessible across class, can be funneled into interpersonal attacks. Even as these dilemmas arise, the groups in this study have done generative work to navigate them and arrive at new lessons and analyses.

Taking a step back from the specificity of white antiracist organizing, it is also worth identifying a mutual interest approach as holding broad sociological appeal. An orientation grounded in mutual interest cultivates a social-systemic way of seeing. People who have been socialized under hypercompetitive individualism, taught to understand their lived experiences and interests as divergent and conflicting, are instead encouraged to identify a common power structure that does them harm, if in disparate ways.[1] Moreover, for those who join social change efforts from a stance of heightened privileges and protections, the mutual interest approach provides a seemingly counterintuitive insight, if not a particularly new one. As theorists of white supremacy, patriarchy, and capitalism have long identified, members of dominant groups are not mere beneficiaries of the systems of dominance they authorize and labor to maintain. They are also harmed by these very systems, often materially, but also psychosocially and spiritually.[2]

The mutual interest approach can also be understood as a useful political principle, and one that shows up across struggles for collective liberation. Important factions of the Black Freedom Struggle, for example, identified U.S. intervention in Vietnam, racial violence at home, and the treatment of poor people the world over as the inseparable operations of U.S. imperialist capitalism.[3] The work to demonstrate how seemingly distinct political contests are shaped by the same set of powerbrokers, institutions, and policies continues today, such as in efforts to connect the plight of student debtors in the United States to those under siege in Gaza.[4] The groups in this book, whether they work to block the construction of a new jail in Los Angeles or to enshrine tenants' rights in rural Kentucky, likewise understand themselves as confronting different nodes of the same systems of racial capitalism and white supremacy. Indeed, in the time after data collection, some of these groups continued their abolitionist and economic justice commitments by prioritizing work to end the genocide in Gaza.

At both the psychosocial as well as political-strategic level, then, mutual interest organizing creates the experiential contexts and interpretive frameworks by which to more deeply grasp our collective and unquestionable interdependence. In turn, it directs the power of collective grief, rage, and a sense of abandonment away from those desperately trying to survive under systems that harm and, instead, towards a set of common targets in the power structure. This study demonstrates how the far-reaching and layered principle of mutual interest might be enacted, what it accomplishes in practice, and where it faces complications

Assessing the ultimate efficacy of the approaches in this study will only be possible in the decades to come. The groups in this book likewise understand that they are in this for the long haul. As their work continues to evolve, there will be new questions to consider. As Pam McMichael reminds us, the efforts in this study come out of a context; they must be flexible and adaptable as conditions shift. The piece of strategy explored in this book that has been most subject to external criticism—that of white affinity organizing—was adopted contextually. The goal was never to build all-white organizations as a movement fixture, but to organize the predominantly white flank of a larger multiracial movement for collective liberation. Organizers' own assessments as to the utility of race-based organizing may also be shifting since the height of previous mobilizations in the Movement for Black Lives (2014–2020). Will race-based organizing continue to make sense moving forward, and if so, under what conditions? These are matters that future movement participants will have to determine.

I conclude the writing of this book in the immediate aftermath of the 2024 U.S. elections, which have made devastatingly clear that organizing against patriarchal white supremacy and for working people remains as urgent as ever. The liberal establishment has failed to recruit rural white communities and the poor and working classes at great peril while the Right has demonstrated its extreme efficacy in organizing white majorities around their suffering. A belief that demographic changes and a growing "minority majority" would be sufficient to usher in more emancipatory politics and possibilities looks as naive at this moment as did predictions of a post-racial presidency over fifteen years ago.

No one has complete answers for how to prevent a descent into authoritarianism and outright fascism. What the groups in this study demonstrate is that trying to dismantle white supremacy by teaching white people that they are white and have therefore done harm, while important in many contexts, is also insufficient to the task at hand. Rather, they are clear that this is a "fight for our people," as many of the white organizers in this study routinely proclaim. Theirs is a fight grounded in love, in an acknowledgment of our thoroughgoing interdependence as a species and as a planet. Theirs is a fight to change the systems and political arrangements that got us here in the first place. Theirs is a fight for a different social contract, for the realization of actual multiracial democracy.

Appendix: Methods

CASE SELECTION

I first heard about Showing Up for Racial Justice at the group's inception in 2009 through my involvement in movement work. Like some of my study participants, however, it was not until 2016 that I familiarized myself much more with the organization, or at least their website. I had just taken a job teaching classes on race and racism with a majority white, wealthy, and self-identified liberal student body. This coincided with having moved to a predominantly white and poor rural region in central New York state, a place very different from any in which I had lived before. It was also the final months of the 2016 U.S. presidential campaign. SURJ's publicly available resources helped me to prepare some generative student learning activities and later afforded me tools for helping students make sense of Donald Trump's first election to the presidency.

By late 2020, as I once again consulted various organizational websites in search of teaching materials for a remote course in the pandemic, I realized that a movement friend from over a decade prior had been working at SURJ for a few years and now lived in Buffalo, New York. That initial conversation with Anne Dunlap in February 2021 was deeply illuminating and revealed that the organization's actual structure and activities were much more layered than I had understood. Without Anne

Dunlap generously agreeing to speak with me, and later introducing and vouching for me with a range of movement participants, I am not sure that this research could have happened.

The overarching question animating the study is how U.S.-based movement efforts might bring more white people into politically impactful, antiracist action. The concept of political impact here requires some definition, particularly given that assessing a movement's precise influence on any sphere of society is a complex endeavor. My definition is quite broad. There are certainly clear and specific metrics that one might turn to, particularly with regard to traditional processes of state governance. Political impact might be measured by voter turnout and candidate outcomes, legislation introduced and policies passed. In the life of an organization, the potential to make a political impact can also hinge on how many members are recruited or the amount of donations secured. Many of the groups in this study can certainly count success along these traditional lines. But for this research, I have spent more time exploring and analyzing features of movement life that are often less obvious and more difficult to measure, though they are no less important for long-term efficacy. These include learning and skill building, forging intra- and intergroup relationships, cultivating commitment, and navigating setbacks, both political and interpersonal. These matters are key in order for movements to build a broader and more diverse base of support, which in turn are crucial prerequisites for being able to effect change at multiple levels of society.[1]

My first year of research was largely spent identifying and gaining entrance to the three urban groups in this study, which I selected because they appeared to be doing what I wished to study—bringing more white people into politically impactful, antiracist action. In other words, I identified groups that had endured through multiple movement cycles and were operating in at least one cross-racial, cross-organizational partnership. Given that my initial interviews with the organization's founders and staff reiterated how mutual interest organizing was a cornerstone approach at the national level, I also wished to examine how a wider range of participants understood the idea and what it looked like in practice. Therefore, in consultation with Anne

Dunlap and others she introduced to me, I selected groups that minimally: (1) had been around since at least the Ferguson uprisings (2014); (2) had maintained a multiyear relationship with at least one BIPOC-led organization; and (3) understood themselves to be doing mutual interest organizing. While the efforts in Louisville, Los Angeles, and Buffalo all adhered to these basic parameters, there were other good reasons to select them as well. I outline specific group dynamics in greater detail at the end of Chapter 2.

As a general overview, the cities in which these chapters organized are obviously quite different in terms of population size, racial composition, and local politics, which all have an important bearing on group assessments and strategies. It was valuable that Los Angeles and Louisville participants had been central to forming the national SURJ network in 2009 and so had institutional memory as well as a sense of evolution over time. Both groups also traced significant histories, with the AWARE-LA network being one of the oldest continuing efforts of its kind in the country. Louisville likewise had deep movement roots, shaped by strands of the Black Freedom Struggle that also helped birth the national network. Moreover, Louisville was home to Pam McMichael and Carla Wallace, the co-founders of SURJ, throughout data collection and writing. Buffalo was likewise important for a number of reasons. It is a rust belt city, and the chapter's makeup was understood as being more working class than many other SURJ chapters. It was also where some key national staff were based when I began the project. Logistically speaking, Buffalo was fairly close to me geographically, making it feasible to more regularly attend in-person meetings and actions.

Given that a comparative study of three groups in distinct cities seemed fairly robust unto itself, I had not initially assumed the parameters of the research would go beyond that. It was only through conversations with national founders and staff, particularly about mutual interest organizing, that I realized I needed to understand the organization's efforts to organize poor and working-class white communities in Appalachia. With that said, it took a bit more time and a broader range of methods to get a sufficient picture of these more rural formations.

Bedford County Listening Project is SURJ's oldest rural formation and had inspired a good deal of print journalism when I began this project. Moreover, the group came up often in interviews with SURJ founders, staff, and partners. For myriad logistical reasons, it was not until the end of data collection in 2024 that I was finally able to connect with lead organizer Kelly Sue Waller, who had worked with the group for seven years.

Kentucky People's Union (KPU) actually formed during the course of my research. I learned about the early steps to organize in eastern Kentucky during my interview with Beth Howard in 2022. Alicia Hurle, with whom I spoke a few months later, was in the process of launching the partnered Black Leadership Action Coalition of Kentucky (BLACK), and we also discussed KPU's first activities. Once KPU was holding regular membership meetings in 2023, I was able to join in group activities and later interviewed group leaders in early 2024.

I followed a few pathways to identify and interview Black and Latinx partners across the sites in this study. Five of the partners I interviewed were introduced to me by Carla Wallace alone, all of whom were based in Louisville. While the groups in Los Angeles and Buffalo were a bit more hands off in connecting me with their partner organization(s), which were understood to be operating at capacity already, they did point me to the appropriate contact information. This method yielded conversations with two partners in each city, fewer than I ultimately wished, and I hope that future studies might continue to push this line of inquiry. Nevertheless, I believe the quality, detail, and candor of the conversations I had with partners compensate some for the lack of quantity.

There is also the question of openness and transparency, which should be considered across all of my interviews but has a racialized dimension in my conversations with Black and Latinx organizers. A skeptical reader might wonder if I was only introduced to partners who had good things to say. Moreover, would politically conscious organizers, particularly those organizing Black and Latinx communities, really open up to a white researcher? I cannot fully account for or correct for this of course, and this may partially explain why some partners never responded to my interview request. I can report that, among those who did speak with me, partners were quite frank about their relationships with SURJ groups over time as well as what they identified as organizational areas for growth. They also sometimes discussed live struggles in their own efforts, which I saw as an indication of some level of openness, even as I was quite clear that my aims were not to evaluate BIPOC-led organizing.

DATA COLLECTION

The primary source of data for this project is interviews with fifty-eight antiracist activists, following a purposive sampling procedure, using my own networks, followed by snowball sampling. I sought to identify long-term antiracist organizers both within and outside of SURJ. Of those interviewed, twelve included SURJ founders (2), paid rural organizers (2), and other staff (8). Eleven were with Black (10) and non-Black Latinx (1) organizers who partner with one of the groups in this study, or the national organization. Twenty-eight were participants in the three urban groups and Kentucky People's Union. I also spoke to seven activists engaged in antiracist organizing but who were not involved with SURJ efforts. This subgroup included: participants in Catalyst Project (3), AWARE-LA (2), an early SURJ founder no longer involved with the organization (1), and a former SNCC participant deeply familiar with SURJ who had helped mentor SURJ participants (1). I interviewed these seven activists in order to gain important additional history, context, and commentary regarding the approaches this book explores from people I understood as movement experts. The table at the end of this appendix offers a visual overview of my interview participants.

Interviews were semi-structured and usually lasted an hour and a half, though six (with founders of SURJ, AWARE and Catalyst Project) were much longer—between three and five total hours, conducted over several sessions. I provided participants with a list of written questions ahead of time, so as to make the interview process as inviting and accessible as possible. This also allowed some participants time to consult their own records and send me helpful documents they might have saved, such as minutes from SURJ's first phone convening. Given that

TABLE A.1 Interview Participants*

	Name	Location	Role	Race/Ethnicity	Gender and Sexuality	Class
1	Anne Dunlap	Buffalo, NY	SURJ staff	white	woman, queer	middle
2	Erin Heaney	Buffalo, NY	SURJ staff	white	woman, queer	raised working, currently middle
3	Linnea Brett	Buffalo, NY	SURJ staff	white	woman, queer	working
4	Josie Diebold	Buffalo, NY	chapter member	white	woman, queer	middle
5	Steph	Buffalo, NY	chapter member	white	woman, straight	working
6	Tiffany	Buffalo, NY	chapter member	white	woman, queer	middle
7	Jill	Buffalo, NY	chapter member	white	woman, straight	working
8	Richard	Buffalo, NY	chapter member	white	man, straight	middle
9	Connor	Buffalo, NY	chapter member	white	man, straight	middle
10	Shontay Barnes	Buffalo, NY	chapter member and partner (to SURJ Buffalo)	Black	woman, queer	middle
11	Phylicia Brown	Buffalo, NY	partner (to SURJ Buffalo)	Black	woman, unspecified	raised poor, currently unspecified†
12	Carla Wallace	Louisville, KY‡	SURJ founder	white	woman, queer	raised mixed class, currently owning
13	Pam McMichael	Louisville, KY	SURJ founder	white	woman, queer	working
14	Z! Haukness	Louisville, KY	SURJ staff	white	nonbinary, queer	mixed
15	Sonja DeVries	Louisville, KY	chapter member	white	woman, queer	raised working, currently some precarity
16	David Horvath	Louisville, KY	chapter member	white	man, straight	raised poor, currently owning
17	Kate	Louisville, KY	chapter member	white	woman, unspecified	middle
18	Shameka Parrish-Wright	Louisville, KY	partner (to LSURJ)	Black	woman, straight	extreme precarity for much of life (including homelessness)

19	Karina Barillas	Louisville, KY	partner (to LSURJ)	Latina	woman, unspecified	raised poor, currently unspecified
20	Attica Scott	Louisville, KY	partner (to LSURJ)	Black	woman, straight	raised poor, currently middle
21	Alicia Hurle	Louisville, KY	partner (to LSURJ)	Black	woman, queer	middle
22	Ashanti Scott	Louisville, KY	partner (to LSURJ)	Black	woman, straight	working
23	Beth Howard	Lexington, KY	SURJ staff	white	woman, queer	working
24	Elliot Frederick	Ashland, KY	KPU member	white	nonbinary, queer	working
25	Amelia	Ashland, KY	KPU member	Mixed race, Black/white	woman, straight	working
26	Sean Farrington	Ashland, KY	KPU member	white	man, queer	working
27	Kelly Sue Waller	Shelbyville, TN	SURJ staff	white	woman, queer	raised poor, currently working
28	Dahlia Ferlito	Los Angeles, CA	chapter member	white	nonbinary, queer	raised working, currently middle
29	Liz Sutton	Los Angeles, CA	chapter member	white	woman, queer	middle
30	Hannah Jurs-Allen	Los Angeles, CA	chapter member	white	woman, queer	working
31	Halle Bills	Los Angeles, CA	chapter member	white	nonbinary, queer	middle
32	Kristen Brock-Petroshius	Los Angeles, CA	chapter member	white	woman, queer	raised working, currently middle
33	Jason David	Los Angeles, CA	chapter member	white	man, straight	upper middle
34	Kristina Lear	Los Angeles, CA	chapter member	white	woman, queer	middle
35	Ella	Los Angeles, CA	chapter member	white	woman, straight	middle
36	Rebecca	Los Angeles, CA	chapter member	white	woman, unspecified	middle
37	Naomi	Los Angeles, CA	chapter member	white	woman, straight	upper middle
38	Allen	Los Angeles, CA	chapter member	white	man, straight	working
39	Joe	Los Angeles, CA	chapter member	white	nonbinary, queer	upper middle

	Name	Location	Role	Race/Ethnicity	Gender and Sexuality	Class
40	Eric	Los Angeles, CA	chapter member	white	man, straight	working
41	Kit	Los Angeles, CA	chapter member	white	nonbinary, queer	working
42	Mary	Los Angeles, CA	chapter member	white	woman, unspecified	upper middle
43	Mark	Los Angeles, CA	chapter member	white	man, unspecified	middle
44	Nana Gyamfi	Los Angeles, CA	mentor/ supporter; partner (between BLM LA and WP4BL)	Black	woman, unspecified	unspecified
45	Michael Williams	Los Angeles, CA	partner (to WP4BL)	Black	man, straight	middle
46	Grace Aheron	Charlottesville, VA	SURJ staff	mixed race, Asian/white	woman, queer	upper middle
47	Misha Viets VanDyk	western MA	SURJ staff	white	woman, queer	working
48	Taryn Hallweaver	Boston metro area, MA	SURJ staff	white	woman, queer	middle
49	Julia Daniel	Bronx, NY	SURJ staff	white	woman, unspecified	raised working, some upward mobility
50	Jerome Scott	Atlanta, GA	partner (to SURJ national)	Black	man, straight	working
51	Paige Ingram	Minneapolis, MN	partner (to SURJ national)	Black	woman, unspecified	raised poor, currently middle
52	Shelly Tochluk	Los Angeles, CA	outside SURJ (AWARE LA)	white	woman, straight	upper middle
53	Cameron Levin	Los Angeles, CA	outside SURJ (formerly of AWARE LA)	white	man, unspecified	middle
54	Scott Winn	Seattle, WA	outside SURJ (though helped found network)	white	man, queer	raised working, currently middle

55	Elisabeth Long	San Franciso Bay Area, CA	outside SURJ (Catalyst)	white	woman, queer	working
56	Clare Bayard	San Francisco Bay Area, CA	outside SURJ (Catalyst)	white	nonbinary, queer	raised owning, currently mixed
57	Rochelle Watson	San Francisco Bay Area, CA	outside SURJ (Catalyst)	white	woman, unspecified	working
58	Penny Patch	Lyndonville, VT	outside SURJ (worked for SNCC)	white	woman, straight	raised owning, currently middle

*This table only includes study participants whom I formally interviewed. It is therefore not inclusive of everyone I write about in the book, as some research participants I met during fieldwork were never interviewed.

†"Unspecified" can mean that the participant did not want this information shared publicly or that the participant did not report the information.

‡The Louisville participants do not include the eight LSURJ chapter members who participated in Court Watch and were part of the focus group.

this study commenced in early 2021, when few had been vaccinated against the deadly coronavirus, Zoom or phone interviews were my only option. As this worked well, and as some participants reported, made it more feasible for them to participate, I continued to conduct interviews in this fashion.

Interviews broadly followed a similar course. I began by collecting basic demographic information and proceeded by asking what had brought participants into their movement work; how they had witnessed group practices evolve over time; the features of movement work that they saw as promising as well as challenges they believed they faced. For most participants, I also asked what their group was doing at present and why. Because different participants held distinct forms of knowledge, interviews were tailored and focused on those areas that each participant could treat with the greatest detail. Thus, an interview with a SURJ founder might focus on the network's early formation, while an interview with a Black partner would likely examine coalition dynamics.

In addition to interviews, I conducted just over a hundred hours of participant observation in meetings, trainings, and campaign activities, primarily though not exclusively with the three urban groups in this study. Fieldwork allowed me to connect the experiences and interpretations reported in interviews to more coordinated campaign efforts and to see a wider range of participants in interactive contexts. The hundred hours tally does not include time doing informal activities with participants, such as getting tours of cities to identify key protest locations, which I did in Louisville, or meeting with participants over coffee and meals to get updates on group dynamics, campaigns, and the like, which I did in both Los Angeles and Louisville. There is also no easy category in which to situate a focus group I conducted with eight members of LSURJ's Court Watch program. This hour-long session was one they offered and organized in early 2022 after I had myself participated in Court Watch.

The third form of data—particularly important to enhancing my research on SURJ's rural groups—included written, audio, and video media created by and about the groups in this study. These data included webinars hosted by the national organization, text-based information available on websites, and print and audio journalism about the various campaigns explored in this research. This range of video recordings, podcasts, and published writing allowed me to further contextualize participant observation as well as verify the accuracy of participant reports.

The naming conventions in this book are driven by participant preference. Early in the course of conducting interviews, many expressed feeling quite strongly about being named in association with their words. All of SURJ's staff, for instance, requested I use their full names whether I interviewed them formally or just witnessed them in action during fieldwork. There were also, however, study participants who did not want to be named. Some requested that I use only their first name, understanding that they would be recognizable to other movement participants but not to the general public. A smaller group affirmatively requested I assign them a pseudonym. There are two additional cases in which the participant did not make a clear decision and so is given a pseudonym out of prudence: (1) any participant whom I encountered only during fieldwork but never spoke with directly; and (2) those who left their naming preferences unclear during our interview and could not be reached again afterwards.

CHALLENGES

As a final note, I wish to acknowledge some of the challenges and potential pitfalls of doing research on white involvement in racial justice efforts. It is always a difficult time to write about race, racism, and antiracist efforts. Our current moment, however, is arguably particularly charged. On the political Right, the lane for argumentation has been so narrowed that, in some circles the very act of trying to accurately describe race socially and historically has been recast as itself "racist" and hateful. Meanwhile, on the political Left, what Olúfẹ́mi Táíwò terms "deference politics" can overdetermine who is permitted to speak or write about the dynamic social matters we face.[2]

Many of the white participants in this study are quite aware of this context, and getting access to the groups in this study was not always easy. As but one indicative example, one of the SURJ groups I approached early on seemed to struggle for months before deciding they could not be part of this research. Their concern was that allowing themselves to be studied and written about risked recentering whiteness and taking the focus away from BIPOC organizing, what Zachary Sunderman identifies as a common moral and epistemological dilemma faced by "white allies."[3] This logic is not unfamiliar, nor is it completely ill-founded. I too have faced the range of moments in which I have been riddled with doubt and deliberation regarding my ability to complete this project with sufficient nuance and clarity.

That said, the structure of self-doubt has shifted some as I have been at school with the people in this book. I have certainly pondered if I, particularly as someone raced white and with class privilege, could do this work with the integrity and clarity of vision required. As the project progressed, my concerns transitioned towards the slightly more generic. When I make the mistakes I am bound to make in this book, what is the likelihood of harm, and to what or whom? Perhaps such questions will be recognizable to some readers and are useful to keep tucked in a back pocket, to review every once and again, even as we continue to roll up our sleeves and, to quote Louisville organizer Shameka Parrish-Wright, "keep it moving."

Notes

Acknowledgments

1. Roscoe, Ayesha. 2024, October 13. "Ta-Nehisi Coates on Why Books Scare People: Up First from NPR." *NPR*. https://www.npr.org/transcripts/1211596752

Chapter 1

1. Jill is a pseudonym, as I only encountered her during fieldwork, as opposed to formally interviewing her, and we never communicated directly. I elaborate on naming conventions in the Appendix.

2. Britton-Purdy, Jedediah. 2016, March 21. "The Violent Remaking of Appalachia." *The Atlantic*. https://www.theatlantic.com/technology/archive/2016/03/the-violent-remaking-of-appalachia/474603/; Spencer, Naomi. 2015, November 26. "Ashland, Kentucky Steel Furnace Idled." *World Socialist Web Site*. https://www.wsws.org/en/articles/2015/11/26/appa-n26.html; Stein, Jeff. 2019, October 25. "Trump Boosted the U.S. Steel Industry. But in Kentucky, It Didn't Last." *Washington Post*. https://www.washingtonpost.com/business/economy/as-a-kentucky-mill-shutters-steelworkers-see-the-limits-of-trumps-intervention/2019/10/25/a27d3bb2-f02f-11e9-89eb-ec56cd414732_story.html

3. Nopper, Tamara (Kil Ja Kim). 2003, February 24. "The White Anti-Racist Is an Oxymoron." *The Anarchist Library*. https://theanarchistlibrary.org/library/tamara-k-nopper-the-white-anti-racist-is-an-oxymoron

4. Anderson, Carol. 2016. *White Rage: The Unspoken Truth of Our Racial Divide*. Bloomsbury; McVeigh, Rory, and Kevin Estep. 2019. *The Politics of Losing: Trump, the Klan, and the Mainstreaming of Resentment*. Columbia University Press; Fording, Richard, and Sanford Schram. 2020. *Hard White: The Mainstreaming of Racism in American Politics*. Oxford University Press.

5. Alexander, Michelle. 2020. *The New Jim Crow: Mass Incarceration in the Age of Colorblindness*, 10th anniversary ed. New Press; Ioanide, Paula. 2015. *The Emotional Politics of Racism: How Feelings Trump Facts in an Era of Colorblindness*. Stanford University Press.

6. HoSang, Daniel Martinez, and Joseph E. Lowndes. 2019. *Producers, Parasites, Patriots: Race and the New Right-Wing Politics of Precarity*. University of Minnesota Press.

7. Gest, Justin. 2016. *The New Minority: White Working Class Politics in an Age of Immigration and Inequality*. Oxford University Press; Metzl, Jonathan M. 2019. *Dying of Whiteness: How the Politics of Racial Resentment Is Killing America's Heartland*. Basic Books.

8. HoSang, Daniel Martinez. 2021. *A Wider Type of Freedom: How Struggles for Racial Justice Liberate Everyone*. University of California Press.

9. Barker, Joanne. 2021. *Red Scare: The State's Indigenous Terrorist*. University of California Press.

10. Paik, A. Naomi. 2020. *Bans, Walls, Raids, Sanctuary: Understanding U.S. Immigration for the Twenty-First Century*. University of California Press.

11. Maira, Sunaina. 2018. *Boycott!: The Academy and Justice for Palestine*. University of California Press.

12. Taylor, Keeanga-Yamahtta. 2016. *From #BlackLivesMatter to Black Liberation*. Haymarket Books; Ransby, Barbara. 2018. *Making All Black Lives Matter: Reimagining Freedom in the Twenty-First Century*. University of California Press.

13. Jardina, Ashley. 2019. *White Identity Politics*. Cambridge University Press; Torkelson, Jason, and Douglas Hartmann. 2021. "The Heart of Whiteness: On the Study of Whiteness and White Americans." *Sociology Compass* 15(11). doi:10.1111/soc4.12932; McDermott, Monica, and Annie Ferguson. 2022. "Sociology of Whiteness." *Annual Review of Sociology* 48(1):257–276. doi:10.1146/annurev-soc-083121-054338

14. Aptheker, Herbert. 1993. *Anti-Racism in U.S. History: The First Two Hundred Years*. Praeger; Thompson, Becky. 2001. *A Promise and a Way of Life: White Antiracist Activism*. University of Minnesota Press.

15. Du Bois, W. E. B. 1998 [1935]. *Black Reconstruction in America, 1860–1880*. Free Press; Mills, Charles W. 1997. *The Racial Contract*. Cornell University Press; Lipsitz, George. 2018. *The Possessive Investment in Whiteness: How White People Profit from Identity Politics*, 20th anniversary ed. Temple University Press; McGhee, Heather. 2021. *The Sum of Us: What Racism Costs Everyone and How We Can Prosper Together*. One World.

16. Sheppard, Barry. 1965. "Interview with Malcolm X." *Young Socialist* 5(3). https://blackagendareport.com/interview-malcolm-x-and-young-socialist-1965]]; Carmichael, Stokely. 1966, September 22. "What We Want." *New York Review of Books*. https://www.nybooks.com/articles/1966/09/22/what-we-want/; Anony-

mous. 1968, August. "Huey Newton Talks to the Movement About the Black Panther Party, Cultural Nationalism, SNCC, Liberals and White Revolutionaries." *The Movement*, 8–11; Middlebrook, Jeb. 2010. "The Ballot Box and Beyond: The (Im)Possibilities of White Antiracist Organizing." *American Quarterly* 62(2):233–252; Benally, Klee. 2013. "Klee Benally on Decolonization." *Unsettling America*. https://unsettlingamerica.wordpress.com/2013/07/26/klee-benally-on-decolonization/; Mott, Carrie. 2019. "Precious Work: White Anti-Racist Pedagogies in Southern Arizona." *Social & Cultural Geography* 20(2):178–197. doi:10.1080/14649365.2017.1355067

17. SNCC Position Paper for the Vine City Project. 1966. freedomarchives.org/Documents/Finder/DOC513_scans/SNCC/513.SNCC.black.power.summer.1966.pdf, p. 1.

18. Jeffries, Hasan Kwame. 2009. *Bloody Lowndes: Civil Rights and Black Power in Alabama's Black Belt*. NYU Press.

19. McAdam, Doug. 1988. *Freedom Summer*. New York: Oxford University Press; Carson, Clayborne. 1995. *In Struggle: SNCC and the Black Awakening of the 1960s*, 2nd ed. Cambridge: Harvard University Press.

20. SNCC Position Paper 1966, 2.

21. Robnett, Belinda. 1997. *How Long? How Long? African American Women in the Struggle for Civil Rights*. Oxford University Press.

22. Cited in Carson 1995, 102.

23. Carson 1995; Forman, James. 1997. *The Making of Black Revolutionaries*, illustrated ed. University of Washington; Holsaert, Faith S., Martha Prescod Norman Noonan, Judy Richardson, Betty Garman Robinson, Jean Smith Young, and Dorothy M. Zellner, eds. 2012. *Hands on the Freedom Plow: Personal Accounts by Women in SNCC*. University of Illinois Press.

24. McAdam 1988; Carson 1995; Robnett 1997.

25. Ibid.

26. Robnett 1997; Payne, Charles M. 2007. *I've Got the Light of Freedom: The Organizing Tradition and the Mississippi Freedom Struggle*, 2nd ed., with a new preface. University of California Press.

27. McAdam 1988; Thompson 2001.

28. Sonnie, Amy, and James Tracy. 2011. *Hillbilly Nationalists, Urban Race Rebels, and Black Power: Community Organizing in Radical Times*, illustrated ed. Melville House, 28.

29. Carmichael 1966; King Jr., Martin Luther. 2010 [1968]. *Where Do We Go from Here: Chaos or Community?* Beacon Press.

30. Carson 1995; Randolph, A. Philip, and Bayard Rustin. 1967, January. "The Civil-Rights Movement's Plan to End Poverty, Annotated." *The Atlantic*. https://www.theatlantic.com/magazine/archive/2018/02/a-freedom-budget-for-all-americans-annotated/557024/; Clemons, Jared. 2022. "From 'Freedom Now!' to

'Black Lives Matter': Retrieving King and Randolph to Theorize Contemporary White Antiracism." *Perspectives on Politics* 1–15. doi:10.1017/S1537592722001074

31. Le Blanc, Paul, and Michael D. Yates. 2013. *A Freedom Budget for All Americans: Recapturing the Promise of the Civil Rights Movement in the Struggle for Economic Justice Today.* NYU Press, 33; for something of a counterargument, see: O'Dell, Jack. 2010. "On the Transition from Civil Rights to Civil Equality," in *Climbin' Jacob's Ladder, The Black Freedom Movement Writings of Jack O'Dell*, ed. N. P. Singh. University of California Press, 222–254.

32. Du Bois 1998; Baldwin, James. 2021. *The Price of the Ticket: Collected Nonfiction: 1948–1985*, reprint ed. Beacon Press; Sullivan, Shannon. 2014. *Good White People: The Problem with Middle-Class White Anti-Racism.* SUNY Press.

33. Smedley, Audrey. 2011. *Race in North America: Origin and Evolution of a Worldview*, 4th ed. Oxford: Taylor & Francis; Allen, Theodore. 1997. *The Invention of the White Race, Vol. 2: Racial Oppression and Social Control.* Verso.

34. Alexander 2020.

35. Mills 1997.

36. Du Bois 1998, 700.

37. Melamed, Jodi. 2015. "Racial Capitalism." *Critical Ethnic Studies* 1(1):79,

38. Robinson, Cedric. 1983. *Black Marxism: The Making of the Black Radical Tradition.* Zed Books; HoSang and Lowndes 2019.

39. Robinson 1983; Eddins, Crystal Nicole. 2022. "Racial Capitalism and Black Social Movements," in *Race and Space, Vol. 46: Research in Social Movements, Conflicts and Change*, ed. L. Leitz. Emerald Publishing, 11–36.

40. Roediger, David R. 1994. *The Wages of Whiteness: Race and the Making of the American Working Class.* Verso.

41. Ignatiev, Noel. 1995. *How the Irish Became White.* Routledge; Brodkin, Karen. 1998. *How Jews Became White Folks and What That Says About Race in America.* Rutgers University Press.

42. Lipsitz 2018.

43. Harris, Cheryl. 1993. "Whiteness as Property." *Harvard Law Review* 106(8): 1707–1791.

44. Katznelson, Ira. 2006. *When Affirmative Action Was White: An Untold History of Racial Inequality in Twentieth-Century America*, reprint ed. Norton; Lipsitz 2018.

45. Quadagno, Jill. 1996. *The Color of Welfare: How Racism Undermined the War on Poverty.* Oxford University Press; Haney López, Ian. 2015. *Dog Whistle Politics: How Coded Racial Appeals Have Reinvented Racism and Wrecked the Middle Class*, reprint ed. Oxford University Press; McGhee 2021.

46. Ioanide 2015, 15; see too: Fanon, Frantz. 2008 [1952]. *Black Skin, White Masks*, revised ed. Grove Press.

47. Anderson 2016.

48. Gest 2016; Metzl 2019.

49. On education: Dhaliwal, Tasminda K., Mark J. Chin, Virginia S. Lovison, and David M. Quinn. 2020. *Educator Bias Is Associated with Racial Disparities in Student Achievement and Discipline.* Brookings Institute.

On socially structured health outcomes: Brown, Lauren, and Reginald Tucker-Seeley. 2018. "Commentary: Will 'Deaths of Despair' Among Whites Change How We Talk About Racial/Ethnic Health Disparities?" *Ethnicity & Disease* 28(2):123–128. doi:10.18865/ed.28.2.123

On wealth: Oliver, Melvin, and Thomas M. Shapiro. 2006. *Black Wealth / White Wealth: A New Perspective on Racial Inequality,* 2nd ed. Routledge.

On housing market: Korver-Glenn, Elizabeth. 2018. "Compounding Inequalities: How Racial Stereotypes and Discrimination Accumulate Across the Stages of Housing Exchange." *American Sociological Review* 83(4): 627–656. doi:10.1177/0003122418781774.

On voting: Bentele, Keith G., and Erin E. O'Brien. 2013. "Jim Crow 2.0? Why States Consider and Adopt Restrictive Voter Access Policies." *Perspectives on Politics* 11(4):1088–1116. doi:10.1017/S1537592713002843; Codrington III, Wilfred. 2019, November 17. "The Electoral College's Racist Origins." *The Atlantic.* https://www.theatlantic.com/ideas/archive/2019/11/electoral-college-racist-origins/601918/

On state violence: Pierson, Emma, Camelia Simoiu, Jan Overgoor, Sam Corbett-Davies, Daniel Jenson, Amy Shoemaker, Vignesh Ramachandran, Phoebe Barghouty, Cheryl Phillips, Ravi Shroff, and Sharad Goel. 2020. "A Large-Scale Analysis of Racial Disparities in Police Stops Across the United States." *Nature Human Behaviour* 4(7):736–745. doi:10.1038/s41562-020-0858-1; Soss, Joe, Richard C. Fording, and Sanford F. Schram. 2011. *Disciplining the Poor: Neoliberal Paternalism and the Persistent Power of Race.* University of Chicago Press; Alexander 2020.

On "slow violence": Nixon, Rob. 2011. *Slow Violence and the Environmentalism of the Poor.* Harvard University Press.

On water: Deitz, Shiloh, and Katie Meehan. 2019. "Plumbing Poverty: Mapping Hot Spots of Racial and Geographic Inequality in U.S. Household Water Insecurity." *Annals of the American Association of Geographers* 109(4):1092–1109. doi:10.1080/24694452.2018.1530587

On air: Dillon, Lindsey, and Julie Sze. 2016. "Police Power and Particulate Matters: Environmental Justice and the Spatialities of In/Securities in U.S. Cities." *English Language Notes* 54(2):13–23.

50. Du Bois 1998; Sullivan 2014; HoSang 2021; Baldwin, James. 2021. *The Price of the Ticket: Collected Nonfiction: 1948–1985,* reprint ed. Beacon Press.

51. HoSang and Loundes 2019; McDermott, Monica. 2020. *Whiteness in America.* Polity; Torkelson and Hartmann 2021; Ioanide, Paula. 2021. "Apocalyptic

Fears in a Time of Dying (of) Whiteness." *Journal of Speculative Philosophy* 35(4): 323–48. doi: 10.5325/jspecphil.35.4.0323

52. Barnes, Shailly Gupta. 2015, June 17. "50 Years of Poor People's Organizing: An Interview with Bob Zellner." *Kairos Center*. https://kairoscenter.org/50-years-of-poor-peoples-organizing-an-interview-with-bob-zellner/; Holsaert et al. 2012.

53. Sonnie and Tracy 2011.

54. Williams, Jakobi. 2013. *From the Bullet to the Ballot: The Illinois Chapter of the Black Panther Party and Racial Coalition Politics in Chicago*. University of North Carolina Press.

55. Breines, Wini. 1989. *Community and Organization in the New Left, 1962–1968: The Great Refusal*, new ed. Rutgers University Press; Thompson 2001.

56. Berger, Dan. 2005. *Outlaws of America: The Weather Underground and the Politics of Solidarity*. AK Press; Sonnie and Tracy, 2011.

57. Portelli, Alessandro. 1991. *The Death of Luigi Trastulli and Other Stories: Form and Meaning in Oral History*. SUNY Press; Hill, Herbert. 1996. "The Problem of Race in American Labor History." *Reviews in American History* 24(2):189–208; Santow, Mark. 2023. *Saul Alinsky and the Dilemmas of Race: Community Organizing in the Postwar City*. University of Chicago Press.

58. Hill, Herbert. 1982. "The AFL-CIO and the Black Worker: Twenty-Five Years After the Merger." *Journal of Intergroup Relations* 19(1):193.

59. Inouye, Mie. 2022. "Starting with People Where They Are: Ella Baker's Theory of Political Organizing." *American Political Science Review* 116(2):533–546. doi:10.1017/S0003055421001015

60. Dobbie, David, and Katie Richards-Schuster. 2008. "Building Solidarity Through Difference: A Practice Model for Critical Multicultural Organizing." *Journal of Community Practice* 16(3):317–337; Beeman, Angie. 2022. *Liberal White Supremacy: How Progressives Silence Racial and Class Oppression*. University of Georgia Press.

61. Forman, James. 1997. *The Making of Black Revolutionaries: Illustrated Edition*. University of Washington; Holsaert et al. 2012.

62. McAdam 1988.

63. Taylor, Verta. 1989. "Social Movement Continuity: The Women's Movement in Abeyance." *American Sociological Review* 54(5):761–775. doi:10.2307/2117752; Oliver, Pamela, Chaeyoon Lim, Morgan Matthews, and Alex Hanna. 2022. "Black Protests in the United States, 1994 to 2010." *Sociological Science* 9: 275–312. doi:10.15195/v9.a12

64. Warren, Mark. 2010. *Fire in the Heart: How White Activists Embrace Racial Justice*. Oxford University Press, 209.

65. Gilmore, Ruth Wilson. 1998. "Globalisation and US Prison Growth: From Military Keynesianism to Post-Keynesian Militarism." *Race & Class* 40(2/3):171–

188. doi:10.1177/030639689904000212; Camp, Jordan T. 2016. *Incarcerating the Crisis: Freedom Struggles and the Rise of the Neoliberal State*. University of California Press.

66. Bonilla-Silva, Eduardo. 2021. *Racism Without Racists: Color-Blind Racism and the Persistence of Racial Inequality in America*, 6th ed. Rowman & Littlefield.

67. Haney López 2015; Ioanide 2015.

68. Maxwell, Angie, and Todd Shields. 2019. *The Long Southern Strategy: How Chasing White Voters in the South Changed American Politics*, illustrated ed. Oxford University Press.

69. Cited in Alexander 2020, 56.

70. Gilmore, Ruth Wilson. 2007. *Golden Gulag: Prisons, Surplus, Crisis, and Opposition in Globalizing California*. University of California Press.

71. Duggan, Lisa. 2004. *The Twilight of Equality? Neoliberalism, Cultural Politics, and the Attack on Democracy*. Beacon Press; Harvey, David. 2005. *A Brief History of Neoliberalism*. Oxford University Press; Giroux, Henry A. 2008. *Against the Terror of Neoliberalism: Politics Beyond the Age of Greed*. Routledge.

72. Dylan Rodriquez defines the carceral state as a form of governance that "institutionalizes various forms of human capture"; Rodriquez, Dylan. 2019. "Abolition as Praxis of Human Being: A Foreword." *Harvard Law Review* 132:1576.

73. Wacquant, Loïc. 2009. *Punishing the Poor: The Neoliberal Government of Social Insecurity*. Duke University Press.

74. Davis, Angela Y. 2003. *Are Prisons Obsolete?* Seven Stories Press; Gilmore 2007.

75. Tyler, Imogen. 2013. *Revolting Subjects: Social Abjection and Resistance in Neoliberal Britain*. Zed Books; Ioanide 2015.

76. Denning, Michael. 1997. *The Cultural Front: The Laboring of American Culture in the Twentieth Century*. Verso; Kelley, Robin D. G. 2003. *Freedom Dreams: The Black Radical Imagination*, new ed. Beacon Press; Widener, Daniel. 2010. *Black Arts West: Culture and Struggle in Postwar Los Angeles*. Duke University Press; Ontiveros, Randy J. 2014. *In the Spirit of a New People: The Cultural Politics of the Chicano Movement*. NYU Press; Camp 2016; Burris, Greg. 2019. *The Palestinian Idea: Film, Media, and the Radical Imagination*. Temple University Press.

77. Scott, James C. 1987. *Weapons of the Weak: Everyday Forms of Peasant Resistance*. Yale University Press; Bayat, Asef. 2013. *Life as Politics: How Ordinary People Change the Middle East*, 2nd ed. Stanford University Press.

78. See, for instance: Taylor 2016; Ransby 2018; Woodly, Deva R. 2021. *Reckoning: Black Lives Matter and the Democratic Necessity of Social Movements*. Oxford University Press.

79. Ransby 2018, 70.

80. Board Jr., Marcus. 2022. *Invisible Weapons: Infiltrating Resistance and Defeating Movements*. Oxford University Press; Simpson, Chaniqua D., Avery

Walter, and Kim Ebert. 2021. "'Brainwashing for the Right Reasons with the Right Message': Ideology and Political Subjectivity in Black Organizing." *Mobilization: An International Quarterly* 26(4):401–20. doi: 10.17813/1086-671X-26-4-401

81. Ransby 2018, 2.

82. BlackPast, B. 2012, November 16. "(1977) The Combahee River Collective Statement." *BlackPast.org*. https://www.blackpast.org/african-american-history/combahee-river-collective-statement-1977/

83. Garza, Alicia. 2014, October 7. "A Herstory of the #BlackLivesMatter Movement by Alicia Garza." *The Feminist Wire.* https://thefeministwire.com/2014/10/blacklivesmatter-2/

84. Jung, Moon-Kie, and João H. Costa Vargas. 2021. *Antiblackness*. Duke University Press.

85. Case, Kim A. 2012. "Discovering the Privilege of Whiteness: White Women's Reflections on Anti-Racist Identity and Ally Behavior." *Journal of Social Issues* 68(1):18.

86. Kelly, Erin, and Frank Dobbin. 1998. "How Affirmative Action Became Diversity Management: Employer Response to Anti-Discrimination Law, 1961 to 1996." *American Behavioral Scientist* 41(7):960–984. doi:10.1177/0002764298041007008; Berrey, Ellen. 2015. *The Enigma of Diversity: The Language of Race and the Limits of Racial Justice*. University of Chicago Press; Mayorga-Gallo, Sarah. 2019. "The White-Centering Logic of Diversity Ideology." *American Behavioral Scientist* 63(13):1789–1809. doi:10.1177/0002764219842619

87. Srivastava, Sakita. 1996. "Song and Dance? The Performance of Antiracist Workshops." *Canadian Review of Sociology/Revue Canadienne de Sociologie* 33(3):291–315. doi:10.1111/j.1755-618X.1996.tb02454.x; Blake, Felice, Paula Ioanide, and Alison Reed. 2019. *Antiracism Inc.: Why the Way We Talk About Racial Justice Matters*. Punctum Books; Thomas, James M. 2020. *Diversity Regimes: Why Talk Is Not Enough to Fix Racial Inequality at Universities*. Rutgers University Press.

88. Scott, Ellen K. 2000. "Everyone Against Racism: Agency and the Production of Meaning in the Anti-Racism Practices of Two Feminist Organizations." *Theory and Society* 29(6):785–818.

89. Bell, Joyce M., and Douglas Hartmann. 2007. "Diversity in Everyday Discourse: The Cultural Ambiguities and Consequences of 'Happy Talk.'" *American Sociological Review* 72(6):895–914. doi:10.1177/000312240707200603; Ahmed, Sara. 2007. "The Language of Diversity." *Ethnic and Racial Studies* 30(2):235–256. doi:10.1080/01419870601143927

90. Gordon, Avery F., and Christopher Newfield, eds. 1996. *Mapping Multiculturalism*. University of Minnesota Press.

91. Sivanandan, A. 1985. "RAT and the Degradation of Black Struggle." *Race & Class* 26(4):1–33; Middlebrook 2010; Aouragh, Miriyam. 2019. "'White Privi-

lege' and Shortcuts to Anti-Racism." *Race & Class* 61(2):3–26. doi:10.1177/0306396819874629

92. Sullivan 2014; Beeman 2022.

93. Segrest, Mab. 1999. *Memoir of a Race Traitor*. South End Press; Warren 2010; Ball, Amanda C. 2022. "I Know Why the White Lady Cries: Growing Pains of an Antiracist Cleft Habitus." *Social Problems* 70(3): 598–615; Sunderman, Zachary. 2023. *Dilemmas of Allyship: White Anti-Racists and the Challenges of Social Justice*. Routledge.

94. Middlebrook 2010, 237–238.

95. Hazelbaker, Taylor, Christa Spears Brown, Lindsey Nenadal, and Rashmita Mistry. 2022. "Fostering Anti-Racism in White Children and Youth: Development Within Contexts." *American Psychologist* 77(4):497–509.

96. Ford, Kristie A., and Josephine Orlandella. 2015. "The 'Not-So-Final Remark': The Journey to Becoming White Allies." *Sociology of Race and Ethnicity* 1(2):287–301.

97. Srivastava 1996; Srivastava, Sarita. 2005. "'You're Calling Me a Racist?' The Moral and Emotional Regulation of Antiracism and Feminism." *Signs: Journal of Women in Culture and Society* 31(1):29–62. doi:10.1086/432738; McKinney, Karyn D. 2005. *Being White: Stories of Race and Racism*. Routledge; Boatright-Horowitz, Su, Marisa Marraccini, and Yvette Harps-Logan. 2012. "Teaching Antiracism: College Students' Emotional and Cognitive Reactions to Learning About White Privilege." *Journal of Black Studies* 43(8):893–911; Evans-Winters, Venus E., and Dorothy E. Hines. 2020. "Unmasking White Fragility: How Whiteness and White Student Resistance Impacts Anti-Racist Education." *Whiteness and Education* 5(1):1–16. doi:10.1080/23793406.2019.1675182

98. Sue, Derald Wing. 2017. "The Challenges of Becoming a White Ally." *Counseling Psychologist* 45(5):713. doi:10.1177/0011000017719323

99. McIntosh, Peggy. 1989. "White Privilege: Unpacking the Invisible Knapsack." *Peace and Freedom Magazine* (July/August):10–12.

100. Bonilla-Silva 2021.

101. Leonardo, Zeus. 2004. "The Color of Supremacy: Beyond the Discourse of 'White Privilege.'" *Educational Philosophy and Theory* 36(2):138.

102. Blum, Lawrence. 2008. "'White Privilege': A Mild Critique." *Theory and Research in Education* 6(3):309–321.

103. Ibid.; Lensmire, Timothy, Shannon McManimon, Jessica Tierney, Mary Lee-Nichols, Zachary Casey, Audrey Lensmire, and Bryan Davis. 2013. "McIntosh as Synecdoche: How Teacher Education's Focus on White Privilege Undermines Antiracism." *Harvard Educational Review* 83(3):410–431.

104. Levine-Rasky, Cynthia. 2000. "Framing Whiteness: Working Through the Tensions in Introducing Whiteness to Educators." *Race Ethnicity and Education* 3(3):271–292. doi:10.1080/713693039; Lensmire et al. 2013.

105. Srivastava 1996; Mott 2019; Táíwò, Olúfẹ́mi O. 2022. *Elite Capture: How the Powerful Took over Identity Politics.* Haymarket Books.

106. Felice Blake and Paula Ioanide, cited in Lipsitz, George. 2014. "'Standing at the Crossroads': Why Race, State Violence, and Radical Movements Matter Now," in *The Rising Tide of Color: Race, State Violence, and Radical Movements Across the Pacific,* ed. M.-H. Jung. University of Washington Press, 62.

107. Tuck, Eve, and K. Wayne Yang. 2012. "Decolonization Is Not a Metaphor." *Decolonization: Indigeneity, Education & Society* 1(1):10.

108. Ibid., 19.

109. Hanisch, Carol. 1969. "The Personal Is Political." *Carol Hanisch.* http://www.carolhanisch.org/CHwritings/PIP.html

110. Sumerau, J. E., TehQuin D. Forbes, Eric Joy Denise, and Lain A. B. Mathers. 2021. "Constructing Allyship and the Persistence of Inequality." *Social Problems* 68(2):358–373. doi:10.1093/socpro/spaa003

111. Perry, Samuel L., Kenneth E. Frantz, and Joshua B. Grubbs. 2021. "Who Identifies as Anti-Racist? Racial Identity, Color-Blindness, and Generic Liberalism." *Socius: Sociological Research for a Dynamic World* 7:237802312110529. doi:10.1177/23780231211052945

112. Ray, Ranita. 2023. "Race-Conscious Racism: Alibis for Racial Harm in the Classroom." *Social Problems* 70(3):683. doi:10.1093/socpro/spac009

113. Sullivan 2014, 102.

114. Ibid.

115. McDermott, Monica. 2006. *Working-Class White: The Making and Unmaking of Race Relations.* University of California Press; Wray, Matt. 2006. *Not Quite White: White Trash and the Boundaries of Whiteness.* Duke University Press; HoSang and Lowndes 2019.

116. See Beeman 2022, 44, for extended discussion.

117. Hughey, Matthew. 2012. *White Bound: Nationalists, Antiracists, and the Shared Meanings of Race.* Stanford University Press.

118. Sharp, Gene. 2011. *Sharp's Dictionary of Power and Struggle: Language of Civil Resistance in Conflicts.* Oxford University Press; Shafi, Azfar, and Ilyas Nagdee. 2020, October. "*Recovering Antiracism: Reflections on Collectivity and Solidarity in Antiracist Organizing.*" Transnational Institute. https://www.tni.org/files/publication-downloads/antiracism_online.pdf

119. Haider, Asad. 2018. *Mistaken Identity: Mass Movements and Racial Ideology.* Verso; Táíwò 2022.

120. Woodly 2021; Reed, Allison S. 2023. "Repertoires of Care and Activist Sustainability in U.S. Social Justice Organizing." *Mobilization: An International Quarterly* 28(2):209–228.

121. Thompson 2001; Warren 2010.

122. Sheppard 1965; Carmichael 1966; Anonymous 1968; Middlebrook 2010; Benally 2013; Mott 2019.

123. Gorski, Paul C., and Noura Erakat. 2019. "Racism, Whiteness, and Burnout in Antiracism Movements: How White Racial Justice Activists Elevate Burnout in Racial Justice Activists of Color in the United States." *Ethnicities* 19(5): 784–808.

124. Ball 2022, 6.

125. Garza, Alicia. 2020, October 19. "When Movements Are Guilty of What They Are Trying to Challenge." *The Atlantic*. https://www.theatlantic.com/ideas/archive/2020/10/how-to-build-a-multiracial-movement/616762/

126. Garcia, Ruben J. 2002. "New Voices at Work: Race and Gender Identity Caucuses in the U.S. Labor Movement." *Scholarly Works*, 659. https://scholars.law.unlv.edu/facpub/659

127. Du Bois 1998; Carson 1995; Le Blanc and Yates 2013; Clemons 2022.

128. Sullivan 2014; al-Gharbi, Musa. 2019. "Resistance as Sacrifice: Toward an Ascetic Antiracism." *Sociological Forum* 34(S1):1197–1216. doi:10.1111/socf.12544; Beeman 2022.

129. Wing, Bob. 2018. *Toward Racial Justice and a Third Reconstruction*. Lulu Press.

130. Rodden, Jonathan A. 2019. *Why Cities Lose: The Deep Roots of the Urban-Rural Political Divide*. Basic Books.

131. Maxwell and Shields 2019.

132. Codrington 2019.

133. Ross II, Bertrall L. 2020. "Partisan Gerrymandering as a Threat to Multiracial Democracy." *Southwestern Law Review* 50(3):509–525.

134. Anderson 2016; Alexander 2020.

135. Bentele and O'Brien 2013.

136. Rosenblum, April. 2024. "How to Vote Like a Radical." *April Rosenblum*. https://www.aprilrosenblum.com/longgameblog/how-to-vote-like-a-radical; Morales, Aurora Levins. 2024, September 11. "Midnight in the Latrines, Again." *Convergence Magazine*. https://convergencemag.com/articles/midnight-in-the-latrines-again/

137. Tatum, Beverly Daniel. 1994. "Teaching White Students About Racism: The Search for White Allies and the Restoration of Hope." *Teachers College Record* 95(4):462–472; O'Brien, Eileen. 2001. *Whites Confront Racism: Antiracists and Their Paths to Action*. Rowman & Littlefield; Thompson 2001; Torkelson and Hartmann 2021.

138. Thompson 2001, xv.

139. O'Brien 2001; Burnett, Lynn. 2022, May 20. "White Antiracist History; White Antiracist Mobilization: The Vision Statement for the White Antiracist

Ancestry Project." *Medium*. Retrieved August 1, 2023. https://burnett-lynn.medium.com/white-antiracist-history-white-antiracist-mobilization-the-vision-statement-for-the-white-1a6ff4f86d43

140. Rodriguez, Dylan. 2006. *Forced Passages: Imprisoned Radical Intellectuals and the U.S. Prison Regime*. University of Minnesota Press.

141. Estes, Nick. 2019. *Our History Is the Future: Standing Rock Versus the Dakota Access Pipeline, and the Long Tradition of Indigenous Resistance*. Verso.

142. Kauanui, J. Kēhaulani. 2008. "Colonialism in Equality: Hawaiian Sovereignty and the Question of U.S. Civil Rights." *South Atlantic Quarterly* 107(4):635–650. doi:10.1215/00382876-2008-010; Mott 2019.

143. Whaley, Rick, and Walter Bresette. 1993. *Walleye Warriors: An Effective Alliance Against Racism and for the Earth*. New Society; Grossman, Zoltán. 2017. *Unlikely Alliances: Native Nations and White Communities Join to Defend Rural Lands*. University of Washington Press; Powell, Dana E., and Ricki Draper. 2020. "Making It Home: Solidarity and Belonging in the #NoDAPL/Standing Rock Encampments." *Collaborative Anthropologies* 13(1):1–45. doi:10.1353/cla.2020.0003

144. Jung and Vargas 2021.

145. BlackPast 2012; Garza 2014; Hannah-Jones, Nikole. 2019, August 14. "The 1619 Project." *New York Times*.

146. O'Brien 2001: Thompson 2001: Warren 2010.

147. Hughey 2012; Sullivan 2014; Beeman 2022.

148. Burley, Shane. 2017. *Fascism Today: What It Is and How to End It*. Oakland: AK Press; Fording and Schram 2020; Blee, Kathleen M., Robert Futrell, and Pete Simi. 2023. *Out of Hiding: Extremist White Supremacy and How It Can Be Stopped*. Routledge.

Chapter 2

1. Taylor, Keeanga-Yamahtta. 2016. *From #BlackLivesMatter to Black Liberation*. Haymarket Books; Anderson, Carol. 2016. *White Rage: The Unspoken Truth of Our Racial Divide*. Bloomsbury; McVeigh, Rory, and Kevin Estep. 2019. *The Politics of Losing: Trump, the Klan, and the Mainstreaming of Resentment*. Columbia University Press.

2. Bonilla-Silva, Eduardo, and Victor Ray. 2015. "Getting over the Obama Hope Hangover," in *Theories of Race and Ethnicity: Contemporary Debates and Perspectives*, eds. K. Murji and J. Solomos. Cambridge University Press.

3. Heaney, Erin. 2023. "Winning White People to the Fight Against the MAGA Right." *The Forge*. https://forgeorganizing.org/article/winning-white-people-fight-against-maga-right

4. Preskill, Stephen. 2021. *Education in Black and White: Myles Horton and the Highlander Center's Vision for Social Justice*. University of California Press.

5. Morris, Aldon. 1984. *The Origins of the Civil Rights Movements: Black Communities Organizing for Change*. Free Press, 140.

6. While I later learned that Horton termed the school's pedagogy "yeasty education," Pam was not aware of this connection when she used this phrase. See: Inouye, Mie. 2019, April 3. "The Highlander Idea." *Jacobin*. https://jacobin.com/2019/04/highlander-folk-school-tennessee-organizing-movements

7. Fosl, Catherine. 2002. *Subversive Southerner: Anne Braden and the Struggle for Racial Justice in the Cold War South*. Palgrave Macmillan; Burnett, Lynn. 2022, May 20. "White Antiracist History; White Antiracist Mobilization: The Vision Statement for the White Antiracist Ancestry Project." *Medium*. https://burnett-lynn.medium.com/white-antiracist-history-white-antiracist-mobilization-the-vision-statement-for-the-white-1a6ff4f86d43

8. Fosl 2002.

9. Burnett 2018.

10. Morris, Aldon. 1984. *The Origins of the Civil Rights Movements: Black Communities Organizing for Change*. Free Press; Carson, Clayborne. 1995. *In Struggle: SNCC and the Black Awakening of the 1960s*, 2nd ed. Harvard University Press; Payne, Charles M. 2007. *I've Got the Light of Freedom: The Organizing Tradition and the Mississippi Freedom Struggle,* 2nd ed., with a new preface. University of California Press; Ransby, Barbara. 2003. *Ella Baker and the Black Freedom Movement: A Radical Democratic Vision*. University of North Carolina Press; HoSang, Daniel Martinez. 2021. *A Wider Type of Freedom: How Struggles for Racial Justice Liberate Everyone*. University of California Press.

11. Ransby 2003, 233.

12. Payne 2007; Hosang 2021.

13. Fosl 2002; Payne 2007; Hosang 2021; Inouye, Mie. 2022. "Starting with People Where They Are: Ella Baker's Theory of Political Organizing." *American Political Science Review* 116(2):533–546. doi:10.1017/S0003055421001015

14. Ransby 2018, 19.

15. Thompson, Becky. 2001. *A Promise and a Way of Life: White Antiracist Activism*. University of Minnesota Press, 384.

16. Hosang 2021, 57.

17. Martinas, Sharon, and Mickey Ellinger. 2010. "'Passing It On': Reflections of a White Anti-Racist Solidarity Organizer," in *Accountability and White Anti-Racist Organizing: Stories from Our Work*, eds. B. B. Cushing, L. Cabbil, M. Freeman, J. Hitchcock, K. Richards, and R. Chisom. Crandall, Dostie & Douglass Books, 141–168.

18. https://www.corpwatch.org/article/where-was-color-seattle

19. Ford, Kristie A. 2012. "Shifting White Ideological Scripts: The Educational Benefits of Inter- and Intraracial Curricular Dialogues on the Experiences of

White College Students." *Journal of Diversity in Higher Education* 5(3):138–158. doi:10.1037/a0028917; Blitz, Lisa V., and Benjamin G. Kohl. 2012. "Addressing Racism in the Organization: The Role of White Racial Affinity Groups in Creating Change." *Administration in Social Work* 36(5):479–498. doi:10.1080/03643107.2011.624261

20. Goldberg, Susan, and Cameron Levin. 2009. "Towards a Radical White Identity." *Square Space*. https://static1.squarespace.com/static/581e9e06ff7c509a5ca2fe32/t/588d4ff3414fb55621d5d0f1/1485656053135/Toward+a+Radical+White+Identity.pdf

21. Tochluk, Shelly, and Cameron Levin. 2010. "Powerful Partnerships: Transformative Alliance Building," in *Accountability and White Anti-Racist Organizing*, 190–219.

22. Warren, Mark. 2010. *Fire in the Heart: How White Activists Embrace Racial Justice*. Oxford University Press, 209.

23. Archibold, Randal C. 2010, April 23. "Arizona Enacts Stringent Law on Immigration." *New York Times*. https://www.nytimes.com/2010/04/24/us/politics/24immig.html

24. Cohn, Marjorie. 2012. "Racial Profiling Legalized in Arizona." *Columbia Journal of Race and Law* 1(2):168–186.

25. Heaney 2023.

26. Engler, Paul. 2009. "The US Immigrant Rights Movement (2004–Ongoing)." *ICNC*. https://www.nonviolent-conflict.org/us-immigrant-rights-movement-2004-ongoing/; Zepeda-Millán, Chris. 2017. *Latino Mass Mobilization: Immigration, Racialization, and Activism*. Cambridge University Press.

27. Nicholls, Walter J., and Justus Uitermark. 2021. "A Virtuous Nation and Its Deserving Immigrants. How the Immigrant Rights Movement Embraced Nationalism." *Social Movement Studies* 20(4):382. doi:10.1080/14742837.2019.1677459

28. Dunbar-Ortiz, Roxanne. 2021. *Not "A Nation of Immigrants": Settler Colonialism, White Supremacy, and a History of Erasure and Exclusion*. Beacon Press.

29. Engler, Mark, and Paul Engler. 2016. *This Is an Uprising: How Nonviolent Revolt Is Shaping the Twenty-First Century*. Bold Type Books; Chenoweth, Erica. 2021. *Civil Resistance: What Everyone Needs to Know*. Oxford University Press. There are important debates as to whether this principle holds in non-autocratic contexts.

30. Olson, Joel. 2005. "What Is a Cadre Organization?" *Bring the Ruckus*. joelolson.net/political

31. Dorsey, Cheryl, Jeffrey Bradach, and Peter Kim. 2020. "Racial Equity and Philanthropy." *Bridgespan*. https://www.bridgespan.org/insights/disparities-nonprofit-funding-for-leaders-of-color

32. Arnold, Gretchen. 2011. "The Impact of Social Ties on Coalition Strength and Effectiveness: The Case of the Battered Women's Movement in St Louis."

Social Movement Studies 10(2):131–150. doi:10.1080/14742837.2011.562360; Van Dyke, Nella, and Bryan Amos. 2017. "Social Movement Coalitions: Formation, Longevity, and Success." *Sociology Compass* 11(7):e12489. doi:10.1111/soc4.12489

33. Publicly available tax filings suggest that annual organizational revenue went from being between $100,000 and $300,000 between 2016 and 2019 to between $1 million and $3 million beginning in 2020.

34. Haber, Michael. 2019. "The New Activist Non-Profits: Four Models Breaking from the Non-Profit Industrial Complex." *University of Miami Law Review* 73:863–954.

35. Thompson 2001.

36. Fenwick, Ryan, and Cassia Herron. 2015. "Group Denounces Methane Plant Agreement." *Courier-Journal*. https://www.courier-journal.com/story/opinion/2015/11/24/group-denounces-methane-plant-agreement/76302536/

37. Watkins, Morgan. 2017. "Bevin Signs Contentious Blue Lives Matter Law." *Courier-Journal*. https://www.courier-journal.com/story/news/politics/2017/03/22/bevin-signs-contentious-blue-lives-matter-law/99514820/

38. Fortson, Jobina. 2018. "Community Leaders, Lawmakers Oppose 'Gang Bill.'" *Wave 3*. https://www.wave3.com/story/37933438/community-leaders-lawmakers-oppose-gang-bill

39. Kalla, Joshua L., and David E. Broockman. 2020. "Reducing Exclusionary Attitudes Through Interpersonal Conversation: Evidence from Three Field Experiments." *American Political Science Review* 114(2):410–425. doi:10.1017/S0003055419000923

40. Phillips, Steve. 2023. "White People and the Fight for Racial Justice with SURJ's Erin Heaney." *Democracy in Color*. https://oliviaxe.podbean.com/e/democracy-in-color

41. Ibid.

42. Ibid.

43. Ibid.

Chapter 3

1. Woolston, Bryan. 2017, October 28. "White Nationalists Stage Anti-Refugee Protests in Tennessee." *Reuters*. https://www.reuters.com/article/us-tennessee-protests-idUSKBN1CX0BZ

2. Lind, Dara. 2017, August 14. "Unite the Right, the Violent White Supremacist Rally in Charlottesville, Explained." *Vox*. https://www.vox.com/2017/8/12/16138246/charlottesville-nazi-rally-right-uva

3. Ong, Linda. 2020. "Local Group in Bedford County Calls for Change to Squalid Renters Conditions." *WKRN*. https://www.wkrn.com/news/local-news/local-group-in-bedford-county-calls-for-change-to-squalid-renters-conditions/

4. Leonardo, Zeus. 2004. "The Color of Supremacy: Beyond the Discourse of

'White Privilege.'" *Educational Philosophy and Theory* 36(2):138; Blum, Lawrence. 2008. "'White Privilege': A Mild Critique." *Theory and Research in Education* 6(3):309–321; Lensmire, Timothy, Shannon McManimon, Jessica Tierney, Mary Lee-Nichols, Zachary Casey, Audrey Lensmire, and Bryan Davis. 2013. "McIntosh as Synecdoche: How Teacher Education's Focus on White Privilege Undermines Antiracism." *Harvard Educational Review* 83(3): 410–431.

5. Du Bois, W. E. B. 1998 [1935]. *Black Reconstruction in America, 1860–1880*. Free Press; Roediger, David R. 1994. *The Wages of Whiteness: Race and the Making of the American Working Class*. Verso; Ioanide, Paula. 2015. *The Emotional Politics of Racism: How Feelings Trump Facts in an Era of Colorblindness*. Stanford University Press.

6. On schools: Garcia, Emma. 2017. "Poor Black Children Are Much More Likely to Attend High-Poverty Schools Than Poor White Children." *Economic Policy Institute*. https://www.epi.org/publication/poor-black-children-are-much-more-likely-to-attend-high-poverty-schools-than-poor-white-children/

On housing: Desilver, Drew, and Kristen Bialik. 2017. "Blacks and Hispanics Face Extra Challenges in Getting Home Loans." *Pew Research Center*. https://www.pewresearch.org/fact-tank/2017/01/10/blacks-and-hispanics-face-extra-challenges-in-getting-home-loans/; Korver-Glenn, Elizabeth. 2021. *Race Brokers: Housing Markets and Segregation in 21st Century Urban America*. Oxford University Press.

On polluting facilities: Mikati, Ihab, Adam F. Benson, Thomas J. Luben, Jason D. Sacks, and Jennifer Richmond-Bryant. 2018. "Disparities in Distribution of Particulate Matter Emission Sources by Race and Poverty Status." *American Journal of Public Health* 108(4):480–485. doi:10.2105/AJPH.2017.304297

On voting power: Rodden, Jonathan A. 2019. *Why Cities Lose: The Deep Roots of the Urban-Rural Political Divide*. Basic Books; Codrington III, Wilfred. 2019. "The Electoral College's Racist Origins." *The Atlantic*. https://www.theatlantic.com/ideas/archive/2019/11/electoral-college-racist-origins/601918/; Ross II, Bertrall L. 2020. "Partisan Gerrymandering as a Threat to Multiracial Democracy." *Southwestern Law Review* 50(3):509–525; Anderson, Carol. 2016. *White Rage: The Unspoken Truth of Our Racial Divide*. Bloomsbury; Alexander, Michelle. 2020. *The New Jim Crow: Mass Incarceration in the Age of Colorblindness*, 10th anniversary ed. New Press; Bentele, Keith G., and Erin E. O'Brien. 2013. "Jim Crow 2.0? Why States Consider and Adopt Restrictive Voter Access Policies." *Perspectives on Politics* 11(4):1088–1116.

7. Braden, Anne. 1966, November 13. "Black Power and White Organizing." From Key List Mailing, by Friends of SNCC, 3. https://collectiveliberation.org/wp-content/uploads/2013/01/Braden_Black_Power_White_Organizing.pdf

8. Benford, Robert D., and David A. Snow. 2000. "Framing Processes and Social Movements: An Overview and Assessment." *Annual Review of Sociology*

26(1): 611–639.

9. McGhee, Heather. 2021. *The Sum of Us: What Racism Costs Everyone and How We Can Prosper Together.* One World.

10. Carson, Clayborne. 1995. *In Struggle: SNCC and the Black Awakening of the 1960s,* 2nd ed. Harvard University Press; McAdam, Doug. 1988. *Freedom Summer.* Oxford University Press; Ture, Kwame, and Charles V. Hamilton. 1992. *Black Power: The Politics of Liberation,* 2nd ed. Vintage.

11. On what I have termed "solidarity activists," see: Russo, Chandra. 2018. *Solidarity in Practice: Moral Protest and the US Security State.* Cambridge University Press; as well as Sundberg, Juanita. 2007. "Reconfiguring North–South Solidarity: Critical Reflections on Experiences of Transnational Resistance." *Antipode* 39(1):144–166. Other literature uses different terms. McCarthy, John D., and Mayer N. Zald. 1977. "Resource Mobilization and Social Movements: A Partial Theory." *American Journal of Sociology* 82(6):1212–1241, discuss "conscience constituents." Munkres, Susan. 2008. "Being 'Sisters' to Salvadoran Peasants: Deep Identification and Its Limits," in *Identity Work in Social Movements,* eds. J. Reger, D. J. Myers, and R. L. Einwohner. University of Minnesota Press, 199–212, uses "privileged outsiders."

For discussions on risk aversion, see for example: Marx, Gary T., and Michael Useem. 1971. "Majority Involvement in Minority Movements: Civil Rights, Abolition, Untouchability." *Journal of Social Issues* 27(1):81–104; Myers, Daniel J. 2008. "Ally Identity: The Politically Gay," in *Identity Work in Social Movements,* 167–188.

12. Korver-Glenn 2021.

13. Du Bois 1998.

14. Bell, Derrick. 1980. "Brown v. Board of Education and the Interest-Convergence Dilemma." *Harvard Law Review* 93(3):523.

15. While many associate a narrow conceptualization of self-interest with storied organizer and movement intellectual Saul Alinsky, even he emphasized that self-interest was rarely fixed. See: Alinsky, Saul. 1971. *Rules for Radicals: A Practical Primer for Realistic Radicals.* Vintage.

16. Hirsch, Eric L. 1986. "The Creation of Political Solidarity in Social Movement Organizations." *Sociological Quarterly* 27(3): 373–387.

17. Wilson, James Q. 1973. *Political Organizations.* Basic Books.

18. Jackson, Taharee Apirom. 2011. "Which Interests Are Served by the Principle of Interest Convergence? Whiteness, Collective Trauma, and the Case for Anti-Racism." *Race Ethnicity and Education* 14(4):442.

19. Myers, Katie. 2020. "Community Takes Down Neo-Nazis and Slumlords in Rural Tennessee." *Scalawag Magazine.* http://scalawagmagazine.org/2020/03/bedford-county-listening-project/

20. There is clearly a critique to be made about this signage, in that creating

"more refugees," as a legal category, is likely not a liberatory political project, insofar as this would indicate people needing to flee their homes. It is clear, however, that this message was intended to index a specific group of Shelbyville residents. Reading it otherwise in this context seems rather academic and cynical.

21. Melson, David. 2020, November 5. "County Backs Trump; Isaacs Wins City Council Seat." *Shelbyville Times-Gazette.* https://www.t-g.com/stories/county-backs-trump-isaacs-wins-city-council-seat,4450?

22. Farmer, Blake. 2020. "Shelbyville Residents Report More KKK Activity." *WPLN.* https://wpln.org/post/shelbyville-residents-report-more-kkk-activity/

23. Haggard, Amanda. 2023, September 27. "Rural Renters: Part One of a Series on Fighting for Renters Rights in Rural Communities." *The Contributor.* https://thecontributor.org/rural-renters-part-one-of-a-series-on-fighting-for-renters-rights-in-rural-communities/

24. Belew, Kathleen, and Ramon A. Gutierrez. 2021. *Field Guide to White Supremacy.* University of California Press.

25. Huber, Patrick. 2006. "Red Necks and Red Bandanas: Appalachian Coal Miners and the Coloring of Union Identity, 1912–1936." *Western Folklore* 65(1/2):195–210.

26. On the Battle of Blair Mountain, see: https://www.smithsonianmag.com/history/battle-blair-mountain-largest-labor-uprising-american-history-180978520/; https://www.nps.gov/articles/000/the-battle-of-blair-mountain.htm

27. Howard, Beth. 2021, June 4. "Rednecks for Black Lives." *Medium.* https://fight4thesouth.medium.com/rednecks-for-black-lives-edddd51cf95b

28. The contemporary reclamation of the term "redneck," the red bandana, and the story of Blair Mountain, among white working-class communities pursuing antiracist ends is not unique to KPU. See for instance the recently disbanded Redneck Revolt: Rothschild, Teal. 2019. "Multiplicity in Movements: The Case for Redneck Revolt." *Contexts* 18(3):57–59. doi:10.1177/1536504219864964

29. There is a rich literature on the importance of listening, as well as its historic devaluation, in democratic processes: Bickford, Susan. 2000. *The Dissonance of Democracy: Race and Victorian Women's Fiction.* Cornell University Press; Dobson, Andrew. 2014. *Listening for Democracy: Recognition, Representation, Reconciliation.* Oxford University Press. This is notable insofar as grassroots organizing has itself been theorized as a practice of democracy: Han, Hahrie, Matthew Baggetta, and Jennifer Oser. 2024. "Organizing and Democracy: Understanding the Possibilities for Transformative Collective Action." *Annual Review of Political Science* 27(1):245–262. doi:10.1146/annurev-polisci-041322-043040; Woodly, Deva R. 2021. *Reckoning: Black Lives Matter and the Democratic Necessity of Social Movements.* Oxford University Press. Democratic theorists certainly conceptualize different kinds of listening: Hendriks, Caro-

lyn M., Selen A. Ercan, and Sonya Duus. 2019. "Listening in Polarised Controversies: A Study of Listening Practices in the Public Sphere." *Policy Sciences* 52(1): 137–151. doi:10.1007/s11077-018-9343-3. Yet the ethos of listening is generally one of curiosity, collective empowerment, and even co-creation: Crisman, Jonathan Jae-an. 2022. "Co-Creation from the Grassroots: Listening to Arts-Based Community Organizing in Little Tokyo." *Urban Planning* 7(3). doi:10.17645/up.v7i3.5336

30. Baker, Ella. 1972. "Developing Community Leadership," in *Black Women in White America: A Documentary History*, ed. G. Lerner. Vintage, 345–352; Alinsky 1971; McAlevey, Jane. 2016. *No Shortcuts: Organizing for Power in the New Gilded Age*. Oxford University Press; Inouye, Mie. 2022. "Starting with People Where They Are: Ella Baker's Theory of Political Organizing." *American Political Science Review* 116(2):533–546. doi:10.1017/S0003055421001015

31. Disability and socioeconomic class have a complex and interdependent relationship. See: Leondar-Wright, Betsy. 2005. *Class Matters: Cross-Class Alliance Building for Middle-Class Activists*. New Society Publishers.

32. On dehumanization regardless of class, see: Dow, Dawn Marie. 2019. *Mothering While Black: Boundaries and Burdens of Middle-Class Parenthood*. University of California Press. On psychic and material benefits: Du Bois 1998; Ioanide 2015; McGhee 2021. On cross-racial alliances: Norrell 1986 cited in Hill, Herbert. 1996. "The Problem of Race in American Labor History." *Reviews in American History* 24(2):189–208; Portelli, Alessandro. 1991. *The Death of Luigi Trastulli and Other Stories: Form and Meaning in Oral History*. SUNY Press; Santow, Mark. 2023. *Saul Alinsky and the Dilemmas of Race: Community Organizing in the Postwar City*. University of Chicago Press.

33. On resisting the presumption that poor people are more racist: Sullivan, Shannon. 2014. *Good White People: The Problem with Middle-Class White Anti-Racism. Albany*: SUNY Press; al-Gharbi, Musa. 2019. "Resistance as Sacrifice: Toward an Ascetic Antiracism." *Sociological Forum* 34(S1):1197–1216. doi:10.1111/socf.12544; Beeman, Angie. 2022. *Liberal White Supremacy: How Progressives Silence Racial and Class Oppression*. University of Georgia Press.

34. On ignoring white racism in social justice organizations: Dobbie, David, and Katie Richards-Schuster. 2008. "Building Solidarity Through Difference: A Practice Model for Critical Multicultural Organizing." *Journal of Community Practice* 16(3):317–337; Beeman 2022.

35. See for example: Adams, Emmie Schrader. 2012. "An Interracial Alliance of the Poor?" in *Hands on the Freedom Plow: Personal Accounts by Women in SNCC*, eds. Faith S. Holsaert, Martha Prescod Norman Noonan, Judy Richardson, Betty Garman Robinson, Jean Smith Young, and Dorothy M. Zellner. University of Illinois Press, 424.

36. Braden 1966, 3.

37. Rein, Marcy. 2023, February 27. "Election Wins Fuel Long Push to End Cash Bail." *Convergence*. https://convergencemag.com/articles/election-wins-fuel-long-push-to-end-cash-bail/

38. Critical resistance definitions: https://criticalresistance.org/mission-vision/not-so-common-language/. On complexity of putting abolition into policy and practice: Ben-Moshe, Liat. 2020. *Decarcerating Disability: Deinstitutionalization and Prison Abolition*. University of Minnesota Press; Akbar, Amna A. 2023. "Non-Reformist Reforms and Struggles over Life, Death, and Democracy." *Yale Law Journal* 132(8): 2497–2577.

39. Brock-Petroshius, Kristen, and Laura Wray-Lake. 2022. "Organizing Through Stories: The Role of Emotions in Increasing Support for Decarceration." *Journal of Community Practice* 30(1):89. doi:10.1080/10705422.2022.2033376

40. In the end, the multiracial coalition collected close to 250,000 total signatures, about 100,000 more than needed to certify.

41. Brock-Petroshius and Wray-Lake 2022.

42. Du Bois, W. E. B. 1999 [1910]. "The Souls of White Folk," in *Darkwater: Voices from Within the Veil*. Harcourt Brace, 923–938; Baldwin, James. 2021. *The Price of the Ticket: Collected Nonfiction: 1948–1985*, reprint ed. Beacon Press.

43. On moral shocks: Jasper, James M. 1997. *The Art of Moral Protest: Culture, Biography, and Creativity in Social Movements*. Chicago: University of Chicago Press. On "seminal experiences" for white antiracists: Warren 2010. On "approximating experiences": O'Brien, Eileen. 2001. *Whites Confront Racism: Antiracists and Their Paths to Action*. Rowman & Littlefield.

Chapter 4

1. Stein, Jeff. 2019, October 25. "Trump Boosted the U.S. Steel Industry. But in Kentucky, It Didn't Last." *Washington Post*. https://www.washingtonpost.com/business/economy/as-a-kentucky-mill-shutters-steelworkers-see-the-limits-of-trumps-intervention/2019/10/25/a27d3bb2-f02f-11e9-89eb-ec56cd414732_story.html

2. McAlevey, Jane. 2016. *No Shortcuts: Organizing for Power in the New Gilded Age*. Oxford University Press; Han, Hahrie. 2014. *How Organizations Develop Activists: Civic Associations and Leadership in the 21st Century*. Oxford University Press.

3. Morris, Aldon. 1984. *The Origins of the Civil Rights Movements: Black Communities Organizing for Change*. Free Press; Taylor, Verta. 1989. "Social Movement Continuity: The Women's Movement in Abeyance." *American Sociological Review* 54(5):761–775. doi:10.2307/2117752; Polletta, Francesca. 2006. *It Was Like a Fever: Storytelling in Protest and Politics*. University of Chicago Press.

4. On impacts of protest: Meyer, David S. 2003. "How Social Movements Matter." *Contexts* 2(4):30–35. On importance of broad and enduring movements:

Oakes, Jeannie, John Rogers, and Martin Lipton. 2006. *Learning Power: Organizing for Education and Justice*. New York: Teachers College Press; Chenoweth, Erica. 2021. *Civil Resistance: What Everyone Needs to Know*. Oxford University Press. For organizing's origins: Sen, Rinku. 2003. *Stir It Up: Lessons in Community Organizing and Advocacy*. Jossey-Bass; Bretherton, Luke. 2014. *Resurrecting Democracy: Faith, Citizenship, and the Politics of a Common Life*. Cambridge University Press.

5. Ganz, Marshall. 2004. "Organizing as Leadership," in *Encyclopedia of Leadership*, eds. G. Goethals, G. Sorenson, and J. M. Burns. SAGE Publications, 1134–1144; Han 2014.

6. Warren, Mark R., Karen L. Mapp, and the Community Organizing and School Reform Project. 2011. *A Match on Dry Grass: Community Organizing as a Catalyst for School Reform*. Oxford University Press.

7. Woodly, Deva R. 2021. *Reckoning: Black Lives Matter and the Democratic Necessity of Social Movements*. Oxford University Press, 140.

8. Du Bois, W. E. B. 1999 [1910]. "The Souls of White Folk," in *Darkwater: Voices from Within the Veil*. Harcourt Brace, 923–938; Baldwin, James. 2021. *The Price of the Ticket: Collected Nonfiction: 1948–1985*, reprint ed. Beacon Press; Lipsitz, George. 2018. *The Possessive Investment in Whiteness: How White People Profit from Identity Politics*, 20th anniversary ed. Temple University Press; Metzl, Jonathan M. 2019. *Dying of Whiteness: How the Politics of Racial Resentment Is Killing America's Heartland*. Basic Books.

9. Examples from the labor movement: Hill, Herbert. 1996. "The Problem of Race in American Labor History." *Reviews in American History* 24(2):193; see too Portelli, Alessandro. 1991. *The Death of Luigi Trastulli and Other Stories: Form and Meaning in Oral History*. SUNY Press. Examples from community organizing: Sen, Rinku. 2003. *Stir It Up: Lessons in Community Organizing and Advocacy*. Jossey-Bass; Santow, Mark. 2023. *Saul Alinsky and the Dilemmas of Race: Community Organizing in the Postwar City*. University of Chicago Press.

10. Piven, Frances Fox, and Richard Cloward. 1977. *Poor People's Movements: Why They Succeed, How They Fail*. Vintage.

11. Woodly 2021, 138.

12. Polletta, Francesca. 2002. *Freedom Is an Endless Meeting: Democracy in American Social Movements*. University of Chicago Press, 209.

13. This is very much in the model of Paolo Freire's popular education and Myles Horton's learning for social change. See for example: Horton, Myles, and Paulo Freire. 1990. *We Make the Road by Walking: Conversations on Education and Social Change*, reprint ed., eds. B. Bell, J. Gaventa, and J. Peters. Temple University Press; Inouye 2019 cited in Woodly 2021.

14. Ganz, Marshall. 2010. "Leading Change: Leadership, Organization, and Social Movements," in *Handbook of Leadership Theory and Practice: A Harvard Business School Centennial Colloquium*, eds. N. Nohria and R. Khurana. Harvard

Business Press, 31.

15. Smith, Jordan. 2022. "Kentucky Voters Reject Amendment 2 in 'Repudiation of Extreme Anti-Choice Agenda.'" *The Intercept*. Retrieved September 18, 2023. https://theintercept.com/2022/11/09/abortion-rights-kentucky-election/; Epling, Mary Jane. 2023, June 21. "Locals Push Back Against Anti-Trans Legislation." *The Daily Independent*. https://www.dailyindependent.com/news/locals-push-back-against-anti-trans-legislation/article_83b9d820-108d-11ee-b17e-bb35b277a6ca.html?emci=0b445579-db11-ee11-a9bb-00224832eb73&emdi=529cdecb-e111-ee11-a9bb-00224832eb73&ceid=617700

16. Donaghue, Erin. 2019, February 8. "India Cummings Case: Lawsuit Claims Deputies 'Literally Watched' Inmate Die in New York Jail." *CBS News*. https://www.cbsnews.com/news/india-cummings-case-lawsuit-claims-deputies-literally-watched-inmate-die-in-new-york-jail/; Lipsitz, Raina. 2023, March 31. "Why Do People Keep Dying in Erie County's Jails?" *The New Republic*. https://newrepublic.com/article/171009/erie-county-sheriff-garcia-howard

17. Howard's 2017 reelection was ultimately determined by a few thousand votes out of nearly 600,000 ballots cast. See: Anstey, Evan. 2017, November 8. "Tim Howard Re-Elected Erie County Sheriff." *WIBV Channel 4*. https://www.wivb.com/news/local-news/tim-howard-re-elected-erie-county-sheriff/. Actual election returns can be found here: elections.ny.gov/system/files/documents/2023/11/erieed_nov17.pdf; on 2021 outcome: Buehler, Hannah. 2021, November 2. "Zellner: Erie County Sheriff Race Too Close to Call." *WKBW 7 Buffalo*. https://www.wkbw.com/news/local-news/zellner-erie-county-sheriff-race-too-close-to-call

18. Woodly 2021, 147.

19. Piven and Cloward 1977.

20. On campaign priorities: Chun, Jennifer Jihye, George Lipsitz, and Young Shin. 2010. "Immigrant Women Workers at the Center of Social Change: AIWA Takes Stock of Itself." *Kalfou* 1(1):127–132. On regression: Kim, Mimi E. 2020. "The Carceral Creep: Gender-Based Violence, Race, and the Expansion of the Punitive State, 1973–1983." *Social Problems* 67(2):251–269. doi:10.1093/socpro/spz013

21. Morris 1984; Payne, Charles M. 2007. *I've Got the Light of Freedom: The Organizing Tradition and the Mississippi Freedom Struggle*, 2nd ed., with a new preface. University of California Press.

22. It is worth noting that not all electoral organizing is centrally about candidates. In 2022, SURJ members would speak with tens of thousands of white voters as part of the multiracial coalition Protect Kentucky Access, which helped to defeat a near total ban on abortion in the state. See: Wagoner, Arwen, and Phoebe Donahue. 2022, December 14. "Beating Anti-Abortion Bills in a Red State." *Scalawag Magazine*. http://scalawagmagazine.org/2022/12/kentucky-abortion-vote/; Culver, Celina. 2022, December 8. "View from the Grassroots:

SURJ." *The Forge*. https://forgeorganizing.org/article/view-grassroots-surj

23. Brock-Petroshius, Kristen. 2023. "Changing Dominant Carceral Attitudes: A Community Organizing Field Experiment." Unpublished dissertation, UCLA.

24. Brown, Trevor, Suzanne Mettler, and Samantha Puzzi. 2021. "When Rural and Urban Become 'Us' Versus 'Them': How a Growing Divide Is Reshaping American Politics." *The Forum* 19(3):365–393. doi:10.1515/for-2021-2029

25. See too: Wing, Bob. 2018. *Toward Racial Justice and a Third Reconstruction*. Lulu Press.

26. Melson, David. 2020, November 5. "County Backs Trump; Isaacs Wins City Council Seat." *Shelbyville Times-Gazette*. https://www.t-g.com/stories/county-backs-trump-isaacs-wins-city-council-seat,4450?

27. At the national level, SURJ played an important role in the race to defeat Daniel Cameron, the Kentucky attorney general who termed Breonna Taylor's murder "justified." See: Nichols, John. 2023, May 18. "The Man Who Called Breonna Taylor's Killing 'Justified' Could Be Kentucky's Next Governor." *The Nation*. https://www.thenation.com/article/politics/daniel-cameron-governor-kentucky/. Some in KPU did individually choose to participate in the campaign.

28. Oppenheimer, Martin, and George Lakey. 1965. *A Manual for Direct Action: Strategy and Tactics for Civil Rights and All Other Nonviolent Protest Movements*. Quadrangle.

29. Plec, Julie. 2021. *"Dahlia Ferlito Interviewed by Julie Plec."* Instagram.

30. Mills, Charles W. 1997. *The Racial Contract*. Cornell University Press; Tuana, Nancy, and Shannon Sullivan, eds. 2007. *Race and Epistemologies of Ignorance*. SUNY Press; Mueller, Jennifer C. 2017. "Producing Colorblindness: Everyday Mechanisms of White Ignorance." *Social Problems* 64(2):219–238. doi:10.1093/socpro/spw061

31. Ford, Kristie A. 2012. "Shifting White Ideological Scripts: The Educational Benefits of Inter- and Intraracial Curricular Dialogues on the Experiences of White College Students." *Journal of Diversity in Higher Education* 5(3):138–158. doi:10.1037/a0028917; Ball, Amanda C. 2022. "I Know Why the White Lady Cries: Growing Pains of an Antiracist Cleft Habitus." *Social Problems* 70(3):598–615.

32. Plec 2021.

33. On the civil rights movement: Warren and Mapp 2011; on the formerly enslaved: Du Bois, W. E. B. 1998 [1935]. *Black Reconstruction in America, 1860–1880*. Free Press; Woods, Clyde Adrian. 1998. *Development Arrested: The Blues and Plantation Power in the Mississippi Delta*. Verso; on worker organizations: Denning, Michael. 1997. *The Cultural Front: The Laboring of American Culture in the Twentieth Century*. Verso; on the Highlander Center: Inouye, Mie. 2019, April 3. "The Highlander Idea." *Jacobin*. https://jacobin.com/2019/04/highlander-folk-school-tennessee-organizing-movements

34. Inouye 2019.

35. Ransby, Barbara. 2003. *Ella Baker and the Black Freedom Movement: A Radical Democratic Vision*. University of North Carolina Press; Inouye, Mie. 2022. "Starting with People Where They Are: Ella Baker's Theory of Political Organizing." *American Political Science Review* 116(2):533–546. doi:10.1017/S0003055421001015; HoSang, Daniel Martinez. 2021. *A Wider Type of Freedom: How Struggles for Racial Justice Liberate Everyone*. University of California Press.

36. Page, Joshua, and Christine S. Scott-Hayward. 2022. "Bail and Pretrial Justice in the United States: A Field of Possibility." *Annual Review of Criminology* 5(1):91–113. doi:10.1146/annurev-criminol-030920-093024

37. Rein, Marcy. 2023, February 27. "Election Wins Fuel Long Push to End Cash Bail." *Convergence*. https://convergencemag.com/articles/election-wins-fuel-long-push-to-end-cash-bail/

38. Ibid.

39. For evidence around growing political polarization and the tendency among Americans to "self-sort" along ideological lines, see for instance: Geiger, Abigail. 2014. "Political Polarization in the American Public." *Pew Research Center*. https://www.pewresearch.org/politics/2014/06/12/political-polarization-in-the-american-public/; Boxell, Levi, Matthew Gentzkow, and Jesse Shapiro. 2024. "Cross-Country Trends in Affective Polarization." *Review of Economics and Statistics* 106(2):557–565. For evidence that Americans believe themselves to be more ideologically divided than they actually are, see: Populace Research. 2021. "The American Aspirations Index." *Populace.org*. https://populace.org/research

40. Payne 2007, 178.

41. Clemons, Jared. 2022. "From 'Freedom Now!' to 'Black Lives Matter': Retrieving King and Randolph to Theorize Contemporary White Antiracism." *Perspectives on Politics*, 7. doi:10.1017/S1537592722001074

42. Marx, Karl, and Friedrich Engels. 1845. *The German Ideology, Including Theses on Feuerbach*. Prometheus Books.

43. Ganz 2004, 1134.

44. On Movement for Black Lives: Taylor, Keeanga-Yamahtta. 2016. *From #BlackLivesMatter to Black Liberation*. Chicago: Haymarket Books; Ransby, Barbara. 2018. *Making All Black Lives Matter: Reimagining Freedom in the Twenty-First Century*. University of California Press; Woodly 2021.

On consolidating fascism: Robinson, William, and Mario Barrera. 2011. "Global Capitalism and Twenty-First Century Fascism: A US Case Study." *Race & Class* 53(3):4–29; Fording, Richard, and Sanford Schram. 2020. *Hard White: The Mainstreaming of Racism in American Politics*. Oxford University Press; Carnaghi, Benedetta. 2024, October 25. "Is Donald Trump a Fascist? Here's What an Expert Thinks." *The Conversation*. http://theconversation.com/is-donald-trump-a-fascist-heres-what-an-expert-thinks-242243; Snyder, Timothy. 2024,

November 8. "What Does It Mean That Donald Trump Is a Fascist?" *New Yorker* https://www.newyorker.com/magazine/dispatches/what-does-it-mean-that-donald-trump-is-a-fascist; Burley, Shane. 2017. *Fascism Today: What It Is and How to End It*. Oakland: AK Press; Blee, Kathleen M., Robert Futrell, and Pete Simi. 2023. *Out of Hiding: Extremist White Supremacy and How It Can Be Stopped*. Routledge.

45. Formal data collection ended in 2024, and so I cannot comment on the organization's growth following the 2024 election results.

46. Boggs, Grace Lee. 2016. *Living for Change: An Autobiography*, reprint ed. University of Minnesota Press; Woodly 2021; Cannady, Emmanuel. In press. *Black Lives Matter University: How Activist Knowledge Generates Organizational Sustainability*. NYU Press.

47. On absorption: "The Momentum Model: A Living Model for Hybrid Organizing." *Momentum*. Retrieved November 18, 2024. https://www.momentumcommunity.org/momentum-model; Momentum's origins: Kingkade, Tyler. 2019. "These Activists Are Training Every Movement That Matters." *VICE*. https://www.vice.com/en/article/these-activists-are-training-every-movement-that-matters-v26n4/. For theories and research from which Momentum draws: Sharp, Gene. 2011. *Sharp's Dictionary of Power and Struggle: Language of Civil Resistance in Conflicts*. Oxford University Press; Chenoweth 2021.

48. Burke, Minyvonne. 2022, June 16. "Buffalo Shooting Suspect Said He Carried Out Attack 'For the Future of the White Race,' Federal Complaint Says." *NBC News*. https://www.nbcnews.com/news/us-news/buffalo-shooting-suspect-said-carried-attack-future-white-race-federal-rcna33886

Chapter 5

1. Jacobs, Michelle R., and Tiffany Taylor. 2011. "Challenges of Multiracial Antiracist Activism: Racial Consciousness and Chief Wahoo." *Critical Sociology* 38(5):687–706. doi:10.1177/0896920511407357; Gorski, Paul C., and Noura Erakat. 2019. "Racism, Whiteness, and Burnout in Antiracism Movements: How White Racial Justice Activists Elevate Burnout in Racial Justice Activists of Color in the United States." *Ethnicities* 19(5):784–808.

2. Beamish, Thomas D., and Amy J. Luebbers. 2009. "Alliance Building Across Social Movements: Bridging Difference in a Peace and Justice Coalition." *Social Problems* 56(4):647–676. doi:10.1525/sp.2009.56.4.647; Dixon, Marc, William Danaher, and Ben Kail. 2013. "Allies, Targets, and the Effectiveness of Coalition Protest: A Comparative Analysis of Labor Unrest in the U. S. South." *Mobilization: An International Quarterly* 18(3):331–350. doi:10.17813/maiq.18.3.a95k861nr14j5810

3. Gawerc, Michelle I. 2021. "Coalition-Building and the Forging of Solidarity Across Difference and Inequality." *Sociology Compass* 15(3). doi:10.1111/soc4

.12858; Bandy, Joe, and Jackie Smith. 2005. "Factors Affecting Conflict and Cooperation in Transnational Movement Networks," in *Coalitions Across Borders: Transnational Protest and the Neoliberal Order*, eds. Joe Bandy and Jackie Smith. Rowman & Littlefield, 231–252.

4. Williams, Bethanni. 2015, December 21. "'Louisville Showing up for Racial Justice' Holds Methane Plant Protest." *Whas11*. https://www.whas11.com/article/news/community/louisville-showing-up-for-racial-justice-holds-methane-plant-protest/417-29003403

5. Ryan, Jacob. 2016. "Metro Council Sets Limits on New Biodigesters in Louisville." *Louisville Public Media*. https://www.lpm.org/news/2016-09-09/metro-council-sets-limits-on-new-biodigesters-in-louisville

6. Watkins, Morgan. 2017, March 22. "Bevin Signs Contentious Blue Lives Matter Law." *Courier-Journal*. https://www.courier-journal.com/story/news/politics/2017/03/22/bevin-signs-contentious-blue-lives-matter-law/99514820/

7. Fortson, Jobina. 2018, April 11. "Community Leaders, Lawmakers Oppose 'Gang Bill.'" *Wave 3*. https://www.wave3.com/story/37933438/community-leaders-lawmakers-oppose-gang-bill

8. brown, adrienne maree. 2017. *Emergent Strategy: Shaping Change, Changing Worlds*. AK Press.

9. Haskell, Josh, and Anabel Muñoz. 2022, October 21. "Black Lives Matter Group Camped Near Kevin de León's Home Say They Won't Leave Until He Resigns." *ABC7 Los Angeles*. https://abc7.com/los-angeles-city-council-kevin-de-leon-gil-cedillo-racist-remarks/12357336/

10. I defer here to the terms BLRR used to describe its work: https://blackloveresistsintherust.org/about-us/

11. Arnold, Gretchen. 2011. "The Impact of Social Ties on Coalition Strength and Effectiveness: The Case of the Battered Women's Movement in St Louis." *Social Movement Studies* 10(2):131–150. doi:10.1080/14742837.2011.562360; Van Dyke, Nella, and Bryan Amos. 2017. "Social Movement Coalitions: Formation, Longevity, and Success." *Sociology Compass* 11(7):e12489. doi:10.1111/soc4.12489

12. Sharp, Gene. 2011. *Sharp's Dictionary of Power and Struggle: Language of Civil Resistance in Conflicts*. Oxford University Press.

13. On John Brown, see Du Bois, W. E. B. 2024. *John Brown: A Biography*. Westholme Publishing. On the Weather Underground, see: Berger, Dan. 2005. *Outlaws of America: The Weather Underground and the Politics of Solidarity*. AK Press; Varon, Jeremy Peter. 2004. *Bringing the War Home: The Weather Underground, the Red Army Faction, and Revolutionary Violence in the Sixties and Seventies*. University of California Press. On Student Nonviolent Coordinating Committee, see: McAdam, Doug. 1988. *Freedom Summer*. Oxford University Press; Carson, Clayborne. 1995. *In Struggle: SNCC and the Black Awakening of the 1960s*, 2nd ed. Harvard University Press.

14. Nepstad, Sharon Erickson. 2004. *Convictions of the Soul: Religion, Culture, and Agency in the Central America Solidarity Movement.* Oxford University Press; Nepstad, Sharon Erickson. 2008. *Religion and War Resistance in the Plowshares Movement.* Cambridge University Press; Russo, Chandra. 2018. *Solidarity in Practice: Moral Protest and the US Security State.* Cambridge University Press; Stanger, Anya. 2022. *Incarcerated Resistance: How Identity, Gender, and Privilege Shape the Experiences of America's Nonviolent Activists.* Lexington Books.

15. Nichols, John. 2023, May 18. "The Man Who Called Breonna Taylor's Killing 'Justified' Could Be Kentucky's Next Governor." *The Nation.* https://www.thenation.com/article/politics/daniel-cameron-governor-kentucky/

16. On racial disparities in protest policing: Davenport, Christian, Sarah A. Soule, and David A. Armstrong. 2011. "Protesting While Black? The Differential Policing of American Activism, 1960 to 1990." *American Sociological Review* 76(1):152–178. doi:10.1177/0003122410395370. On the bias among white audiences of such policing: Davenport, Christian, Rose McDermott, and David Armstrong. 2018. "Protest and Police Abuse: Racial Limits on Perceived Accountability," in *Police Abuse in Contemporary Democracies*, eds. Michelle Bonner, Guillermina Seri, Mary Rose Kubal, and Michael Kempa. Palgrave Macmillan, 165–192.

17. Meador, Jonathan. 2018, July 2. "Updated: Encampment Aims to 'Abolish ICE,' Pressure Mayor." *Insider Louisville.* https://web.archive.org/web/20181230223539/https://insiderlouisville.com/government/local/encampment-aims-to-abolish-ice-pressure-mayor/

18. Martin, Glenn. 2017, September 22. "Those Closest to the Problem Are Closest to the Solution." *The Appeal.* https://theappeal.org/those-closest-to-the-problem-are-closest-to-the-solution-555e04317b79/; see too: Woodly, Deva R. 2021. *Reckoning: Black Lives Matter and the Democratic Necessity of Social Movements.* New York: Oxford University Press, 138 for the M4BL version. For a critique of this position, see Táíwò, Olúfẹ́mi O. 2022. *Elite Capture: How the Powerful Took over Identity Politics.* Haymarket Books.

19. Many scholars treat the dilemmas of white overreach as well as white deference in racial justice work. For a typology of approaches and concerns, see: Thurber, Amie, Kelley Frances Fenelon, and Leah Marion Roberts. 2015. "Staying Off the Megaphone and in the Movement: Cultivating Solidarity and Contesting Authority Among White Antiracist Activists." *Understanding and Dismantling White Privilege* 5(2):1–20. Other helpful literature: Tochluk, Shelly, and Cameron Levin. 2010. "Powerful Partnerships: Transformative Alliance Building," in *Accountability and White Anti-Racist Organizing: Stories from Our Work*, eds. B. B. Cushing, L. Cabbil, M. Freeman, J. Hitchcock, K. Richards, and R. Chisom. Crandall, Dostie & Douglass Books, 190–219; Jacobs and Taylor 2011; Jonsson, Terese. 2016. "The Narrative Reproduction of White Feminist Racism." *Feminist Review* 113(1):50–67. doi:10.1057/fr.2016.2; Gorski and Erakat 2019.

20. On fragility: DiAngelo, Robin. 2011. "White Fragility." *International Journal of Critical Pedagogy* 3(3):54–70. See too: Srivastava, Sakita. 1996. "Song and Dance? The Performance of Antiracist Workshops." *Canadian Review of Sociology/Revue Canadienne de Sociologie* 33(3):291–315. doi:10.1111/j.1755-618X.1996.tb02454.x; Jonsson 2016; Gorski and Erakat 2019.

21. Barlas, Carole, Elizabeth Kasl, Alec MacLeod, Doug Paxton, Penny Rossenwasser, and Linda Sartor. 2012. "White on White: Communicating About Race and White Privilege with Critical Humility." *Understanding and Dismantling Privilege* 2(1):2.

22. Participants listed the three most central criticisms: (1) white people should not be organizing on their own; (2) white people should not be "paid to be antiracist" (see Middlebrook, Jeb. 2010. "The Ballot Box and Beyond: The (Im)Possibilities of White Antiracist Organizing." *American Quarterly* 62(2):233–252); and (3) white people are reading rather than taking action.

23. Collins, Patricia Hill. 2005. *Black Sexual Politics: African Americans, Gender, and the New Racism*. Routledge; Sumerau, J. E., TehQuin D. Forbes, Eric Joy Denise, and Lain A. B. Mathers. 2021. "Constructing Allyship and the Persistence of Inequality." *Social Problems* 68(2):358–373. doi:10.1093/socpro/spaa003

24. Brock-Petroshius, Kristen. 2023. "Changing Dominant Carceral Attitudes: A Community Organizing Field Experiment." Unpublished dissertation, UCLA.

25. Van Dyke and Amos 2017.

26. Corrigall-Brown, Catherine, and David Meyer. 2010. "The Prehistory of a Coalition: The Role of Social Ties in Win Without War," in *Strategic Alliances: Coalition Building and Social Movements*, eds. N. Van Dyke and H. McCammon. University of Minnesota Press, 3–21.

27. Moore, Hilary, and James Tracy. 2020. *No Fascist USA! The John Brown Anti-Klan Committee & Lessons for Today's Movements*. City Lights Publishers.

28. Thurber et al. 2015, 15

29. Sullivan, Shannon. 2014. *Good White People: The Problem with Middle-Class White Anti-Racism*. SUNY Press; Mayorga-Gallo, Sarah. 2019. "The White-Centering Logic of Diversity Ideology." *American Behavioral Scientist* 63(13):1789–1809. doi:10.1177/0002764219842619; Underhill, Megan R. 2019. "'Diversity Is Important to Me': White Parents and Exposure-to-Diversity Parenting Practices." *Sociology of Race and Ethnicity* 5(4):486–499. doi:10.1177/2332649218790992

30. Ibid.

31. Gawerc 2021, 4.

32. Thompson, Becky. 2001. *A Promise and a Way of Life: White Antiracist Activism*. University of Minnesota Press.

33. Dobbie, David, and Katie Richards-Schuster. 2008. "Building Solidarity

Through Difference: A Practice Model for Critical Multicultural Organizing." *Journal of Community Practice* 16(3):317–337.

Chapter 6

1. Varon, Jeremy Peter. 2004. *Bringing the War Home: The Weather Underground, the Red Army Faction, and Revolutionary Violence in the Sixties and Seventies.* University of California Press; Berger, Dan. 2005. *Outlaws of America: The Weather Underground and the Politics of Solidarity.* AK Press; Machtinger, Howard. 2009, February 18. "You Say You Want a Revolution." *In These Times.* https://inthesetimes.com/article/you-say-you-want-a-revolution

2. Middlebrook, Jeb. 2010. "The Ballot Box and Beyond: The (Im)Possibilities of White Antiracist Organizing." *American Quarterly* 62(2):233–252.

3. Machtinger 2009.

4. Levine-Rasky, Cynthia. 2000. "Framing Whiteness: Working Through the Tensions in Introducing Whiteness to Educators." *Race Ethnicity and Education* 3(3):271–292. doi:10.1080/713693039; Lensmire, Timothy, Shannon McManimon, Jessica Tierney, Mary Lee-Nichols, Zachary Casey, Audrey Lensmire, and Bryan Davis. 2013. "McIntosh as Synecdoche: How Teacher Education's Focus on White Privilege Undermines Antiracism." *Harvard Educational Review* 83(3):410–431; Mott, Carrie. 2019. "Precious Work: White Anti-Racist Pedagogies in Southern Arizona." *Social & Cultural Geography* 20(2):178–197. doi:10.1080/14649365.2017.1355067

5. Sunderman, Zachary. 2023. *Dilemmas of Allyship: White Anti-Racists and the Challenges of Social Justice.* Routledge.

6. O'Brien, Eileen. 2001. *Whites Confront Racism: Antiracists and Their Paths to Action.* Rowman & Littlefield; Warren, Mark. 2010. *Fire in the Heart: How White Activists Embrace Racial Justice.* Oxford University Press.

7. Bennett, Jessica. 2020, November 19. "What If Instead of Calling People Out, We Called Them In?" *New York Times.* https://www.nytimes.com/2020/11/19/style/loretta-ross-smith-college-cancel-culture.html; Ross, Loretta J. 2025. *Calling In: How to Start Making Change with Those You'd Rather Cancel.* Simon & Schuster.

8. Ball, Amanda C. 2022. "I Know Why the White Lady Cries: Growing Pains of an Antiracist Cleft Habitus." *Social Problems* 70(3):598–615.

9. McAdam, Doug. 1986. "Recruitment to High-Risk Activism: The Case of Freedom Summer." *American Journal of Sociology* 92(1):70. doi:10.1086/228463; Pérez, Marcos E. 2022. *Proletarian Lives: Routines, Identity, and Culture in Contentious Politics.* Cambridge University Press; Fingerhut, Adam W., and Emma R. Hardy. 2020. "Applying a Model of Volunteerism to Better Understand the Experiences of White Ally Activists." *Group Processes & Intergroup Relations* 23(3):344–360. doi:10.1177/1368430219837345

10. Malott, Krista M., Scott Schaefle, Tina R. Paone, Jennifer Cates, and

Breyan Haizlip. 2019. "Challenges and Coping Mechanisms of Whites Committed to Antiracism." *Journal of Counseling & Development* 97(1):86–97. doi:10.1002/jcad.12238

11. DiAngelo, Robin. 2011. "White Fragility." *International Journal of Critical Pedagogy* 3(3):54–70.

12. Plec, Julie. 2021. "Dahlia Ferlito Interviewed by Julie Plec." Instagram.

13. On the role of white affinity, see Ball 2022. On emotional challenges, see Sunderman 2023. On isolation, see: Segrest, Mab. 1999. *Memoir of a Race Traitor*. South End Press; Thompson, Becky. 2001. *A Promise and a Way of Life: White Antiracist Activism*. University of Minnesota Press; Malott et al. 2019.

14. For an extended discussion of the perils of modeling political relationships after more personal and intimate ones, see Polletta, Francesca. 2020. *Inventing the Ties That Bind: Imagined Relationships in Moral and Political Life*. Chicago: University of Chicago Press.

15. brown, adrienne maree. 2020, August 12. "Strategy and Kamala Feels." *Adriennemareebrown*. https://adriennemareebrown.net/2020/08/12/strategy-and-kamala-feels/

16. Jasper, James M. 1997. *The Art of Moral Protest: Culture, Biography, and Creativity in Social Movements*. University of Chicago Press, 1997; Corrigall-Brown, Catherine. 2011. *Patterns of Protest: Trajectories of Participation in Social Movements*. Stanford University Press; Pérez 2022.

17. Schulman, Sarah. 2021. *Let the Record Show: A Political History of ACT UP New York, 1987–1993*. Farrar, Straus and Giroux.

18. Ball 2022, 1.

19. Leondar-Wright discusses the important overlaps of disability and socioeconomic class. See Leondar-Wright, Betsy. 2005. *Class Matters: Cross-Class Alliance Building for Middle-Class Activists*. New Society Publishers.

20. Srivastava, Sarita. 2005. "'You're Calling Me a Racist?' The Moral and Emotional Regulation of Antiracism and Feminism." *Signs: Journal of Women in Culture and Society* 31(1):29–62; Cadet, Akilah. 2020, July 17. "White Centering." *Change Cadet*. https://www.changecadet.com/blog/2020/7/17/white-centering

21. Bennett 2020; Ross 2025.

22. While this wording is broadly recognized, it is not actually consistent with the original text: Antonini, Francesca. 2019. "Pessimism of the Intellect, Optimism of the Will: Gramsci's Political Thought in the Last Miscellaneous Notebooks." *Rethinking Marxism* 31(1):42–57. doi:10.1080/08935696.2019.1577616

23. King Jr., Martin Luther. 1963. *Strength to Love*. Beacon Press, 46.

24. Sandoval, Chela. 2000. *Methodology of the Oppressed*. University of Minnesota Press, 139.

Chapter 7

1. This is not so dissimilar from C. Wright Mill's articulation of the sociological imagination: being able to categorize as well as connect one's personal troubles to socially structured, public issues. Mills, C. Wright. 1959. *The Sociological Imagination*, 40th anniversary ed. Oxford University Press.

2. Du Bois, W. E. B. 1998 [1935]. *Black Reconstruction in America, 1860–1880*. New York: Free Press; Baldwin, James. 2021. *The Price of the Ticket: Collected Nonfiction: 1948–1985*, reprint ed. Beacon Press; hooks, bell. 2004. *The Will to Change: Men, Masculinity, and Love*. Simon & Schuster.

3. Carmichael, Stokely. 1966, September 22. "What We Want." *New York Review of Books*. https://www.nybooks.com/articles/1966/09/22/what-we-want/; King Jr., Martin Luther. 1967. "Beyond Vietnam: A Time to Break Silence." *American Rhetoric Online Speech Bank*. Retrieved May 22, 2024. https://www.americanrhetoric.com/speeches/mlkatimetobreaksilence.htm; Randolph, A. Philip, and Bayard Rustin. 2018, April 2. "How the Civil-Rights Movement Aimed to End Poverty" [1967]. *The Atlantic*. https://www.theatlantic.com/magazine/archive/2018/02/a-freedom-budget-for-all-americans-annotated/557024/; Carson, Clayborne. 1995. *In Struggle: SNCC and the Black Awakening of the 1960s*, 2nd ed. Harvard University Press; Le Blanc, Paul, and Michael D. Yates. 2013. *A Freedom Budget for All Americans: Recapturing the Promise of the Civil Rights Movement in the Struggle for Economic Justice Today*. NYU Press; Clemons, Jared. 2022. "From 'Freedom Now!' to 'Black Lives Matter': Retrieving King and Randolph to Theorize Contemporary White Antiracism." *Perspectives on Politics*, 7. doi:10.1017/S1537592722001074

4. Appel, Hannah, and Astra Taylor. 2024, July 23. "'You Are Not a Loan!' Introducing the Nation's First Debtors' Union." *In These Times*. https://inthesetimes.com/article/debt-collective-takeover-debtors-union

Appendix

1. See Gawerc, Michelle I. 2020. "Diverse Social Movement Coalitions: Prospects and Challenges." *Sociology Compass* 14(1). doi: 10.1111/soc4.12760

2. Táíwò, Olúfẹ́mi O. 2022. *Elite Capture: How the Powerful Took over Identity Politics*. Haymarket Books.

3. Sunderman, Zachary. 2023. *Dilemmas of Allyship: White Anti-Racists and the Challenges of Social Justice*. New York: Routledge.

Index

Page references with a *t* refer to tables.

abolition, prisons, and police: campaigns for abolitionist action, 100–104, 179; ending cash bail, 136–39; mass incarceration, 13–16, 230; Measure R ballot campaign (Los Angeles, CA), 102–4, 126–28, 175, 178–79, 216

abolitionist action, 100–104, 179. *See also specific causes*

absorption framework (Momentum training institute), 147–49

accountability: Alicia on, 186–87; as alternative to locking people up, 212; balancing with kindness and support, 217; to BIPOC-led movement, 233–34; Diebold on, 161–62; Dunlap on types of, 65; fundraising for partners, 169–70; Gyamfi on, 63; Halle on, 202; Liz on, 187; LSURJ and, 182, 186–87; one-sided, 49; relationships across race, 175; SURJ Buffalo and, 160; SURJ interpretation of, 55, 62, 64, 65, 66, 192, 196–97; Wallace on, 66, 119; WP4BL and, 159, 176

ACLU-KY, 155

activism. *See also* organizing: activist wing of civil rights movement, 7; high-risk, 163–69

ACT UP, 209

Affordable Care Act, 38

African American. *See* Black people

Aheron, Grace, 61–62, 64–65, 117, 177–78, 224–26, 250*t*

Alerta Roja network (in Louisville, KY), 164–65, 169, 178

Alinsky, Saul, 12

Allen, 183–84, 249*t*

Alliance of White Anti-Racists Everywhere (AWARE) (Los Angeles), 47–50, 51, 67–68, 157, 194–96, 200, 211, 221, 222, 241, 243

Amelia, 118, 128, 135, 144–45, 249*t*

Anne Braden Antiracist Organizer Training Program (Catalyst Project), 45, 52

Anti-Blackness, 16, 34, 52
antiracism, 2, 5, 17, 20–21, 24, 30, 36, 45, 57, 74–76, 82, 144, 192, 229, 232
Anzaldúa, Gloria, 225–26
Appalachian region, 12, 39, 91–92. See also Ashland, Kentucky
Arizona SB1070, 51–52
Ashland, Kentucky, 1–2, 4, 109–10, 113–14, 118, 128, 135, 144–45
Ashland Pride, 135–36
awareness-raising, 16–21

Bail Project, 67. See also cash bail, ending
Baker, Ella, 40–41, 136
Ball, Amanda, 210
Barillas, Karina, 155–56, 164–65, 167, 168, 181–82, 187, 249t
Barlas, Carole, 176
Barnes, Shontay, 188, 248t
base building, 54, 108, 110–12, 147–48. See also organizing
"basket of deplorables" comment (H. Clinton), 20–21
Battle of Blair Mountain (West Virginia), 92
Bayard, Clare, 44, 45, 51, 53, 61, 221, 251t
Beaty, Kim, campaign of, 100–101, 120–21, 124–26, 128–29, 179–80
Bedford County Listening Project (BCLP), 73–74, 88–91, 115, 122–23, 127–28, 132–33, 225, 241–42
Bell, Derrick, 83, 86–87
Beshear, Andy, 128
Bills, Halle, 202–4, 249t
biographical availability, 187
Black, Indigenous, and people of color (BIPOC), 3–4, 10–11, 22, 28, 48–49, 64–66, 73, 80, 83, 173, 198, 216, 221, 224, 234–35, 246; choice of term, 33–34
Black Leadership Action Coalition of Kentucky (BLACK), 171–72, 242
Black Love Resists in the Rust (BLRR) (originally Just Resisting) (Buffalo), 120–21, 142–43, 160–62, 171, 173, 179–80, 188
Black movements: Black affinity groups, 26; Black Freedom Struggle, 34, 50, 236, 241; Black liberation movement, 8, 13; Black Lives Matter (BLM), 16, 26, 47, 67, 124–25, 155, 167, 168; Black Lives Matter Los Angeles (BLM LA), 47, 87, 105, 157–59, 161, 169–70; Black Panthers, 12; civil rights movement, 5–7, 39–41, 43–44, 53–54, 131, 140, 208, 229; Movement for Black Lives (M4BL), 3, 13–16, 23, 26–27, 33, 50, 52, 64–65, 96–97, 99–100, 111, 144, 146, 150–51, 230, 237
Black people: choice of term, 34; data collection, 243; feedback, 178; fundraising and, 169–70; high-risk activism, 168, 189; interviews of, 242; Just Resisting (later Black Love Resists in the Rust), 69–70; leadership, 176; in Louisville, 156–57; political relationships with, 187; in Shelbyville, Tennessee, 73; SURJ Buffalo, 160; WP4BL and, 157
Blair Mountain, Battle of (West Virginia), 92
Blue Lives Matter bill (Kentucky), 155
Braden, Anne, 40–43, 78, 98–99, 153
Braden, Carl, 40–42
Brett, Linnea, 56–58, 106, 121, 160–61, 248t

Brock-Petroshius, Kristen, 45–46, 179, 249*t*
Brown, John, 163–64
Brown, Phylicia, 160–62, 173, 188, 248*t*

calling people in: about, 190–95; down speech and, 198–204; engaging in conflict, 211–14; exclusivity, 229; organizational growth and, 214–20; personal stories of being called in, 195–98, 204–10, 220–27
Cameron, Daniel, 165
capitalism: anticapitalist critique, 15, 83, 96; racial, 28, 34, 131, 133, 170, 236; relationship to white supremacy, 17–18, 28, 106, 236
carceral state, 15. *See also* abolition, prisons, and police
cash bail, ending, 136–39
Catalyst Project, 43–45, 51, 243. *See also* Anne Braden Antiracist Organizer Training Program (Catalyst Project)
Challenging White Supremacy (CWS), 43, 44, 46
civil rights legislation, 7
civil rights movement, 5–7, 39–41, 43–44, 53–54, 131, 140, 208, 229
class, socioeconomic: classism, 20, 27, 29, 77–78, 106–8, 137–38, 171, 188, 204–5, 214–16, 218–19, 234–35; classism in antiracist efforts, 17, 57, 75–76; poor and working class, 2, 28–29, 39, 45, 57, 70–71, 73, 76–78, 80–81, 83, 88, 91, 93, 96–97, 101, 109, 118, 133, 138, 144, 172, 188, 214–15, 234, 237, 241; white working class, 11–12, 70–71, 101, 138
Cloward, Richard, 123

coalition. *See* cross-racial/-organizational partnerships
Coalition of Anti-Racist Whites (CARW) (Seattle), 46, 51
colorblind racism, 14, 16, 18, 20, 229
Combahee River Collective, 16
conflict, engaging in, 211–14. *See also* abolition, prisons, and police
Connor, 149, 248*t*
consciousness-raising. *See* awareness-raising
Court Watch program (Louisville, KY), 136–38, 244
critical humility, 176–77
Critical Resistance, 102. *See also* abolition, prisons, and police
cross-racial/-organizational partnerships: "coalition politics," 5; fundraising, 169–72; high-risk activism, 163–69; holding, 180–89; incorporating feedback, 176–80; Los Angeles, 157–60; Louisville SURJ, 153–57; organizing within, 150–89; roles in, 172–76; SURJ and, 62–66, 150–52; SURJ Buffalo, 160–63
Cullors, Patrisse, 16, 47, 103

Dakota Access Pipeline, 33
Daniel, Julia, 93, 127–28, 250*t*
David, Jason, 47–50, 75, 107–8, 211–12, 217–18, 249*t*
Davis, Angela, 41
DeVries, Sonja, 138–41, 178, 182–83, 190–92, 216, 219–20, 248*t*
DiAngelo, Robin, 194
Diebold, Josie, 161–62, 201, 207–9, 248*t*
door knocking, 139–45. *See also* organizing

Du Bois, W. E. B., 9
Dunlap, Anne, 28, 62, 65, 239–41, 248t

Ehrlichman, John, 14
electoral politics: campaigns, 113–19; debates, 38, 52, 111, 124–25; limitations, 125; organizing, 124–29; SURJ's approach, 110–13
Ella, 208, 249t
Ellinger, Mickey, 43, 44
Eric, 214, 250t
Erie County Holding Center, 100–101
European settlers, white supremacy and, 8–9

Fairness Campaign (Louisville, KY), 42
Fanon, Frantz, 10, 225–26
Farrington, Sean, 249t
feedback, incorporating, 176–80. *See also* cross-racial/-organizational partnerships
feminism, 16, 19–20, 26–28, 34, 35, 62, 75, 105, 230
Ferguson uprisings (2014), 33, 69–70, 146, 240–41
Ferlito, Dahlia, 124, 128, 131, 157–58, 168–70, 175–76, 194–96, 199–200, 207, 249t
Floyd, George (police murder of), 25, 146, 165
Frederick, Elliot, 117–18, 135, 249t
Freedom Summer (1964), 6–7. *See also* civil rights movement
fundraising, 60, 169–72

"gang bill" (Kentucky), 155
Ganz, Marshall, 116
Garza, Alicia, 16, 26, 124–25, 154–55

gay and lesbian rights, 16, 26, 86, 170, 221, 230
gender-based violence, 75, 76, 104, 234
Gilmore, Ruth Wilson, 14
Gramsci, Antonio, 225
grassroots organizing, 5, 31, 35, 61, 82–83, 110–12, 115–18, 123, 132–33, 137, 170–71, 194, 232
Great Depression, 14
Groundwork (Madison, WI), 45–46, 51
Guevara, Che, 225–26
Gyamfi, Nana, 63, 105, 173–74, 222–23, 250t

Hallweaver, Taryn, 146–48, 250t
Haukness, Z!, 46, 51, 248t
healthcare debates, under Obama, 38–39. *See also* Obama, Barack; white supremacy
Heaney, Erin, 28–29, 38, 56–57, 62, 68–71, 76–77, 92–94, 107, 118–19, 124, 133, 146, 160–61, 179–80, 248t
Hernández, Paulina Helm, 221
Heyburn Building (Louisville, KY), 167
Highlander Center, 39–43, 54, 60, 130, 191
high-risk activism, 163–69
Hill, Herbert, 12
hooks, bell, 225–26
Horton, Myles, 39
Horvath, David, 248t
HoSang, Daniel Martinez, 42
Howard, Beth, 77, 80, 93, 97–99, 109–10, 114, 171, 242, 249t; "Rednecks for Black Lives," 91–92
Howard, Tim, 120–21
Hurle, Alicia, 80–82, 154, 186–87, 230–31, 242, 249t

Hurricane Katrina, Catalyst Project and, 45

ICE, 67, 164–68
immigrant rights: migrants, 3; Mijente Louisville, 167; uprisings (2006), 50
immigration enforcement: Alerta Roja network (in Louisville, KY), 164–65, 169, 178; Arizona SB1070, 51–52; ICE, 67, 164–68; immigrant rights mobilizations, 53; Trump on, 156
imperialism, resistance to, 7, 41, 191
Indigenous Resistance. *See also* Black, Indigenous, and people of color (BIPOC): environmental justice struggles, 3; feedback from, 54; "Indian," 8; indigenous communities, 3; Indigenous Solidarity Network, 33; land theft, 8, 33; sovereignty, 4
Ingram, Paige, 96–97, 99–100, 150–51, 250*t*
Ioanide, Paula, 10, 197–98
Isaacs, Stephanie, 90–91, 128
issue campaigns, 113–19. *See also* organizing

Joe, 183, 249*t*
John Brown Anti-Klan Committee (JBAKC), 183
Jones, Van, 38
Jurs-Allen, Hannah, 204–5, 208, 213–15, 249*t*
JusticeLA Coalition, 159
Just Resisting (later Black Love Resists in the Rust), 69–70, 160–61, 209

Kate, 197, 222, 248*t*
Kentucky Alliance, 41–42. *See also* Braden, Anne; Davis, Angela
Kentucky People's Union (KPU), 1–2, 27, 57, 92–93, 95, 109–10, 113–19, 128, 135, 144–45, 171, 235, 242
King, Martin Luther, Jr., 40, 225
Kit, 250*t*
KKK, 145

La Casita Center (Louisville, KY), 155, 181–82
Lacey, Jackie, 175–76
Lakey, George, 129
Latine. *See* Latinx
Latino. *See* Latinx
Latinx: choice of term, 34; data collection, 243; feedback, 178; fundraising and, 169–70; high-risk activism, 168, 189; interviews of, 242; Just Resisting (later Black Love Resists in the Rust), 69–70; leadership, 176, 178; in Louisville, 67, 156–57; millennials, 167; political relationships with, 187; in Shelbyville, Tennessee, 72–73; SURJ Buffalo, 160; WP4BL and, 157
Lear, Kristina, 249*t*
learning. *See also* political education: in action, 136–39; from mutual interest organizing, 230–38
Le Blanc, Paul, 7
León, Kevin de, 158–59
Levin, Cameron, 47, 250*t*
Lipsitz, George, 10
Long, Elisabeth, 44–45, 75–76, 82–83, 97, 104–5, 251*t*
Los Angeles: Alliance of White Anti-Racists Everywhere-Los Angeles (AWARE-LA), 47–50, 157, 194–96,

Los Angeles (*cont.*) 200, 211, 221, 241, 243; cross-racial/-organizational partnerships and, 157–60; Los Angeles White People for Black Lives, 54; Measure R ballot campaign, 102–4, 126–28, 175, 178–79, 216

Louisville SURJ (LSURJ): about, 66–67; Beaty and, 101–2; calling in of, 224; cash bail campaign, 138–39; Court Watch program, 136–38; cross-racial/-organizational partnerships and, 153–57; on defund the police, 222; door knocking and, 144; growth of, 231; Kate on, 107; movement roots in, 241; opportunities for communication in, 181–82; organizing out of mutual interest and, 197; Parrish-Wright on, 133–35; Scott and, 81; Sonja on, 216

Louisville Urban League, 155

love, political, calling people in and, 220–27

Malcolm X, 13

Mark, 250*t*

Martinas, Sharon, 43, 44, 46

Martinez, Elizabeth "Betita," "Where Was the Color in Seattle?," 44

Marx, Karl, 146

Mary, 250*t*

mass incarceration, 13–16, 230. *See also* abolition, prisons, and police

McIntosh, Peggy, 18, 75

McMichael, Pam, 37–40, 42–43, 52–57, 60, 62, 78, 130, 147, 153, 228–29, 237, 241, 248*t*

Measure R ballot campaign (Los Angeles, CA), 102–4, 126–28, 175, 178–79, 216

Methodology of the Oppressed (Sandoval), 225–26

Middlebrook, Jeb, 17

militarism, 3, 4, 36, 41

Mills, Charles, 9

Minh-ha, Trinh, 225–26

Momentum training institute, 147

Moraga, Cherríe, 225–26

Morris, Aldon, 39

Movement for Black Lives (M4BL). *See also* Black movements: about, 3, 13–16, 50; Aheron on, 64–65; as an identity-based movement, 26–27; Attica on, 144; growth of, 23, 52, 230, 237; Ingram on, 99–100, 150–51; political organizing in, 111; rise of, 146; rural organizing, 96–97; SURJ and, 33

mutual interest: as an organizing framework, 73–74, 79–83, 102; approach of, 35; beyond self-interest, 84–88; effects of not talking about race, 97–100; framework complexity, 104–8; learning from, 230–38; rural projects, 91–97

Naomi, 212, 249*t*

National Alliance Against Racist & Political Repression, 41. *See also* Kentucky Alliance

New Left, 11–13

Nixon, Richard, 14

Obama, Barack, 37, 38, 52

Occupy ICE campaign, 166–68

Oppenheimer, Martin, 129

organizing: about, 109–13; Baker's philosophy on, 40–42, 136; within cross-racial/-organizational partnerships, 150–89; door knocking,

139–45; electoral, 124–29; ending cash bail, 136–39; grassroots, 5, 31, 35, 61, 82–83, 110–12, 115–18, 123, 132–33, 137, 170–71, 194, 232; issue campaigns, 113–19; learning in action, 136–39; lessons from, 234–35; in movement times, 146–49; mutual interest, 73–74, 79–83, 102, 104–8, 230–38; political education, 131–32; political love, 220–27; self-interest, complexity, 84–88; training, 129–36; wins and losses, 119–24

Parrish-Wright, Shameka, 133–34, 153, 171, 174–75, 246, 248t
Patch, Penny, 251t
Payne, Charles, 140
People's Institute for Survival and Beyond, 43, 46
Piven, Frances, 123
political education, 19, 22, 42, 45, 47, 126, 129–39, 230–38
political home, 204–10
Polletta, Francesca, 115
"Prison Fix." See abolition, prisons, and police; mass incarceration
privilege confessional, 19
Project South, 96, 143
Puerto Rican Young Lords, 12

queer liberation, 170. See also gay and lesbian rights
questions of study, key, 21–24

race: colorblind racism terminology, 33–34; concept of racial capitalism, 9–10; creation and reification of racial categories, 9; effects of not talking about, 97–100; race-conscious racism, 20

Racial Justice Accountability (RJA) Board, 49
the racial contract, 9
Rainbow Coalition, 12. See also cross-racial/-organizational partnerships
Ransby, Barbara, 15, 41
Ray, Ranita, 20
Rebecca, 249t
"Rednecks for Black Lives" (Howard), 91–92
"redneck" term, 91–92
research methods: author orientation, 30–32; case selection, 21–24, 239–43; data collection, 243–49; interviews, 243–44
restorative justice. See conflict, engaging in
Richard, 197, 248t
rings of engagement model, 129. See also spectrum of allies
Rodriguez, Dylan, 31
Ross, Loretta J., 192, 220
rural projects (SURJ), 91–97
Rustin, Bayard, 6

Sandoval, Chela, *Methodology of the Oppressed*, 225–26
Scott, Ashanti, 249t
Scott, Attica, 81, 116–17, 134–35, 143–44, 153–55, 165–68, 174, 181–82, 223–26, 249t
Scott, Jerome, 96, 143, 250t
self- and collective flagellation, shifting culture of. See calling people in
self-interest, complexity, 84–88. See also mutual interest; organizing
Shelbyville, Tennessee, 72–74, 84, 91, 122, 128

Showing Up for Racial Justice (SURJ). *See also* Louisville SURJ (LSURJ); SURJ Buffalo: about, 2, 4, 23–25, 28–30; Alliance of White Anti-Racists Everywhere in Los Angeles (AWARE-LA), 47–50; approach of, 110–13; calling people in and, 192, 196–97, 201, 219, 220; Catalyst Project, 44–45; Coalition of Anti-Racist Whites (CARW), 45–46; critical humility and, 177–78; cross-racial partnerships, 62–66; data collection and, 243–44; door knocking and, 143–44; electoral campaigns, 124–29; engaging in conflict, 211; first actions, 51–54; fundraising, 59–62, 169–72; as a grassroots power-building effort, 112; Groundwork, 45–46; growth of, 32–33, 37–71, 123, 147; high-risk activism, 164; hiring staff, 59–62; Ingram on, 150–51; Louisville SURJ (LSURJ), 66–67; McMichaels on, 228–29; mutual interest frame, 79–83; organizational structure, 54–55, 58; organizing approach of, 130, 146, 226; origins of, 32–33, 37–71; partnerships with, 187–88; political commitments of, 33; political home and, 210; rings of engagement model, 129; role in Indigenous Solidarity Network, 33; rural projects, 91–97, 127; SURJ Buffalo, 68–71; two-pronged model, 55–59; Wallace on, 38, 66, 74–75, 93–94, 191; White People for Black Lives (WP4BL), 67–68; white privilege analytic and, 74–78

skills training, in conflict resolution, 212–13

slavery, formal abolition of, 9

Sonnie, Amy, 7

Southern U.S.: Southerners On New Ground (SONG), 42, 221; Southern Strategy, 14, 127, 234–35

spectrum of allies, 129

Standing Rock Reservation, 33, 45

Steph, 206, 209–10, 248*t*

Student Nonviolent Coordinating Committee (SNCC), 4–6, 44, 78, 163–64

Students for a Democratic Society (SDS), 12

Sue, Derald Wing, 18

Sullivan, Shannon, 20

Sumerau, J. E., 20

Sunderman, Zachary, 246

SURJ Buffalo: abolitionist action by, 100–102; about, 160–63; Beaty campaign and, 128–29, 132; on calling in, 201; decentralization and, 57–58; door knocking, 141–43; fundraising, 171; goals of, 125; Heaney at, 68–71; one-on-ones, 149; organizing, 188, 206–9, 241; values of, 197; wins and losses, 119–22

Sutton, Liz, 64, 147–48, 159–60, 177, 186–87, 249*t*

Taylor, Breonna (police murder of), 25, 66, 146, 165

Tea Party, 38

terminology, 33–34

Thurber, Amie, 184

Tiffany, 248*t*

Tochluk, Shelly, 48, 221–22, 250*t*

Tometi, Opal, 16

Tracy, James, 7

Trump, Donald, 146, 156, 161, 164, 166–67, 198, 239

Tuck, Eve, 19

United States Social Forum, 52
Unite the Right rally, 72
Unmasking Whiteness Institute (AWARE-LA), 194–95
URLTA housing policy, 113, 115

VanDyk, Misha Viets, 250*t*
voter suppression mechanisms, 29

Wade, Andrew, 40
Wallace, Carla, 24, 38–42, 52, 54–55, 66, 70–71, 74, 78–79, 86, 93–95, 98, 119, 133, 138, 142, 153–54, 164–65, 175, 185–86, 190–93, 241–42, 248*t*
Waller, Kelly Sue, 72, 84–86, 88–90, 94, 115, 122–23, 132–33, 136, 141, 225–26, 242, 249*t*
Warren, Mark, 13
Watson, Rochelle, 251*t*
Weather Underground, 163–64
"Where Was the Color in Seattle?" (Martinez), 44
white affiliate organizing model. *See* white racial affinity model
white fragility, 176
whiteness, as a political project, 8. *See also* white supremacy
white people: choice of term, 34; organizing, 11–13, 24–30; in Shelbyville, Tennessee, 73; which, 28–30; why, 25–28
White People for Black Lives (WP4BL): about, 45–47; door knocking, 139–40; electoral organizing, 124, 126–29; engaging in conflict, 211–18; high-risk activism and fundraising and, 168–70; in Los Angeles, 67–68, 157–59, 175–79; Measure R ballot and, 102–5; organizing, 147–49; origins of, 50; partnerships and, 183–84, 196; political home, 204; space to try, 198–201
"White People Stepping Up," 52–53
white privilege: in abolitionist action, 100–104; about, 19, 72–74; analytic of, 74–78; door knocking and, 142; high-risk activism and, 164; limitations of, 19; white privilege pedagogy, 18–19
White Privilege Conference, 48
white racial affinity model, 25–28, 47, 49, 95, 131, 142, 182–87, 189, 193, 198, 234, 237
whites. *See* white people
white supremacy, 20–21, 35–36, 83. *See also* Alliance of White Anti-Racists Everywhere (AWARE); Catalyst Project; Louisville SURJ (LSURJ); Showing Up for Racial Justice (SURJ); SURJ Buffalo; connection to racial capitalism, 28; European settlers, 8–9; material returns of whiteness, 3; shifts from studies in, 17–18; voter suppression mechanisms and, 29; whiteness in liberation movements, 8–11
Williams, Michael, 87–88, 158–59, 161, 250*t*
Winn, Scott, 46, 191, 250*t*
Woodly, Deva, 111, 122
World Trade Organization (WTO), 44

Yang, K. Wayne, 19
Yates, Michael D., 7
Young Patriots, 12

Zellner, Bob and Dottie, 11